Good Books Matter

How to choose and use children's literature to help students grow as readers

SHELLEY STAGG PETERSON

LARRY SWARTZ

Pembroke Publishers Limited

Pembroke Publishers
538 Hood Road
Markham, Ontario, Canada L3R 3K9
www.pembrokepublishers.com

Distributed in the U.S. by Stenhouse Publishers
480 Congress Street
Portland, ME 04101
www.stenhouse.com

We acknowledge the financial support of the Government of Canada through the Book
Publishing Industry Development Program (BPIDP) for our publishing activities.

We acknowledge the Government of Ontario through the Ontario Media Development
Corporation's Ontario Book Initiative.

Library and Archives Canada Cataloguing in Publication

Peterson, Shelley
    Good books matter : how to choose and use children's literature to help
students grow as readers / Shelley Stagg Peterson and Larry Swartz.

Includes index.
ISBN 978-1-55138-232-6

    1. Children—Books and reading. 2. Children's literature—History and
criticism. I. Swartz, Larry II. Title.

Z1037.P453 2008   028.5'5   C2008-904010-4

Editor: Kat Mototsune
Cover Design: John Zehethofer
Typesetting: Jay Tee Graphics Ltd.

Printed and bound in Canada
9 8 7 6 5 4 3 2 1

Contents

Dedication

For Mary Swartz—LS

For Ed and Alice Peterson, Stan Peterson, and Tena Augustin, with love—SSP

Acknowledgments

To Tinlids, The Source, and Theatrebooks, booksellers who ensure we're up to date and in the know;
To Wendy Geoghegan for knowing which books matter;
To Nancy Steele for her passion and perspective;
To Franki Sibberson for her book talk and book friendship;
To Brenda Halliday and Theo Heras, librarians with an expansive knowledge about children's literature;
To Maria José Botelho for her critical multicultural analysis of literature;
To David Booth for helping us to consider a place for children's literature.

Introduction

The uniqueness of children's literature, then, lies in the audience that it addresses. Authors of children's books are circumscribed only by the experiences of childhood, but these are vast and complex. Children think and feel; they wonder and they dream. Much is known, but little is explained. Children are curious about life and adult activities. They live in the midst of tensions, of balances of love and hate within the family and the neighborhood. The author who can bring these experiences imagination and insight, give them literary shape and structure, and communicate them to children is writing children's literature.
(Huck, Hepler, Hickman & Kiefer, 1997: 8)

Selecting Books for Children

When we choose books for children, we must recognize that children's reading interests change with their growing capacities and the new experiences of each passing year. What is appropriate for one child at a certain age will likely not be appropriate a few years later. What is well-loved by one child may be uninteresting to another.

What is defined as children's literature has changed and will continue to change as time passes. Today, we recognize a wide range of genres as children's literature. Board books, such as Heather Collins's *This Little Piggy*, and wordless picture books, such as David Wiesner's *Flotsam*, are part of the body of children's literature. To that list we add concept books (e.g., Tana Hoban's *So Many Circles, So Many Squares*) and alphabet books (e.g., Wallace Edwards's *Alphabeasts*). For early readers there are beginning-to-read books, such as Tim Wynne-Jones's *Ned Mouse Breaks Away*, and predictable books, such as Mirra Ginsburg's *The Chick and the Duckling*. Elaborate pop-ups are now on the market, as well (e.g., Robert Sabuda's *Alice's Adventures in Wonderland*) and more stories than ever before are moving off the page in three-dimensions. Chapter Books (e.g., Pamela Porter's *The Crazy Man*), poetry books (e.g., David Booth's *Til All the Stars Have Fallen*), and nonfiction books, (e.g., Bill Slavin's *Transformed: How Everyday Things are Made*) are all within the realm of children's literature.

With the proliferation of multimedia and digital technology, literature for children is taking new forms that would not have been widely available in 1997 when Huck, Hepler, Kiefer and Hickman wrote the definition that begins this book. In today's world, print is nestled among—and is sometimes nudged out by—visual images that appear in graphic novels, video clips, CDs, websites, weblogs, collectors' cards, comic books, magazines, newspapers, multimedia presentations, video games, chat groups, etc. Brought into existence by creators

Children's literature *tends* to have child protagonists and themes that relate to growing up and becoming increasingly independent. Books for children *tend* to have language, plots, and lengths that are accessible and enjoyable to young people. However, there will always be examples of books that large numbers of children enjoy that do not fit these criteria.

who wanted to bring comic books into the mainstream, graphic novels have gained popularity over the past 25 years. Graphic novels may be superhero stories, human interest stories, *manga* (a translated Japanese comic that is read from back to front), adaptations or spin-offs of popular films or television shows, political satire, or nonfiction (Weiner, 2006). These forms have not been so widely available in the past and must be folded into our definition of children's literature.

Mass-produced books based on popular culture figures, comic books, and magazines have something to offer children, as well. Their familiar characters, settings, and storylines are comforting to readers who are continuously honing their literacy skills. These readers need a chance to practice those skills with texts that are entertaining and somewhat predictable. For younger children, picture books based on TV and movies provide the comfort of familiar characters, such as the Berenstain Bears, Dora the Explorer, and Barney the dinosaur. For older readers, series books, which now take up many shelves in bookstores, serve this purpose. These series take on the topics and desires of young people, including teen romance, science fiction, and sports, and often share characters with TV, movies, and video games. Young people eagerly return again and again to the section of the library or bookstore where the series books are shelved. The hard work of selecting a book is lifted from their shoulders and they know what to expect in the book. There is little chance of disappointment because they already know the characters and have a good sense of what the plot's outcome will be.

It is unlikely that such books will endure as classics for future generations, however, as any specific popular culture examples will soon be dated. Although series books of past generations are still on the shelves, they are generally not the first choice of today's young people. Mass-produced books reflect the popular culture of their time, and thus have mass appeal in their time.

Issues for Discussion

How would you define a classic book for children? What books would be on your list of classics? What do all the books on your list have in common?

There are some books, however, that stand the test of time. They can be called classics because their characters, story lines, and themes are timeless. These books truly do say something about the enduring essence of childhood that children recognize regardless of the era in which the book was written. It is important to consider how certain books, such as E.B. White's *Charlotte's Web*, Ludwig Bemelmans's *Madeleine*, C.S. Lewis's *The Lion, the Witch and the Wardrobe*, and A.A. Milne's *Winnie the Pooh*, have continued to find their place as part of children's taken-for-granted growing up experiences. The books appeal to children even though they are set in long-ago times. To some degree, these classics have been kept alive through the generations by being recast as movies. The special effects of today's multimedia world have given the characters a contemporary sheen. The honoring of these books by previous generations of children does not automatically give them classic status for today's children, however, as Huck, Hepler, Hickman, and Kiefer (1997: 28) explain:

> Most adults remember with nostalgia the books they read as children. They tend to think that what they read was best and ignore the possibility that any better books might be produced. It is easy to forget that every 'classic' was once a new book, that some of today's new books will be tomorrow's classics.

It is important that adults who put these books in children's hands are open to the possibility that the books will not speak to the new generation. They must be able to hold their own as they sit side-by-side with the best of the contemporary literature.

Why Good Books Matter

For Jonathan Culler (1997), what leads readers to treat something as literature is that they find it in a context that identifies it as literature—in a library or a bookstore, a book of poems, a section of a magazine.

Over the past three decades, the literature in our classrooms has included a wide array of picture books, novels, poetry, scripts, folklore, and nonfiction materials. Why some texts earn the merit of being called literature and others do not is, of course, arguable. We value stories that offer the imaginative recreation of experience—both that of others and one's own. We consider a written text to be literature when students are engaged and a response is evoked.

We value teaching through good books because we hope to help children develop into independent, purposeful readers who will think carefully about what they have read. All children need effective comprehension strategies as they grow into independent readers and writers. David Booth (2001: 14) reminds us that as we read, "we build up our store of knowledge, develop insight, think more deeply and critically, question, interpret and evaluate what we are reading." We use the text to stimulate our own thinking so we can engage with the mind of the writer. That is why good books matter.

We teach literature to help students become more human. Much of what we teach in school is based on learning facts and acquiring information. Incorporating literature helps us to inform our feelings and connect them to the intellect, creating a stronger impact. Our students can learn about the lives of others and learn about themselves through the skins of others. Through good books, students can

- Laugh with the kids of Wayside School who watch their teacher turn into an apple, or smile when a little mouse girl tries to sneak her purple plastic purse into the classroom.
- Cry when Little Willy carries his dead dog across the finish line, or when Henry and Zelda bury their science teacher, Miss Applebaum, in a trench in Central Park
- Feel the despair of a mouse named Abel stranded on an island, or relate to Maniac Magee who struggles to survive on the city streets.
- Go on week-long adventure with a very hungry caterpillar, or sail over the world in a giant peach.

We bother to incorporate literature to bring the whole world into our classrooms and to take our classrooms outside to the whole world. Literature gives students vicarious experiences and helps them live more lives than the ones they think they have.

"Why bother so much about children's reading?" Aidan Chambers (1975) asked in a *Horn Magazine* article. In coming to grips with this question, Chambers claims,

> Literature provides us with a unique relationship with language and form, creates the texture of experience through words, brings us to awareness, engages us in imaginary re-enactment and opens up different worlds to us while at the same time showing the relationship of those words to our own.

These functions have vital value for our students as they form attitudes; build concepts, patterns, and images; formulate judgments for understanding; and connect with the human condition. Chambers feels that literary experience

Richard Hoggart (1970: 17) wrote that he values literature "because of the way—the peculiar way—in which it explores, re-creates and seeks for the meanings in human experience." For Hoggart, literature can "make us sense more adequately the fullness, the weight, the inter-relations and the demands of human experience—and the possibilities of order."

feeds the imagination, helping it "to come to grips with the astonishing amount of data and experience which assail children in their lives."

For Charlotte Huck (1990), literature not only has the power to change a reader, but also contains the power to help children become readers. Vivienne Nichols and Victoria Roberts (1993: 7) believe in the power of literature not simply to entertain but "to tell truths about ourselves and to nourish our spirit and imagination."

The craft of the written word found in good books offers a rich foundation for children's language development. Strong readers may not become strong wordsmiths just because they engage with books, but a banquet of stories and poems and tales can help students grow in their grasp of vocabulary and syntactic structures. Shelley Harwayne (1992) contends that, to help children grow as writers, we need to expose them to a variety of genres, styles, and literature themes. The wider the range of vocabulary and language structures children are familiar with, the more likely they are to make choices that best convey their meaning in any context. When children read good books independently, listen to stories read aloud, and discuss what they have read together, their attention can be drawn to the form as well as the content of literature.

Literature nurtures narrative in the classroom. The British educator Harold Rosen (1985) tells us that there are always stories crying to be let out and meanings crying to be let in. Narrative in children's literature invites the children in, as they recreate an author's story for themselves. We believe in the transforming power of good books. Certain books alter us in some way, by disturbing us or by affirming the values and emotions we have but could not express in words.

The word "good" has implications we must consider when working with our children. What is a "good" book to me may not make it on another critic's list. We may find an award-winning book to be outside our students' lives. There are good popular books; good books that are censored; good books for a reluctant reader; good books for a summer's afternoon; good books in a continuing series; good books that talk about our communities, our cultures, our childhoods, or our family situations. For us, the word "good" denotes a book that will have significant impact on a young reader, that will stay with the child long after it has been returned to the shelf. Good books matter, depending on the child, the context, the culture, and the occasion.

About This Book

The Children's Literature Database, an online treasure, can be found at **http://clcd.odyssi.com/member/csearch.htm**

Through reading this book, you will become familiar with the work of many of the finest contemporary authors, poets, and illustrators who have created literature for children in English. These works include picture books, novels, nonfiction, traditional literature, poetry, and multicultural literature by American, Australian, British, and Canadian writers. We recommend these books because we—and young people we know—love reading them and strongly believe they are good books. To select the literature for this textbook, we have used the Children's Choice and Teachers' Choice lists found in the October and November issues of the International Reading Associations' journal, *The Reading Teacher*, and the Canadian Children's Book Centre's publication, *Book News*. We have consulted awards lists, as well as children's librarians and booksellers in bookstores specializing in children's literature, and the Children's Literature Database. We have also revisited and reconsidered all the books on our own

We believe that rather than devoting time, money, and energy to organizing books by reading levels within classrooms and schools, teachers should be reading widely and making a wide variety of texts available for children to read. These texts should take into account the interests, motivations, background experience and knowledge, and cultural identities of the children in the class.

bookshelves in order to consider our final choices in providing this survey of children's literature work.

This book is written for beginning and experienced teachers who want to fill their classroom bookshelves and infuse their teaching with quality children's literature. You will learn about the literature and the features that make it appealing and appropriate for your students. We present the literature in terms of its appropriateness for younger readers (approximately 5–9 years old) and for older readers (approximately 10–14 years old), with the caveat that the choices that children make about what they read should be governed by their interests and desires to learn, not by a grade or reading level.

As you become familiar with the literature, you will also learn about the historical backgrounds and special features of the genres; each illustrated with many examples. Criteria for selecting literature within each genre are an important part of each genre-based chapter. In addition, we include specific suggestions for teaching using the genres, based on the work of McGee and Tompkins (1995), who identify four ways to teach with children's literature. In each genre chapter you will find teaching suggestions for each of the following:

(1) *Responding personally* with emotions, personal connections, remembered experiences, preferences and beliefs, and other responses that reflect the student's individuality.
(2) Teaching *reading and writing skills* through the models of good writing that the literature provides. The literature can be used to teach comprehension skills such as predicting, analyzing, synthesizing, inferring, and evaluating, or to teach children how to write within particular genres.
(3) Raising awareness of *literary elements* (i.e., plot, character, and setting in fiction), as well as the organization of ideas under headings and subheadings, and the tools for seeking information (i.e., indexes and tables of contents in nonfiction; the rhyme, phrasing, and rhythms of poetry).
(4) *Critical reading and writing*, which involves looking at the social, political, and cultural assumptions and power relationships in the literature, and considering the viewpoints of people at different levels of the power relationships in an effort to bring about greater equity for all.

In each chapter you will be introduced to leading research in the fields of children's literature and teaching with children's literature, as we show how the research can be applied in today's classrooms. The titles of all the children's books discussed are in a book list at the end of each chapter. Look to the margins for bits of information, suggestions, and featured writers.

We invite you to use this book as a springboard for your reading of children's literature. We hope you find you can develop and extend your students' love of children's literature through this book. We agree wholeheartedly with Katherine Paterson (1989: 142) who writes:

Perhaps this is the way to teach children. First, we must love music or literature or mathematics or history or science so much that we cannot stand to keep that love to ourselves. Then, with energy and enthusiasm and enormous respect for the learner, we share our love. And we don't give out love in little pieces, we give it full and running over. We don't edit or censor or predigest; we entrust it in its fullness to someone we hope will love it too.

We hope that you will have children by your side or in your heart as you read this book. New discoveries and old favorites await you as you read about the literature, the creative people who made them, and all the ways that the books broaden and enrich children's lives and learning.

Children's Book References

Bemelmans, Ludwig (1939) *Madeline.*

Booth, David (1989) *Til all the stars have fallen.*

Carle, Eric (1969) *The very hungry caterpillar.*

Collins, Heather (1997) *This little piggy.*

Curtis, Christopher Paul (1995) *The Watsons go to Burningham—1963.*

Dahl, Roald (1961) *James and the giant peach.*

Edwards, Wallace (2002) *Alphabeasts.*

Garden, Nancy (2004) *Molly's family*

Ginsburg, Mirra (1988) *The chick and the duckling.*

Henkes, Kevin (1996) *Lilly's purple plastic purse.*

Hoban, Tana (1999) *So many circles, so many squares.*

Lewis, C.S. (1950) *The lion, the witch and the wardrobe.*

Lowry, Lois (1993) *The giver.*

Porter, Pamela (2005) *The Crazy Man.*

Sabuda, Robert (2003) *Alice's adventures in wonderland.*

Sachar, Louis (1989) *Sideways stories from Wayside School.*

Slavin, Bill (2005) *Transformed: How everyday things are made.*

Spinelli, Jerry (1990) *Maniac Magee.*

Steig, William (1976) *Abel's Island.*

White, E.B. (1952) *Charlotte's Web.*

Wiesner, David (2006) *Flotsam.*

Wynne-Jones, Tim (2003) *Ned Mouse breaks away.*

Zindel, Paul (1989) *A begonia for Miss Applebaum.*

CHAPTER 1

Teaching with Children's Literature

The use of literature in classrooms has been shown to develop student interest in reading, provide language models for students' own writing, foster critical thinking, develop vocabulary, promote awareness and develop social and cultural understandings, motivate children to read, promote learning, develop literacy, spark readers' imaginations, and develop a sense of story.
(Bainbridge & Pantaleo, 1999: 207–9)

Children's Literature in the Classroom

There is little that teachers can bring to a classroom that matches the rich experience of reading children's literature. Children gain a deeper understanding of the world, of humanity, and of themselves through children's literature, whether it is through listening to adults reading and bringing the literature to life, or through reading independently. The literature gives shape and coherence to children's experiences. Through reading literature, children encounter new ideas and enter worlds that stretch the outermost bounds of their imaginations. They gain "a love of reading and a taste for literature" that travel with them throughout their lives (Huck, Hepler, Hickman, & Kiefer, 1997: 9). All of this is made possible when children have ready access to a wide variety of children's literature.

Intertextuality is the term used to describe the themes and patterns that readers dip into when they read new texts. Stirring together the familiar with the new creates a richer understanding and makes new texts more familiar and accessible, as well.

Many would argue that a lifetime of pleasure is reason enough to bring literature into classrooms. Others would say that this kind of pleasure is not every child's cup of tea—some children would rather play hockey or soccer; others would rather dance or sing. For those children who do not envision curling up with a book when they think about enjoyable pastimes, we add motivation to learn as another powerful reason for bringing children's literature into classrooms. Children's fiction, nonfiction, and poetry, have "the power to lure [children] into learning" (Paterson, 1989: 139). The crafted language, insights, and illustrations of children's literature captivate children's interest and sustain their attention to the information and ideas that are unveiled with each turn of the page. Reading children's literature also deepens the wellsprings of ideas, values, and perspectives that children draw upon when learning something new.

Children's literature models effective writing in the classroom, as well. As such, classroom libraries are filled with on-demand "team-teachers." Books and their authors help illustrate ways for students to develop characters, captivate the interest of readers through foreshadowing, use specific language to create an image, or use conventional punctuation and spelling to communicate ideas more clearly. They also show what writers can achieve when using various genres to communicate their ideas. Teachers can highlight the ideas and writing techniques of these team-teachers to help students become better writers.

The materials that teachers offer children in the learning-to-read process should be the finest children's literature that a bookshelf can hold. Author Katherine Paterson (1989: 163) underlines this important tenet:

> It is not enough simply to teach children to read; we have to give them something worth reading. Something that will stretch their imaginations— something that will help them make sense of their own lives and encourage them to reach out toward people whose lives are quite different from their own.

The texts children read in classrooms should present exciting ideas to stimulate children's learning and imaginations. They should be well-written and formatted to show children the possibilities for using written language and creating texts of their own. Children's reading materials should make the universe of ideas, from the marvelous to the mundane, accessible to children.

Organizing Your Classroom

Huck, Hepler, Hickman, and Kiefer (1997: 630) tell us that "wide reading is directly related to accessibility; the more books available and the more time for reading, the more children will read and the better readers they will become." The classroom library/reading centres, brimming with a wide variety of genres on topics as diverse as the students in the class, provides such access. Teachers and students select the books and all members of the class are invited to help with arrangements for displaying the books. The books and other texts in the reading centre are chosen to build on students' interests, but also to encourage them to branch out and learn about unfamiliar topics. In the reading centre, there may be three to five copies of some books that teachers plan to use in guided reading instruction or in literature discussion groups. There will likely be a core of books that are always in the classroom library. Other books will remain in the classroom library for four to eight weeks, depending on their connections to curriculum objectives and students' interest in the books.

School librarians are helpful in identifying appropriate books that teachers can borrow for the rotating collection of classroom libraries. Trading books with other teachers in the school or school district is a possibility for expanding classroom libraries without having to pay exorbitant amounts of money to fill classroom libraries.

We recommend that you consult with your school librarian or teacher-librarian as much as possible when organizing your classroom for ways to place the spotlight on literature. Here are some of the ways that your school librarian can help you:

- Recommending books for your classroom library
- Booking author or illustrator tours through organizations such as the Canadian Children's Book Centre: go to www.bookcentre.ca
- Identifying and/or purchasing books on particular topics you are teaching

Children's literature opens up a world of ideas and ways of thinking. As author Marion Dane Bauer (1991: 114) explains, bringing children's literature into classrooms is like bringing "another pair of eyes" for students to look at the world and at themselves.

Consider not classifying the books in your classroom library according to reading levels. The difficulty of a book is determined by the reader's background knowledge about the topic as much as it is by the number of syllables in words, the number of words on a page, or other features of the text used to determine reading levels.

- Subscribing to educational journals you would like to read to stay current with developments in teaching and learning
- Co-teaching with you as students carry out inquiry projects

Teaching with Children's Literature

When the spotlight is on children's literature, students' days are filled with reading, listening to, and responding to literature. Writing, drama, visual art, and multimedia projects accompany hands-on activities, listening to guest speakers (either in person or online), and going out into the world on field trips to engage first-hand in the ideas and activities introduced in the literature. The following pages introduce specific teaching practices.

Reading to Children

Children's first encounters with books in their homes are likely to be while listening to a caring adult read books aloud to them. Children are engaged with the book, most often a picture book, through looking at the illustrations and hearing the cadences of the poem, story, or informational text being read aloud. The pleasure of enjoying a book with someone significant in their lives continues throughout the school years. Indeed, students in our teacher-education classes sit back comfortably in their chairs and show in their body language that they enjoy having a book read to them. Teachers can build on the expectations established in many children's preschool years by reading aloud daily to students of any age.

Reading to children models both fluent reading and a love of reading. Students are introduced to texts they might not otherwise encounter when teachers read aloud to them. Hearing a book read expands children's vocabulary and their familiarity with a variety of sentence structures and ideas. When reading aloud, teachers should be familiar with the content of the text and communicate their enthusiasm for it. The primary goal of reading aloud is to foster children's enjoyment and understanding of the text. Any questions you ask should deepen children's understanding, clarify difficult concepts or relationships, or encourage their emotional response to the book, rather than simply check to see if students can identify more superficial features, such as character and plot.

The selection of literature to read to children depends on the children's ages and attention spans, and on their interests and abilities. Read-aloud time provides an opportunity to stretch children's reading tastes and abilities; books that children can read independently are not the best choice. As the years progress, children are able to sit for longer books with more complex plots. By Grade 3, for example, chapter books are popular read-alouds. The quality of the book is also a consideration: "a book selected for reading aloud should be worthy of the time spent by the readers and listeners" (Norton, 2007: 194). Although there has been a tendency to choose fiction for reading aloud to students, when teachers include narrative nonfiction and poetry, they have no trouble engaging their students in all types of literature (Kozak, 2005). Because students are aware of a wider variety of texts, their independent reading selections are broadened, as well.

See pages 26–27 for Books for Reading Aloud, a list of tried and true picture book, novel, poetry, and nonfiction literature that works well for reading aloud to children.

Students' Independent Reading

As with any new endeavor, the more often students read, the more familiar the processes of reading become. Having ample opportunities to read in a day provides the experience that students need to develop and refine the literacy knowledge and practices they are learning during classroom instruction. In every day, set aside time for students to read texts of their own choice independently. Such opportunities develop students' sense of ownership and responsibility for their reading.

The classroom or school libraries are good sources of texts for students' independent reading. Younger students will likely need to choose two or three books to read during the 8–10 minutes of silent reading time. Older students will probably keep a chapter book or nonfiction book with them, so they can read a chapter or two during the longer silent reading sessions—usually 15–25 minutes. Some teachers believe that free choice should be extended to students' selection of comic books, magazines, and graphic novels for independent reading.

Students may read alone or in soft voices with a partner. Buddy reading is a good learning strategy for students who need assistance with their reading, as the partners help each other make sense of the text. Whenever possible, read books of your own choice during silent reading time to demonstrate the importance of reading. After silent reading, talk to your students about the books they are reading and about the reasons for choosing the books, stimulating them to discuss criteria that they use for making book selections for independent reading. Silent reading time is also a good opportunity for you to listen to individual students read, to gain a sense of students' fluency and their monitoring of their reading.

Students' monitoring of their reading is determined by identifying whether or not students make corrections when their reading does not make sense or does not match the letters on the page.

Shared Reading

Shared reading is an extension of teachers reading aloud to students. This teaching strategy invites greater student participation, as students can see the pages that you read and read along with you. Together with you, students read the text a number of times to become familiar with the text, and then you provide formal instruction by identifying reading concepts and strategies. The students might echo read (reading slightly behind you as they repeat what you say) or they might join in unison with the reader, depending on their fluency in reading the text. When working with Kindergarten or Grade 1 students, you might read from big books with large print that can be seen by children from afar. Point to the lines of text as you read, highlighting concepts about print (Clay, 2000), such as left-to-right and top-to-bottom progression, word or sentence breaks, and letter–sound relationships. The books chosen for shared reading in primary grades tend to be rollicking verses or traditional tales with predictable plots that are easier to read along with the teacher.

Shared reading for older students may take the form of the teacher reading text that students would find difficult while students read silently, a process that models fluent reading. It may also take the form of choral speech, where a poem, story, or informational piece is read in unison or broken up into parts, often with accompanying gestures, actions, and sound effects. Readers theatre, where stories with a lot of dialogue are made into scripts, or where scripts are used by individual readers who read aloud the parts of particular characters, is another form of shared reading. These shared reading practices become highly motivational ways to develop students' fluency.

BOOKS FOR SHARED READING

Carle, Eric (2002) *"Slowly, Slowly, Slowly," said the sloth.*

Cousins, Lucy (2005) *Hooray for fish!*

Erhardt, Karen (2006) *This jazz man.*

Fox, Mem (2004) *Where is the green sheep?* (also: *Hattie and the fox; Time for bed; Time to go!*)

Gilman, Phoebe (1992) *Something from nothing.*

Little, Jean (1999) *I know an old laddie.*

MacDonald, Margaret Read (2005) *A hen, a chick and a string guitar: Inspired by a Chilean folktale.*

Taback, Sims (2002) *This is the house that Jack built.* (also: *There was an old lady who swallowed a fly; Joseph had an overcoat*)

Wood, Audrey (1994) *Silly Sally.*

BOOKS FOR CHORAL DRAMATIZATION

Booth, David (ed.) (1995) *Images of nature: Canadian poets and the Group of Seven.*

Bouchard, David (2006) *Nokum is my teacher.*

Fleischman, Paul (1988) *Joyful noise: Poems for two voices.*

Hall, Donald (1994) *I am the dog / I am the cat.*

Little, Jean & DeVrie, Maggie (1991) *Once upon a golden apple.*

Lottridge, Celia Barker (1989) *The name of the tree.*

Most, Bernard (1993) *The cow that went oink!*

Smith, Charles R. (1999) *Rimshots.*

Swados, Elizabeth (2002) *Hey You! C'mere: a poetry slam.*

BOOKS FOR READERS THEATRE

Carle, Eric (1997) *From head to toe.*

Greenfield, Eloise (2006) *The friendly four.*

Hoberman, Mary Ann (2001) *You read to me, I'll read to you.* (also: *You read to me, I'll read to you, Mother Goose; You read to me, I'll read to you, Fairy tales*).

Fitch, Sheree (1992) *There Were Monkeys in my Kitchen.*

Isadora, Rachel (2007) *Yo, Jo!*

Kovalski, Maryann (1999) *Omar on ice.*

Muth, Jon (2005) *Zen Shorts.*

Poulin, Stéphane (1987) *Could you stop Josephine?*

Rinck, M. & van der Linden, M (2006) *The sweetest kiss.*

Scieszka, Jon (1998) *Squids will be squids.*

Starbright Foundation (2001) *Once upon a fairy tale.*

Guided Reading

Introduced by Reading Recovery™ founder, Marie Clay (1991) and Reading Recovery™ trainers, Irene Fountas and Gay Su Pinnell (1996), guided reading is a teacher-directed small-group instructional method. The teacher brings together students who need to learn particular reading strategies or concepts, or are at similar reading levels, as determined by listening to students read and noting their fluency, error rate, and understanding of texts that have been assigned particular levels. Multiple copies of books are needed, as all members of the group read the same book. The books should be at students' instructional levels —challenging for independent reading but not so challenging that students are frustrated because they are unable to make any sense of the text. Generally, the

Round-robin reading presents numerous disincentives to students' engagement with the text (Tompkins, Bright, Pollard, & Winsor, 2005). The anticipation of having to read and the relief at not having to perform again often distract students from making sense of the text. Students who do not read fluently suffer embarrassment; other students find it difficult to listen to non-fluent readers.

books are short enough to be read in one sitting, but chapter books may also be used. Students would likely read a chapter or a few pages at each guided reading group.

Start by acquainting the group of three to five students with the book: introduce characters, ask questions, or give prompts to encourage students' awareness of their background knowledge and experience with the topic/theme/characters/plot of the book, and to give students a purpose to read. Observe your students reading the book to a partner or to you, and provide assistance where needed. Let the students talk about the book, asking questions to clarify incomplete or inaccurate understandings. Then instruct by modeling or guiding students to develop and practice particular reading processes or to apply new knowledge about reading.

Extending Literature through Concrete Experiences

Literature provides vicarious experience with the people and things of the world. For many students, participating in hands-on experiences enriches their understanding of the ideas and concepts in the literature. In addition to providing first-hand experiences with the vocabulary, concrete experiences contribute a context for the ideas:

- Bring in an object related to the book or involve students in an activity related to the book; for example, Na'im brought jelly beans and fortune cookies into class for students to examine as he read from Bill Slavin's *Transformed: How Everyday Things are Made*, and students discovered the materials and processes involved in their creation
- Arrange for a guest speaker to respond to students' questions about the experience and tell his/her story related to literature students are reading; for example, Jeff invited a volunteer from the local Society for the Prevention of Cruelty to Animals to talk to his Grade 4 class about adopting stray animals when one group of students read Kate DiCamillo's Newbery Honor Book *Because of Winn-Dixie* in their literature circle.
- Visit the site of a story/poem/information book; Corrinne took her Grade 3 class to a nearby pond to observe the water boatmen and other water insects in their natural habitat before reading Joyce Sidman's *Song of the Water Boatman and Other Pond Poems*.

Drama Experiences

Although drama experiences are vicarious, they provide a context for the characters, events, and ideas in children's literature. Drama stimulates students' imagination as students take up roles and imagine themselves in situations encountered by characters in the literature.

Here are two drama practices that work well for enriching and extending students' experiences with literature:

- Hot Seat: Hot seating is a useful teaching strategy for developing students' empathy for characters. Students work in small groups or as a whole class. One student takes the role of a character in a story; another

See the list of Drama Resources on page 28 for sources of drama practices that work well for enriching and extending students' experiences with literature.

student or a group of students question the character, acting as journalists or lawyers in a trial. The student in the hot seat uses the information from the book and her/his own experiences and emotions to respond to the questions as the character would.

- Tableau: Students' understanding of the plot and of character relationships in stories can be furthered through the use of a tableau strategy. In small groups, students take the roles of characters in a given scene. They discuss the relationships among the characters in the scene and, when the teacher calls out, "Freeze," the students re-create the scene as still figures. To deepen students' understanding of the characters' motivations and emotions, the teacher might walk by each frozen scene and touch one student on top of the head. This would bring the character to life, and she/he would voice her/his thoughts or talk to another character in the scene. The teacher might also ask one group at a time to *unfreeze*, and the group members would carry out the actions and dialogue that they imagine would be going on in the scene.

Responding to Literature

Discussion Groups

Literature discussion groups (also called book clubs or literature circles) are motivational forums for students to enrich their reading of texts. As students talk about books with a small group of peers, they gain a greater enjoyment of reading and see themselves as successful readers (Daniels, 2006; Gilles, 1990). They take responsibility for their learning because they choose the books and conduct the literature discussions themselves. Being able to hear other perspectives deepens students' comprehension of what they read and may help students to rethink misconceptions they initially had about a text (Burns, 1998).

However, because of the demands that literature circles place on our students in terms of social and communication skills, sometimes the outcomes for students are far from what we expect. Students might talk about anything but the book, and the conversations may not greatly extend students' understandings of the book. For this reason, it is important to scaffold students' interaction skills (e.g., paying attention, staying on the subject, referring to a previous topic) and to demonstrate how to accept diverse perspectives, so that all students' contributions are valued. Roser and Martinez (1995: 145) suggest that teachers meet with each literature discussion group periodically and are present the first time that a group meets in order to get the group started. Sometimes students should be free "to explore their own agenda and issues from 'kid culture'" and other times they may need the intervention of a teacher to introduce new ideas and to foster more equitable group dynamics. The size of the group influences group dynamics, as well. Harvey Daniels (2002: 76) recommends four or five students per group to allow for "a good variety of voices and perspectives without the group's getting so big that distractions and inefficiencies take over." In the lower grades, three or four students per group is more manageable; fewer people to work with using developing social and communication skills makes the group dynamics less complex.

Choosing one class text for all students to read and discuss in literature circles may not create the optimum learning experience. The diverse interests and wide range of reading abilities in every classroom work against the possibility that one

Some students cause their literature circle peers distress when they read ahead of the assigned reading for each discussion. Having each group determine which pages will be read for each discussion might deter students who are inclined to read ahead. Or all students in the group might choose to read the novel from beginning to end before they start meeting in their literature circles.

text could ever be appropriate for all students. However, it is also difficult to hold a discussion if all group members have read a different text. For these reasons, we recommend providing a selection of books, introducing the books by reading the flyleaf and the first two pages, and inviting students to select a book from the assortment. Availability of books in the school will likely be a factor in teachers' selection of texts for literature discussions. When searching for titles, consult with the school librarian, colleagues, websites with databases of books appropriate for literature discussions, and, of course, books such as this one.

Book talks are helpful for introducing the selection of books that students may choose to read for their literature discussions. Faye Brownlie (2005) recommends giving a quick overview of the book, talking about why you thought the book was worthwhile, and reading an excerpt from the book. Ensure that students know that their groups can be changed with each new round of literature circles, so they choose the book that they want to read, rather than a book that will enable them to be in a group with their friends. Brownlie also suggests that students identify their first and second choices of book, in case no one else wants to read the same book, or in case the group reading the book is already too large and there are not enough students to make two groups.

In discussions of literature circles, teachers are often encouraged to assign roles to students to focus their attention on particular aspects of the book and facilitate group management. These explanations frequently cite Harvey Daniels (2002), who suggests that students be assigned a variety of roles, including discussion director, connector, summarizer. Our experience and reading shows us that the roles sometimes get in the way of interesting, thoughtful, from-the-heart conversation. Harvey Daniels (2006) himself has written a cautionary article saying that the roles were meant to be used on a temporary basis until students became familiar with the routines and expectations of literature circles. Shelley Peterson and Michelle Belizaire, a Grade 8 teacher, found that the size of the group, the relative social popularity and confidence of group members, the range of reading levels, and the type of book that students read all contributed to students' learning and their satisfaction with their literature group discussions. Consider all these factors when making decisions about whether to assign roles or to allow students to take them up as needed.

Text- and Reader-Based Responses

When inviting students to respond to literature, teachers may encourage responses that are primarily text-based or primarily reader-based. We find that retellings, at the *efferent* end of the spectrum, do not lead to the thoughtful, inspired discussions that are possible when students are encouraged to respond *aesthetically*. The range of possible responses is as wide as the range of experiences of the readers in the group.

SAMPLES OF EFFERENT (TEXT-BASED) QUESTIONS

1. What is the topic of the book? What do you know about this topic? What would you like to find out by reading this book?
2. Describe the setting for the story. Why do you think the author chose this setting?
3. Who are the main characters? What are their goals? their problems?
4. How did their problems arise? How did they solve their problems?

While the author and the text are important elements in the reading process, the reader's experiences, background knowledge, values, beliefs, intentions, and aspirations, as well as the context in which they are reading, are equally important. Louise Rosenblatt (1978) uses the term "poem" to explain what is created when individuals read a text. Every time a reader reads a text, a new poem is created—the reader has new experiences and will likely be in a new environment.

5. Why do you think the author chose to write from the point of view of _____?
6. What kind of person is _____ (character)? What did this person do or say to make you feel this way?

SAMPLES OF AESTHETIC (READER-BASED) QUESTIONS

1. What images are created in your mind as you read this story?
2. Who do you know who is like one of the characters? What is it about the character that reminds you of this person?
3. Should _____ (character) have done what she/he did? Why or why not?
4. What did you like and what did you dislike about this book?
5. Have you had a problem similar to the character's problem? How did you solve your problem?
6. Would you want to be in _____ (character's) position? Why or why not?

Written and Visual Responses

SHARED AND INTERACTIVE WRITING

Students in Kindergarten and Grade 1 will likely have much to say about the books they read or have read to them. Writing what they think and feel about the books might not be so easy. Often teacher support is needed to help emergent literacy learners use letters and words to write those responses. You can serve as a scribe, writing what the student says to demonstrate how print works. The formal term for this scribing is *shared writing*. The scribing can take place one-on-one, or you might write responses to literature that small groups or the whole class compose together. Along with writing, use this time to point out letter–sound relationships, word spacing, and the direction that the words go across the page.

Gay Su Pinnell and Irene Fountas (1996) worked with primary teachers to find a way to support emergent and early literacy learners who were in the initial stages of learning about print. Interactive writing was the outcome of their work. As in shared writing, teacher and students together compose responses to the literature they have read. In interactive writing, however, the teacher is not the only scribe. You take turns with individual students using a pen/marker to write the responses.

RESPONSE JOURNALS

Response journals are the visible form of students' thoughts about their reading. Sometimes students write as they are reading, and other times they wait until they have finished reading a section or chapter before they write. The process of writing down their thoughts helps students to clarify the meanings that they are making as they read. The written response also gives students a cue to remember their thinking when they participate in literature circles. Students can refer to what they have written to initiate their contributions to the discussions.

Students can respond to each other's journal responses using a format called a dialogue journal. While this written conversation has the potential to be very rich, most students prefer to talk to each other about their reflections on the book. When using a dialogue journal, students often write comments such as "I never thought of that," or "Great idea"; jottings that are very encouraging, but do not extend the student's thinking to any great degree. One way to get around this challenge is for you to be the other written conversation partner in dialogue journals. As a teacher, you can extend students' thinking as expressed in their journals by asking questions and writing your own personal connections to and perceptions of whatever the students have written. Dialogue journals between students and teachers can contribute immensely to students' learning. Reading the students' responses also gives you insight into students' meaning making as they read.

RESPONDING THROUGH MULTIMEDIA COMBINED WITH PRINT

Writing, when combined with video, photography, drawings, collage, sculpture, and any other visual art form, provides rich opportunities for students to create something tangible that represents what the literature means to them. The possibilities are as wide as your and your students' imaginations. Often, we introduce some types of written and visual products to raise students' awareness of the possible genres they might use. We then invite students to be creative in designing their own responses, thinking about choosing the design and the format that best suits their purpose. Sometimes we give students a choice between two or three projects, so that students can work with the media that give them inspiration to create something. Suggest alternatives to students who choose the same form repeatedly, however, so that they expand their repertoires.

Comprehension Assessment

Louise Rosenblatt's (1978) reader-response theory is helpful when assessing the content of students' responses to literature, whether the responses are written or oral. Lower-level responses tend to be restricted to plucking specific details from the text or leaping in huge bounds away from the text; in other words, responses are extremely text-bound, or so far removed from the text that one wonders if the text has been read. A number of researchers have come up with developmental frameworks that provide more specifics. For example, Thomson (1987) identified six process stages that start with the reader's unreflective interest in action, and move toward showing that the student empathizes with characters; can connect events, characters, themes, and actions; and can reflect on their significance.

More recently, Wilhelm (1997) developed a framework of 10 different dimensions of response that students use as they respond to literature. These dimensions are grouped into three categories: evocative, connective, and reflective. Evocative dimensions include

- preparing to read and think about what the reading will be like
- showing interest in the story
- relating to characters
- noticing clues for creating mental images.

The connective dimensions include

- building up clues to create meaning that fills in gaps in the story

• making explicit connections between personal experiences and story experiences.

The reflective dimensions include

• considering the significance of events and behavior to the overall story meaning,
• recognizing literary conventions,
• recognizing the choices authors make
• evaluating these choices in terms of the effectiveness of the story and their influence on the readers' identity construction.

Daniels (2002: 187) recommends literature discussion assessment tools, including open-ended, narrative observational notes, logs, and records; checklists; interviews/conferences and portfolios of students writing; response journals and other artifacts of students' responses to literature.

Students' ownership of and reflection on their learning are goals underpinning the peer- and self-assessment practices recommended by Evans (2001: 91). Students consider how well they cooperate with others in the group using criteria such as sitting in the circle, talking nicely and not arguing or fooling around, listening, not hurting others' feelings, reading the book, and staying with the group. They also assess their participation in the group using the following criteria: talking about the book, helping others in the group, giving opinions and rationales for the opinions, asking questions, responding to others' questions with reasonable answers, and giving details.

On pages 24–25 you will find an assessment tool that was developed in an action research study with Grade 8 teacher Michelle Belizaire. Michelle and Shelley developed the criteria by analyzing four discussions of each of four groups in Michelle's class. We found it useful to have spaces for check marks for a number of discussion group meetings, in order to get a picture of the student's contributions over an extended period of time. One checklist could be used to keep track of a student's contributions over a reporting period or throughout the school year. The checklist has criteria organized within the two overall categories: *Reading/Thinking Processes* and *Social Processes*. The criteria in parentheses are higher-level extensions of the criteria that immediately precede them.

Assessing Reading, Thinking, and Social Processes in Literature Discussion Groups

Name _____   Dates _____

Titles of Books Discussed: _____

Reading/Thinking Processes	Social Processes
Digs into the Book	**Negotiates Understandings**

❑ Identifies characters, their problems/conflicts, roles and actions
❑ Makes judgments about characters' actions
   ❑ (with support from the story/background social, cultural academic knowledge, and experiences/values, etc.)
❑ Infers sources of the characters' problems/conflicts and motivations for their actions
   ❑ (with support from the story/background social, cultural and academic knowledge, and experiences/values, etc.)
❑ Summarizes events
   ❑ with connections to overall theme of story)
❑ Describes setting and visual images created while reading
❑ Defines vocabulary with analogies, examples, attributes and functions drawn from book and from background knowledge
❑ Infers theme/what author wanted to say in book
❑ Predicts future events
   ❑ (using background knowledge about the topic and genre, story information, other books read, and personal experience)
	❑ Asks question about vocabulary or a part the student did not understand
	❑ Asks question about characters' motivations and influences on their actions/what student would have done in character's position
	❑ Asks question about accuracy and plausibility of context, actions and details in story and about gaps in the information provided
	❑ Provides evidence from story to clarify a peer's confusion
	❑ Restates what peer said to clarify
	❑ Challenges peer's ideas/assertions with question/statement about a gap, error or inconsistency
	   ❑ (with support from the story/background social, cultural academic knowledge, and experiences/values, etc.)
	❑ Builds on peers' contributions to negotiate understandings about events, characters' motivations, context, topic, related life issue, etc. by contributing general information, evidence from the story, interpretations and opinions, hypothetical and lived experiences, etc.

Notes/Quotes from Discussions	**Notes/Quotes from Discussions**

Reading/Thinking Processes	Social Processes
Makes Personal Connections ☐ Connects event/incident/character to personal experience/someone student knows ☐ Explains how student would act/feel in character's situation ☐ Expresses emotional response to actions/character/theme, etc.	**Builds Relationships** ☐ Affirms what peers have said (sometimes with a qualifier) ☐ Shows interest in peers' contributions by asking questions for more information or inviting elaboration or clarification ☐ Redirects topic when notices a peer or self being embarrassed ☐ Makes peers laugh by exaggerating, using irony, etc.
Evaluates/Extends ☐ Assesses book in one or two words ☐ Assesses parts/whole book with elaboration ☐ States belief/value related to events/themes in book ☐ Draws conclusion/makes generalization about how people interact, their choices and their motivations for their actions ☐ (showing social/emotional/psychological/political insight) ☐ Describes own reading processes while reading the book and how effective the author was in making the book readable and interesting ☐ Makes generalizations about how books of this genre are written and read (may make comparisons with other books of similar genre or books/movies, etc. that have other similarities)	**Moves the Discussion Forward** ☐ Initiates a conversation thread by asking a question ☐ Continues a conversation thread by responding to question ☐ Invites a particular student to contribute ☐ Asserts right to contribute ☐ Negotiates what to read in preparation for next discussion ☐ Invites/confirms closure of the discussion **Holds the Discussion Back** ☐ Puts down a peer ☐ Assesses a peer's contributions negatively ☐ Asks question/raises topic that embarrasses peer or puts peer on defensive ☐ Ignores peer's question/point and talks about another topic ☐ Tells peer what she/he should think or feel ☐ Interrupts peer ☐ Coerces peer into participating ☐ Refuses invitation to participate
Notes/Quotes from Discussions	**Notes/Quotes from Discussions**

(Published in "Literature Discussions and Assessment: Bringing Literary and Social Learning Together" *Ohio Journal of English Language Arts*, 48(1): 48–56)

Book Lists

Books for Reading Aloud

TO PRIMARY READERS: KINDERGARTEN–GRADE 2

Bryan, Sean (2005) *A boy and his bunny* (sequel: *A girl and her gator*). One morning, a boy wakes and discovers a bunny on his head. He convinces his mother that the rabbit would be worth keeping because of all the things they can do together.

Burningham, John (2006) *Edwardo: The horriblest boy in the whole wide world.* Edward's behavior grows from bad to worse—until he accidentally does good deeds that get him many compliments.

Cronin, Doreen (2003) *Click, clack, moo: Cows that type* (also: *Thump, quack, moo: a whacky adventure; Giggle, giggle, quack; Duck for president*). When he refuses to comply with their demands, Farmer Brown's cows decide to take action.

Cousins, Lucy (2002) *Jazzy in the jungle.* A baby lemur plays hide and seek with Mama Jojo. Cut-pages and liftable flaps invite participation as readers investigate the world forest fauna and wild creatures.

Grant, Joan (2005) *Cat and fish* (sequel: *Cat and fish go to see*). The adventures of an unlikely pair, from different worlds, who discover that new experiences can bring many pleasures.

Niemann, Christoph (2008) *The pet dragon: A story about adventure, friendship and Chinese characters.* A young Chinese girl searching for her pet dragon meets a witch who helps her with her quest. A bonus feature of this picture book are the Chinese calligraphy characters on each page.

Prelutsky, Jack (1986) *Read-aloud rhymes for the very young.* A collection of more than 200 short poems by both known and anonymous American and British authors.

To Young Readers: Grades 3–5

Avi (2004) *The end of the beginning: Being the adventures of a small snail (and an even smaller ant).* (sequel: *A beginning, a muddle and an end*). A modern fable about a young snail who is convinced that having adventures is the key to a happy life.

Babbitt, Natalie (2007) *Jack Plank tells tales.* When Jack Plank is dismissed from his pirate ship. he sets off to find himself a new job.

Browne, Anthony (2004) *Into the forest.* After his father disappears, a young boy travels through the forest in order to take a cake to his sick grandmother.

Cumyn, Alan (2002) *The secret life of Owen Skye* (sequels: *After Sylvia; Dear Sylvia*). An episodic story of three brothers who keep themselves entertained with a number of wacky adventures.

DiCamillo, Kate (2006) *The miraculous journey of Edward Tulane* (also: *The Tale of Desperaux*). A proud rabbit who loves himself is separated from the little girl who owns him. In his travels he acquires new owners and listens to their histories, their hopes, and their dreams.

Crossley-Holland, Kevin (2000) *Enchantment: Fairy tales, ghost stories and tales of wonder.* A collection of folk and fairy tales, silly, magical, and scary.

Lester, Julius (2005) *Let's talk about race.* In this autobiographical picture book, the author helps readers explore what makes each of us special.

Lowry, Lois (2008) *The Willoughbys.* The four Willhoughby children set out to become "deserving orphans" after their neglectful parents embark on a treacherous around-the-world adventure.

McBratney, Sam (2005/2008) *One voice, please: Favourite read-aloud stories.* There are more than 30 stories in this collection, each taking a few minutes to read out loud imparting bits of wisdom and much amusement.

McLeod, Bob (2006) *Superheroes ABC.* Twenty-six superhero characters are introduced to readers in colorful comic format.

Polacco, Patricia (1998) *Thank you, Mr. Falker* (also: *Chicken Sunday; The keeping quilt; Mr. Lincoln's way*). Trisha loves school until she reaches fifth grade, when her difficulties learning to read make her feel inadequate. A caring teacher gives the young girl support and helps her to overcome her problems.

Scieszka, Jon (1998) *Squids will be squids.* A humorous twist on the world of fables.

Steig, William (1985) *Abel's island.* A mouse is separated from his wife during a terrible storm. In his new life, Abel learns to conquer many challenges and gains insight into his own true self.

Yolen, Jane (1987) *Owl moon.* Late one winter full-mooned night, a young girl and her father trek into the woods to see the Great Horned Owl

Wild, Margaret (2001) *Fox.* Dog and Magpie are friends, but when sly Fox enters the bush, friendship, loyalty, and betrayal are put to the test.

To Older Readers: Grades 6–8

Almond, David (1998) *Skellig.* Michael's world changes when he steps into a crumbling garage and encounters what seems to be a human being, or strange kind of beast.

Bunting, Eve (2001) *Riding the tiger* (also: *Smoky night*). Bored and lonely, Danny hops climbs on the back of a scary tiger who offers him a ride.

Gaiman, Neil (2003) *The wolves in the walls.* Lucy can hear wolves hustling and haunting, crawling and crackling in the walls of the old house where her family lives. This book has been described as being the "stuff of nightmares."

Crossley-Holland, Kevin (2005) *The Outsiders.* A collection of tales that depict communities that encounter an outsider in their midst, some strange, some wild.

Howe, James (2003) *Thirteen.* Thirteen stories that capture the agony and ecstasy of being 13 years old.

Janeczko, Paul (2002) *Seeing the blue between: Advice and inspiration for young poets.* Sample selections, along with advice on writing poetry, from thirty-two renowned poets.

Muth, Jon (2002) *The three questions.* Based on story by Leo Tolstoy, Nikolai asks his animal friends the answer to three important questions.

Nichol, Barbara (2006) *The Tales of Don Quixote (Books 1 and 2).* Barbara Nichol retells stories written by Miguel de Cervantes four centuries ago.

Rylant, Cynthia (2006) *Ludie's life.* The powerful story, told through a series of poems, of one woman's experiences in a mining town in West Virginia.

Yolen, Jane (1998) *Here there be ghosts* (also: *Here there be witches; Here there be dragons; Here there be unicorns; Here there be angels*). A collection of stories, interspersed with poetry, by master storyteller Jane Yolen.

Drama Resources

Baldwin, P., & Fleming, K. (2003) *Teaching literacy through drama.* London, UK: RoutledgeFalmer.

Barton, B. (2000) *Telling stories your way: Storytelling and reading aloud in the classroom.* Markham, ON: Pembroke.

Booth, D. (2005) *Story drama: Creating stories through role playing, improvising, and reading aloud.* Markham, ON: Pembroke.

Booth, D. & Barton, B. (2000) *Story works: How teachers can use shared stories in the new curriculum.* Markham, ON: Pembroke.

Dickinson, R. & Neelands, J. (2006) *Improve your primary school through drama.* London, UK: David Fulton Publishers.

Miller, S. & Saxton, J. (2004) *Into the story.* Portsmouth, NH: Heinemann.

Swartz, L. (2002) *The new dramathemes.* Markham, ON: Pembroke.

Children's Book References

DiCamillo, Kate (2000) *Because of Winn-Dixie.*

Sidman, Joyce (2005) *Song of the water boatman and other pond poems.*

Slavin, Bill (2005) *Transformed: How everyday things are made.*

CHAPTER 2   Poetry

> In our fast-paced, "instant everything" world, we need poetry. It helps children and adults to ponder, to observe, to ask questions, to discover sights, sounds, and feelings that otherwise might remain untapped. It brings balance and beauty to our increasingly complex world. Poetry can awaken our senses or bring the element of surprise into our lives. It makes us laugh, teaches us powerful lessons, and renews our souls.   (Harrison & Holderith, 2003: 6)

Poetry—including nursery rhymes, songs, jingles, word play, and riddles—is often children's first genre. From a very early age, poetry accompanies or is central to children's playful interactions with adults and other children. Of all genres, poetry is also likely to be

> the most ancient. The religious and ceremonial chants of primitive people constituted the earliest poems; in cultures with written languages, major poets have generally appeared before major prose writers; and children's earliest vocal responses are often rhythmic and singsong. (Stott, 1984: 224)

First in children's lives, earliest of literary genres, and first in our hearts, we have placed poetry ahead of the other genre chapters in this book.

There is no straightforward way to define poetry. Carl Leggo (2003: 97) tells us that "a poem is written out of engagement with the world and engagement with words." Verbs seem to be important when defining poetry: David Booth and Bill Moore (2003: 24, 26, 11) rely on verbs when they tell us that "poems paint pictures" and "make ears sing." Poems also "deepen an everyday happening or an ordinary experience and make us see it through a magnifying glass, somehow broadening the experience. . . [Poetry] appeals to both thought and feeling, and has the power to call up rich sensory images in the reader and evoke deep emotional responses." The meanings and images created in poetry go beyond what is possible when gathering words together into the sentences of prose.

Along with verbs, poetry can be defined by explaining where we can find it: "where life hangs out" (Wooldridge, 1996: 4). Poetry appears in expected and unexpected places in every corner of our lives; in jingles in television ads, in the songs that we hear on the radio or sing in the shower, in children's skipping songs or playground games and taunts, in jokes and riddles, and in cards we send to others for special occasions. Along with not being fussy about where it shows up in everyday life, poetry is not particular about the topics it takes up. From the lofty to the mundane, no topic is beyond the reach of poetry. Yet there is nothing ordinary about poetry: Johnson, Sickel, Sayers and Horovitz (1977:

161) tell us that the "age-old glories" of poetry are constant throughout the centuries: "the poet's vision beyond our own, the intensified and distilled emotion, the new dimensions given to words we thought we knew."

In this chapter, we present criteria for selecting poetry and then introduce recommended nursery rhyme collections, classic poetry collections, general poetry collections, poetry that is humorous and celebrates everyday life experiences and themes, poetry that highlights the natural world, classics, multicultural poetry, and poetry that features particular poetry forms. The chapter ends with teaching ideas and questions to stimulate your thinking about teaching poetry in K–8 classrooms.

See Appendix B for more on awards for children's poetry.

Selecting Poetry

Criteria for Selecting Poetry

In a study (Strenski & Esposito, 1980), college students were asked to define poetry. Sadly, most of the students in the study focused on the importance of rhythm, rhyme, and punctuation when defining poetry. Emotions, vision, engagement, painting images, making ears sing—these did not enter into the college students' perceptions of poetry. Furthermore, when students were asked to explain what makes a good poem, they said that the more difficult a poem was to understand, the better the poem!

How impenetrable the poetry is *should not* be a criterion for selecting poetry for your students. Instead, we recommend following Ann Terry's (1984) suggestions, based on a national survey of upper elementary children's poetry preferences. The first is that children are the best judges of what they like and they will not likely recognize the literary merit in poetry in the same way that judges of poetry awards might. Also, teachers should keep in mind that children's preferences change across grades, and there are often gender differences in their preferences. New poems tend to be preferred over poems that have been created in the distant past, though the poems in the Classics section of this chapter that have been republished with contemporary illustrators certainly put the lie to this consideration. Thoughtful, meditative poems tend not to be enjoyed as much as humorous and raucous poems about familiar experiences. The final consideration is likely apparent to all: if children cannot make sense of a poem, they are unlikely to enjoy it.

In addition to these considerations, we have drawn from the criteria for the National Council of Teachers of English Award for Poetry for Children to create a list of five features to guide your poetry selections.

EXCITES THE IMAGINATION AND STIRS FRESH INSIGHTS

Children and adults alike enjoy reading something that stimulates our imagination and shows us something new about ourselves and/or our world. We believe that all of the poetry we highlight in this chapter is fresh and insightful, but feature Ashley Bryan's first book of original poetry that he also illustrated, *Sing to the Sun: Poems and Pictures*, a Lee Bennett Hopkins Award winner. In his poem, "Pretty Is," for example, the beauty of a flower cannot be captured by just saying it is pretty, but rather in this way that gives us a new way to think about "pretty."

Pretty is
How good I feel
When I see it
And say it.

In another example, children benefit from the affectionate and meticulous eyes through which both poet Joyce Sidman and illustrator Beckie Prange have observed the drama of a pond in the Lee Bennett Hopkins Poetry Award winner and Caldecott Honor book, *Song of the Water Boatman and other Pond Poems*. The book's fresh insights lie in bringing science and poetry together with a slight touch of whimsy.

SHOWS CREATIVITY IN USE OF LANGUAGE, SYNTAX, AND FORMAT

Creativity is expected in poetry. It shows up in the ways that words are put together for meaning and for sound, as well as their arrangement on the page. Playing with sounds and rhythms is the forte of William New in *Llamas in the Laundry*, illustrated with Vivian Bevis's cartoon watercolors. A poem about tickling a porcupine and other creatures with rhythmic names, such as a barnacle bug, dances on the tongue, as does a rhythmic list of Canadian place names alongside the days of the week in "Everyday Weekday", ending with: "North Bay Little Bay Saguenay Sunday." The poem for which the book is named plays with the spellings of words with "l": "Lamas in the llaundry/Llamas in the llane."

Award-winning book and magazine designer John Grandits plays with font and form in *Technically, It's Not My Fault*, a book of concrete poems in red, white, and black. These poems are not for the rigid right-to-left, top-to- bottom reader. The words in "My Stupid Day," for example, follow the clock's hands, showing the neverending pattern of each school day from morning to night. In "Skateboard," an example of adolescent ironies, the words lift, cut, and figure-eight in skateboard style, ending with a warning that there's no skateboarding allowed in the parking lot or in the park. With each turn of the page, readers find an innovative twist on expectations for how words, fonts, illustrations, and page layouts can come together to create something refreshingly new and original.

CREATES SHARP, NEW IMAGES

David Booth and Bill Moore (2003: 24) explain that "poets paint pictures with words, as painters do with color and shape." In American Kristine O'Connell George's *The Great Frog Race and Other Poems*, a Lee Hopkins Bennett Award winner readers can see the "Evening Rain" through O'Connell George's words: The porch light shines on rain / Taking thin silken stitches."

This does not mean that only descriptive poetry is good poetry. The images of any topic can be very sharply etched into readers' minds through poets' artful use of language. For example, readers have a vivid image of the lawn mowing handiwork of a "girl failing geometry" in Jane O'Wayne's "In Praise of Zigzags" (in Rosenberg, 1996: 181) as she leaves, along with the lawnmower out of its shed, "a trail of unmown strips and crisscrosses,/her scribbling on the lawn/like a line of thought that's hard to follow."

TOUCHES READERS' EMOTIONS

Poetry is not written simply to stimulate images and show off poets' artistry with language. It is written to evoke emotional responses to the natural and human-created world. Like all good writing, poetry says something that matters. Jean Little shows extraordinary humanity and gentle humor in a book of free-verse poems sprinkled with a few short narratives, *Hey World, Here I Am!* This combination evokes tender and joyful emotional response from readers. We find out that Kate was "being angelic" when she made snow angels alongside a younger girl who had just discovered snow angels, arriving home soaked to the skin because she was not wearing a snowsuit in "About Angels and Age." In "Louisa," Kate shows unconditional love for a friend's baby sister, telling her: "I love you right now, Louisa, before you know anything/Before you even know that you are Louisa." The poems do not drip with sentimentalism, but instead touch readers' emotions through their honesty and their keen sensitivity to young girls' experiences and perspectives.

PRESENTS UNIVERSAL IDEAS THAT RESONATE WITH TODAY'S CHILDREN

Poetry appeals to the musical ear of children, with its lively rhythms and, in many cases, rhymes. It also appeals to children's hearts, with themes that speak to the essence of children's experience and imagination, and often tickle their funny bone. The timelessness of T.S. Eliot's *Old Possum's Book of Practical Cats* is evident in its continuous reprinting across the decades and its role as the libretto of the popular Andrew Lloyd Weber musical *Cats*.

Similarly, the poetry of Shel Silverstein in *Where the Sidewalk Ends* and *Light in the Attic*, written decades ago, still resonates with children in today's classrooms. When we invite teachers to talk about a favorite book of poetry, one or both of these two books is at the top of most of their lists. Guffaws, chuckles, nods, gags, *hmm*s, and *aha*s follow in the wake of a reading of Silverstein's poetry. There is no subject too mundane, too profound, too silly, too serious, or too off-limits for a Silverstein poem: from putting one's sister "For Sale," to a "Me-Stew" served with crackers when there is nothing in the cupboard to make a stew, to spelling out what love is in "Love" when the classmates holding the other letters cannot make it and all that's left is the child holding "V" who is "all of love that could make it today." Silverstein's black-and-white drawings are both the poem and a complement to the poem—poet and illustrator as one person makes for a close symbiosis between words and illustrations.

Carrying on in the tradition of Shel Silverstein, Jack Prelutsky has created a series of black-and-white anthologies, with drawings by James Stevenson, serving a banquet of poems to amuse and ponder. Young readers can open any page of *It's The New Kid on the Block, Something Big Has Been Here,* or *My Dog May be a Genius,* and will likely think about things they may have not have before. We can taste wacky concoctions, such as "Salamander Salmon Slug/ Bat Begonia Barley Bug" at "Gloppe's Soup Shoppe"; we can meet strange characters such as Herman Sherman Thurman, who is "perfect… that's a fact,/ No matter the activity,/ I'm thorough and exact" and Swami Gourami "one of a kind,/ unlocking the past/ with my mystical mind"; we can find weird pets, such as a three-thousand pound cat, a bedraggled gerbil, or a dromedary in a garage "wearing camel-flage"—all in *Pizza the Size of the Sun.*

Douglas Florian is another poet who carries the Silverstein torch. He has won the Lee Bennett Hopkins Poetry Award for his work, which includes a series of books celebrating the animal kingdom (*Beast Feast* and *Lizards, Frogs and Polliwogs*) and a quartet of books that celebrates the four seasons (*Summersaults, Winter Eyes, Autumnblings,* and *Handsprings*). According to Douglas, there is only one rule to follow when writing poetry: There are no rules.

Poetry for Children

Nursery Rhymes as Poetry

We engaged in a tug-of-war when deciding where in this book to include nursery rhymes. They are unquestionably traditional literature; however, when we talk about nursery rhymes, we use the language of poetry. The nursery rhymes seemed to be more at home with other poetry, so we let them stay here.

When selecting nursery rhyme collections, consider the number of verses in the rhymes, and whether there is a mix of well-known rhymes with new and unusual ones. The appeal of the illustrations and how well they elaborate the text are also important considerations. Finally, take into account whether there is a sense of unity to the book, with a thematic arrangement of the verses, or whether they seem to be scattered willy-nilly across the pages.

Ask most adults to recite the first poem that comes to mind and it is likely to be a nursery rhyme. The rhymes that we learn as young children ride along with us throughout our lives. Mother Goose nursery rhymes are part of many English-speaking children's playful interactions with adults; for example, the clapping song, "Pat-a-cake, pat-a-cake, baker's man, Bake me a cake as fast as you can," has been played out with countless young children across the ages.

The content of nursery rhymes is of the everyday; their story lines are short and easy to follow. The musical rhythms and rhymes make them easy to remember. Nursery rhymes are enjoyable to repeat again and again, with clapping and playing that go along with them. These rhymes provide engaging language models for children at a time when they are learning new concepts and playing with the words that describe their world.

Two notable Canadian nursery rhyme books include those of Kady MacDonald Denton and Barbara Reid, both renowned illustrators of children's books. Ink and watercolor illustrations accompany the rhymes in Kady MacDonald Denton's *A Child's Treasury of Nursery Rhymes*. Arranged in four sections, the book begins with familiar verses of discovery for babies (e.g., lullabies and playtime rhymes); it continues with rhymes that follow the pattern of a toddler's day; then it moves into playground chants, verses, and nonsense rhymes; and it ends with rhymes for older children. MacDonald Denton closes the book with Edward Lear's "The Owl and the Pussy-Cat," one of her childhood favorites. In Barbara Reid's *Sing a Song of Mother Goose*, her signature clay illustrations raise the nursery-rhyme characters off the page. The familiar cast of Mother Goose figures is here: Mary and her lamb, Tommy Tucker, Mother Hubbard, Simple Simon, Old King Cole, the old woman in a shoe, and many others.

American nursery rhyme collections of note are Bobbye S. Goldstein's *Mother Goose on the Loose*, Tomie de Paola's *Mother Goose*, and Iona and Peter Opie's *The Oxford Dictionary of Nursery Rhyme*. In Goldstein's book, cheeky cartoons from *The New Yorker* accompany the traditional verses. Tomie de Paola's book, illustrated with brilliant tones and diverse cultural representation of characters, has more than 200 verses, several presented on full spreads. A brand new edition of *the* classic anthology of nursery rhymes, *The Oxford Dictionary of Nursery Rhymes* includes more than 500 rhymes, songs, nonsense jingles, and lullabies for young children. With each piece, Iona and Peter Opie introduce a wealth of information, noting the earliest known publications of the rhyme, describing how it originated, illustrating changes in wording over time, and indicating variations and parallels in other languages. Including reproductions of early art found in ballad sheets and music books, the nearly 100 illustrations highlight the development of children's illustrations over the last two centuries. For this second edition, the notes have been updated and extended in light of recent scholarship. Iona Opie is also the editor of two companion treasures illustrated by Rosemary Wells. *My Very First Mother* Goose and *Here Comes Mother Goose* offer a parade of best-loved nursery rhymes written in bold clear font and illustrated with Wells signature animal characters. Artists Charles Addams, Michael Foreman, Arnold Lobel, and Helen Oxenbury add to the wide spectrum of illustrators of Mother Goose rhymes.

Collections of rhymes from other languages and other lands reveal that engaging young children with language playfully through rhymes is part of family interactions everywhere. Alma Flor Ada and F. Isabel Campoy's *!Pio Peep!: Traditional Spanish Nursery Rhymes* is a bilingual collection of traditional Spanish and Latin American nursery rhymes. The English translations have been reworked so that the verses rhyme. In another Spanish bilingual book, the translations are literal: Margot Griego teams up with noted illustrator and author Barbara Cooney to create *Tortillitas Para Mama*, with Latin American rhymes collected from Spanish-speaking communities in the Americas. Cooney illustrates this dual-language book with authentic settings. Traditional rhymes and riddles selected and edited by Robert Wyndham are written in blue Chinese characters along the side of Ed Young's pebbly illustrations in *Chinese Mother Goose Rhymes*. The English translations are in verse form under the illustrations.

The rhymes of childhood do not all come from the cradleside. In *Doctor Knickerbocker and Other Rhymes*, David Booth has gathered together the folk poetry of childhood: chants, skipping rhymes, jingles, riddles, sayings and superstitions, taunts and teases, tongue twisters, jokes, and other verses of contemporary childhood, along with those of previous generations and long ago. Maryann Kovalski illustrates the book with delightful woodcuts and pen-and-ink drawings.

Classics

Timelessness is certainly a criterion that can be applied to the poetry in this section. The featured poetry has been reprinted many times, as parents and teachers continue to buy them for the children in their lives.

FOR YOUNGER READERS

The familiar phrase, "'Twas the night before Christmas,/when all through the house/not a creature was stirring,/not even a mouse," has been with us since *A Visit from St. Nicholas* was published anonymously in 1823 in the Troy, New York, newspaper. Its author, Clement Moore, later acknowledged his authorship. The first major work of poetry published for children, this poem has been reprinted in a multitude of forms, including a version illustrated by Jan Brett with her signature borders, a board book with illustrations compiled by Cooper Edens, and another illustrated by Matt Tavares, in which the original language, spelling, and punctuation are used.

The poetry of Edward Lear has been part of children's lives since the 19th century, as well. His *Book of Nonsense* contains the four-line limericks associated with Lear, about many an "old man" or "young lady," often from a particular city or country, with quirky behavior or remarkable physical characteristics. The book also contains alphabet rhymes, ballads (such as the well-loved "The Owl and the Pussycat") and other verses.

Classic poetry of the early 20th century for young children includes A.A. Milne's *When we Were Very Young* and *Now We are Six*. A.A. Milne assures readers in *Now We Are Six* that the "name of the book doesn't mean that this is us being six all the time, but that is about as far as we've got at present, and we half think of stopping there." The poems are told from the perspective of a young boy growing up in upper class England in the early 20th century, and many may not resonate with children in today's classrooms. But there are some whimsical, timeless poems, such as "Sneezles", where the adults in Christopher Robin's life confine him to bed and wonder: "If wheezles/Could turn/Into measles,/If sneezles/Would turn/Into mumps." Winnie the Pooh makes an appearance in verse in "Us Two," and throughout the book in Ernest H. Shepard's etchings (identified as "decorations" on the book's cover).

In *The Oxford Illustrated Book of American Children's Poems*, Donald Hall, author of Caldecott Award-winning picture book *The Ox-Cart Man*, brings the child-friendly work of renowned poets whose work is usually directed toward an adult audience—Emily Dickinson, e.e. cummings, Ralph Waldo Emerson, Robert Frost, T.S. Eliot, and Langston Hughes—together with the work of poets familiar to children—Eve Merriam, X.J. Kennedy, Jack Prelutsky, Nikki Giovanni, Sandra Cisneros, and Karla Kuskin. This collection begins with an anonymous Native American "Chant to the Fire-Fly" and moves chronologically from poetry such as John Godfrey Saxe's "The Blind Men and the Elephant" from the late 19th century, to humorous classics such as Shel Silverstein's "Sarah Cynthia Sylvia Stout Would Not Take the Garbage Out" from the late 20th century. The illustrations include archival selections from rare and early editions of children's magazines, recreating the tenor of the times in which the poetry was written.

FOR OLDER READERS

Lewis Carroll's nonsense classic *Jabberwocky* has been given two modern-day interpretations to engage readers who might not readily come to poetry. Artist Christopher Myers takes the pages of this poem from *Through the Looking Glass* and puts them onto the basketball courts in an urban setting. Illustrator Stéphane Jorisch interprets the poem using Governor General's Award- winning pencil, ink, watercolor, and digital drawings in the Visions in Poetry series from Kids Can Press. The mock-heroic ballad is written with portmanteau words (two words packed into one word with hints of both the sounds and the meanings in the new word), such as "slithy," a pairing of "slimy" and "lithe." Jorisch's Jabberwock is a creature of nature, slain by a young man in soldier garb in a stark, Orwellian, über-industrial world devoid of natural beauty. Ubiquitous television cameras picture a military man warning, "Beware the Jabberwock." The young man rids the world of the Jabberwock, but the world does not become a better one—the "borogoves" continue to be "all mimsy" and the "mome raths" continued to "outgrabe."

Another award winner in this series is Alfred, Lord Tennyson's *The Lady of Shalott* with illustrations by Geneviève Côté. The soft blues, greens, golds, and burnt siennas and the flowing lines of water color illustrations are true to the romantic imagery of the poem. In sketchy, modernist art, medieval passersby mix with more contemporary ones traveling toward Camelot's high-rise skyline by horse or automobile. Côté uses a metamorphosis metaphor to show the Lady's escape from imprisonment in the tower through death. The illustrations garnered an Elizabeth Mrazik-Cleaver Canadian Picture Book Award.

Robert Service's *The Creation of Sam McGee* was a *New York Times* Best Illustrated Children's Book of the Year. This ballad about a Tennessee man, spellbound by the North, yet ever griping about the cold, swoops along in a spirited rhythm. From the first line, which promises that there are "strange things done in the midnight sun," to the close of the tale, where Sam's corpse comes to life in the heat of the fire meant to cremate his body, there is a rollicking adventurous humor in the writing. Canadian Ted Harrison uses bold chartreuse, blue, yellow, and orange woodblock-style illustrations to convey the spirit and the beauty of the north.

Other highly recommended books from the KidsCan series are Alfred Noyes's *The Highwayman*, where illustrator Murray Kimber interprets the highwayman as a Harley Davidson-driving robber being tracked by FBI agents; Ernest L. Thayer's *Casey at the Bat*, illustrated by Joe Morse with a modern setting and angular characters in blue and grey hues; and Edward Lear's *The Owl and the Pussycat*, illustrated with Stéphane Jorisch's characteristic playful and fantastic images. Each book ends with a discussion of the poetry and a number of perspectives on their meanings, and the illustrators' explanations of their visual interpretations of the poetry.

Poetry Collections

The poetry collections in this section offer a taste of many poets' work, often organized in themed sections. The person who has gathered the poetry together has done much of the work for teachers—selecting notable poets and their best work—so it is important to identify the collector's qualifications to determine their knowledge of children's poetry. All of the collections identified in this textbook have been gathered by highly regarded poets for children and academics recognized for their work with children's literature.

FOR YOUNGER READERS

The ABC Children's Booksellers Choices Award winning *The 20th Century Children's Poetry Treasury*, compiled by Jack Prelutsky, contains more than 200 poems by 137 poets (mostly American) such as John Ciardi, Georgia Heard, Langston Hughes, Karla Kuskin, Joyce Carol Thomas, and Eve Merriam, with Canadians Jean Little and Dennis Lee, and the British Roald Dahl and A.A. Milne. A riot of poems is knit together by Meilo So's expressive watercolors and by theme on each two-page spread. Themes are wide ranging, from food (including Dennis Lee's "Alligator Pie": "If I don't get some I think I'm gonna die"), and people (e.g., Ogden Nash's "The People Upstairs" whose "living room is a bowling alley") to seasons (e.g., in Marilyn Singer's "April is a Dog's Dream" when there are "no excuses now, we're going to the park").

Paul Janeczko paired poems by highly-regarded American poets on topics ranging from mosquitoes to skyscrapers in *Hey, You!* Emily Dickinson, for example, takes a fly's perspective in "Bee, I'm Expecting You!" while Nikki Grimes advises a bee to "leave me alone, drone/Show yourself the door"; Robert Rayevsky's watercolors fill the two-page spread with bees buzzing in a flower garden and around a young boy's head. The presentation of two perspectives on a topic makes this book stand out from other poetry collections.

Bernice Cullinan, noted children's literature expert, brought together ten NCTE Award winners in her collection *A Jar of Tiny Stars*. This book truly is a "Who's Who" of American children's poets: David McCord, Myra Cohn Livingston, Aileen Fisher, Eve Merriam, Karla Kuskin, John Ciardi, Lilian Moore, Valerie Worth, Arnold Adoff, and Barbara Esbensen. Readers are introduced to the poets through Marc Nadel's black-and-white portraits, short biographies, quotes from each about how they write, and their thoughts on poetry. Of course, their poetry says as much about them as any of the above, and a bibliography of each poet's published collections invites readers to "bite in" to as many poems as we can find, to borrow Eve Merriam's explanation of "How to Eat a Poem." Andi MacLeod's realistic pen-and-ink drawings complement the poems, usually appearing alongside or under the words.

The misfortune of being responsible for the winning run for the *other* team in a baseball game (Joy N. Humlem's "Play Ball") and the tragedy of a pet rabbit's death (Madeleine Comora's "Winger Rabbit") are topics in Lee Bennett Hopkins's edited collection *Oh, No! Where are my Pants and other Disasters: Poems.* Well-known writers, such as Karla Kuskin, Marilyn Singer, Judith Viorst, and Lee Bennett Hopkins himself, write sensitively and with kind-hearted humor about the small and large hardships in children's lives. The eyes, eyebrows, mouth, and body movements of Germany's Wolf Erlbruch's cartoon characters convey the range of emotions associated with everyday disasters.

The lively rhythms, delightful humor, and thoughtful observations of everyday life characterize Jack Prelutsky's poetry and brought him to prominence as the USA's first Children's Poet Laureate. *In Aunt Giraffe's Green Garden*, with watercolors by Petra Mathers, captures settings from Denver and Idaho to Maine and the Everglades.

Author and educator David Booth has collected *Til All the Stars Have Fallen: Canadian Poems for Children*, a one-of-a-kind collection of poetry from Canadian writers known around the world, such as Dennis Lee, Tim Wynne-Jones, Jean Little, and Margaret Atwood, and from other beloved Canadian poets, such as sean o'huigan, George Swede, Fran Newman, and Emily Hearn. Arranged by theme, the collection includes poetry that "sings to the ears," that "whistles in the dark," and that tells "all my secrets." Many poems evoke smiles, as in sean o'huigan's "Yawn" where the words ebb in one- and two-word phrases up and down the page, proposing that it would be hard to keep fights going if people yawned just as they were about to be punched in the face. Other poems bring new awareness of ordinary and extraordinary things, as in Emily Hearn's "Courage," where courage takes the form of saying "no" to an invitation to a sleepover by a friend with a cat when you have allergies to cats. Kady MacDonald Denton's illustrations capture the imagery using media that changes according to the poem—from soft watercolor to bold collage.

Readers come to know poets and their poetry in anthologies that feature commentaries by the poets to accompany their work. *Seeing the Blue Between*, compiled by Paul B. Janeczko, offers advice and inspiration in letters and short essays written to the reader by each poet. Similarly, Janeczko has selected poems on a number of themes in *The Place My Words Are Looking For*, in which poets such as Siv Cedering, Eve Merriam, and Naomi Shihab Nye describe how they came to write the poem included in the book. Liz Rosenberg's edited collection, *Invisible Ladder: An Anthology of Contemporary American Poems for Young Readers*, was a Claudia Lewis Award winner. Short commentaries about links between poetry and childhood in their writing and their lives, along with photographs of each poet, give readers a sense of who the poets are. The diverse group of 38 poets includes Robert Bly, Rita Dove, Martín Espada, Allen Ginsberg, Li-Young Lee, and Nikki Giovanni. The poems range in subject from the power of love, to *Tires Stacked in the Hallways of Civilization* (Martín Espada's poem about a new immigrant tenant who must remove those stacked tires, but is allowed to keep his rodent-controlling cat), to the mysteries of math (from Kyoko Mori's *Barbie Says Math is Hard*: "If x equals y,/is it like putting apples into/cole slaw, the way a tomato/is really a fruit?"). A section called "Ways to Use this Book" precedes biographical notes on the poets. Rosenberg's goal of making contemporary poems written for adults accessible to young adults has succeeded admirably in this collection.

Jan Greenberg commissioned 43 distinguished poets to write poetry inspired by paintings, lithographs, sculpture, mixed media, and photographs representing artistic movements of the 20th century, including American modernism, abstract expressionism, and pop art. The dramatically beautiful and exciting result is *Heart to Heart: New Poems Inspired by Twentieth-Century American Art*. Organized into four sections, the poems conjure a memory or tell an anecdote (stories), take the voice of the object or person depicted in the artwork (voices), examine and comment on elements of the artwork (impressions), and explore aspects of visual form (expressions). Full-page reproductions of the artworks are set alongside free-verse poems, sonnets, rhymed poems, and poetry with experimental forms written by Jane Yolen, Deborah Chandra, Kristine O'Connell George, Angela Johnson, X.J. Kennedy, Constance Levy, Naomi Shihab Nye, Brenda Seabrooke, Nancy Willard, and many others. Biographical notes on the poets and on the artists follow the poetry, with a helpful index of poets, artists, and first lines at the end of the book.

Humor and Everyday Life

Much contemporary poetry for children is light-hearted and playful, incorporating the "oral traditions of playground verse and the cadences of Mother Goose" (Booth & Moore, 2003: 18). The poems in this section bring out the humor in the small and big parts of children's lives.

FOR YOUNGER CHILDREN

We considered including Dennis Lee's *Garbage Delight* (published again with *Another Helping*) in the Classics section because it is so well-known and loved by children and adults alike. Illustrated with Maryanne Kovalski's pencil crayon and watercolors, the collection includes humorous tales, such as "I Eat Kids Yum Yum!" about a girl, not cowed by a mighty monster, who "chomped and t[ook] a chew"; and the poem "Garbage Delight," about one whose talents were wasted "Until I had tasted/ The wonders of Garbage Delight." Children delight in Lee's naughty poem, which flirts with ideas that many children may have considered but would never carry out, about "The Bratty Brother" who was mailed "to a jail in Moosonee" after he had survived every other effort to get rid of him. Another collection, *Bubblegum Delicious*, entertains young readers with its sing-song rhythm and rhyme ("Bubblegum delicious/ Bubblegum delight/ Bubblegum de-lovely in the / middle of the night") and thoughts to ponder ("If lonesome was a pot of gold/ I'd be a millionaire").

Like *Garbage Delight*, another of Dennis Lee's classic books of poetry, *Alligator Pie*, was a Canadian Book of the Year for Children. The rhythms and tongue-tickling rhymes of "Rattlesnake Skipping Song"—"Mississauga rattlesnakes/Eat brown bread./Mississauga rattlesnakes/fall down dead"—have become part of the fabric of children's play in Canadian homes and playgrounds. Lee finds the zing in Canadian place names (e.g., "In Kamloops" and "Kahshe or Chicoutimi") and even in former Prime Minister's names ("William Lyon Mackenzie King"). Frank Newfeld's round-faced drawings are not as lively and bright as the poetry, but they provide some color to each page. All who have ever been introduced to this delightful collection will agree with the sentiment, that you can "Give away the green grass, give away the sky/but don't give away my *Alligator Pie*."

Loris Lesynski's *Cabbagehead*, illustrated in ink, colored pencil, and watercolor cartoons, begins with a plea for a "brain that's brilliant [and] a head that hums" as she accepts that "sometimes I'm a cabbagehead." The opening poem sets up the book for a search for ideas and poems about questions that she is curious about (e.g., "Does my blood taste as good to mosquitoes as pie?") Lesynski has a good time with repeated sounds in poems such as "Below Below Baloney," Nuts and Bolts" with "mutts and molts," and tongue twisters such as "Jazzy Cabbage" where a desire to "camouflage a cabbage" in words is preferred over eating "cabbage fudge." Loris Lesynski also wrote and illustrated *Nothing Beats a Pizza*, this time using a bit of tomato sauce and eye shadow, in addition to watercolors, as her media. Pizza, pets, and school realities are the topics of the 32 poems in this book. Introduced by an invitation to read aloud the poems so one can "hear them leap right off the pages," the poems play with sounds and layout on the page; slippy, slidy pizzas meander across the page in the poem for

Dennis Lee has been a full-time writer since 1972, becoming Toronto's first Poet Laureate in 2001. In between these times, he wrote *Alligator Pie*, one of the best-selling Canadian children's books of all time, *Garbage Delight*, *Jelly Belly*, *The Ice Cream Store*, and *Bubblegum Delicious*. Lee wrote most of the song lyrics for *Fraggle Rock*, a co-production of Jim Henson Associates and CBC-TV in the 1980s. In 1986, Lee won the Vicky Metcalf Award for a body of work written for children, and in 1993 he was made an Officer of the Order of Canada.

which the book is named. Special note should be made of Loris Lesynski's book *I Did It Because…* in which the author shares a number of her favorite rhyming poems and the secrets of how they came to be written.

Sixteen ways to say thank-you are found in Nikki Grimes's *Thanks a Million*. Though the sentiment is the same through the poems, the form ranges from haiku, to a rebus, to a poem for two voices, to a prayer, and a riddle. Teachers, new acquaintances, family members (e.g., the child's dad who plays basketball with him; something that his friend would "love to see the day/my father joined me/ on the court./He be's too busy to play"), neighbors, and an author whose work was a refuge for a grateful child after her/his father's death when the child would, on some nights, "crawl between the pages/of that novel and hide for hours," are among the recipients of the gratitude expressed in the poems. Cabrera's vibrant acrylic paintings radiate the warmth in both dark and light faces when showing gratitude through countless small actions.

The nine poems in Stephen Mitchell's *The Wishing Bone and Other Poems* range from ballads to rhyming quatrains; from imagining what will happen "When I Grow Up" to a "Perpetual Number Song" that gives character to the base-10 system. Tom Pohrt's ink-and-watercolor cartoon illustrations introduce each poem and then scamper across the tops and bottoms of the pages, occasionally making a dash right down the middle.

Robert Heidbreder has taken onomatopoeia to new heights in *Lickety Split*, which follows the imagined adventures of a boy who is "thumpity thumped" by an elephant, who "skippity-skips" across the edge of a waterfall, and "hippity-hops" from two speeding motorcycles, among many other daring deeds. Cartoon illustrations by award-winning illustrator Dusan Petricic tell the story as the print provides the sound effects.

FOR OLDER CHILDREN

Sheree Fitch's *If I Had a Million Onions* is a collection of 26 poems that give "The Most Excellent Advice": "Sing a song of whatyouwish/Sing a song tomorrow"; say "A Prayer" that "no cats get in your sandbox/May your Frisbees always spin"; and pronounce on certain people, like "Aunt Emma and Uncle Nate," that in spite of the love the child narrator has for them, she/he says, "but I wish they'd get TV"). Yayo's pastel cartoon drawings are often outlines with just enough shape and detail to contribute to the wisdom and whimsy of the poetry, but leave lots of space for readers to fill in.

The poems in James Stevenson's *Sweet Corn* speak truths that bring a chuckle about the ordinary things in children's lives—big kids getting to see more because they sit in the front seat whereas their smaller counterparts sitting in the back catch things only when they're over (in "Injustice")—and realizations about important things, such as the smiles and happy relationships depicted in a family photo album where there are no pictures showing any unhappy sides to family life in "Photo Album." The poet is the illustrator, who uses watercolors and pencil drawings. He also uses the page as a canvas for the fonts and word arrangements on the page, such as the italicized "Clothesline Vacation" poem that flaps in the breeze, with only some clothespins preventing the words and the laundry on the clothesline from "flying to Spain."

With the irreverent humor readers have come to associate with Jon Scieszka's writing, *Science Verse* pronounces on physics, biology, and chemistry topics. A boy who was "zapped [] with a curse of SCIENCE VERSE," finds poetry in topics ranging from mealworm life cycles to combustion to the "Water Cycle,"

Nikki Grimes began composing poetry at the age of six and gave her first public poetry reading at the age of 13 at the Countee Cullen Library in Harlem. The turmoil and insecurity of her childhood are reflected in the lives of children in her novels and books of poetry, such as *Jazmin's Notebook* (a Coretta Scott King Honor Book) and the Danitra Brown poetry collections. Grimes received the 2006 NCTE Award for Excellence in Poetry for Children.

Companions to *Sweet Corn* include *Candy Corn, Corn Chowder, Cornflakes, Corn-fed,* and *Popcorn.*

deemed to be "boring" because of the never-ending "Precipitation,/Evaporation… /Evening, night, and morning." Together with original poem forms, Scieszka transforms classic poems, such as Ernest L. Thayer's "Casey at the Bat" to "Scientific Method at the Bat," and Clement Moore's "'Twas the Night Before Christmas" to "'Twas the Night before Any Thing" where a big sneeze expands a dense dot into the universe and it is agreed to "…call it something much grander, all right?/Merry BIG BANG to all! And to all—Gesundheit!" Lane Smith's expressionist illustrations add to the zany, imaginative tone of the poems. Like the words, the pictures unsettle the symmetry and patterns of scientific theory with three-eyed human-like forms made of words like "Phosphoric Acid" and "Lecithin," and blood-like splotches scattered across the page as a boy holds an open cereal box with a cheery clown's face.

McNaughton belongs to the club of humorous British poets that includes Brian Patten (*Gargling with Jelly*), Roger McGough (*Sky in the Pie*), and Michael Rosen (*Mind Your Own Business*).

Colin McNaughton inspires giggles with just the titles of his collections. *Who's Been Sleeping in My Porridge?* contains weird and jokey poems about creatures (and humans) of all shapes and sizes. Such outrageous poems as "Smedley was Deadly" about "A Spitter supreme" and "I Once Saw a Fish Up a Tree" ("And this fish he had legs, believe me"), McNaughton writes (and illustrates) poems that promise readers fun with a twist of rudeness.

The poems in Paul Duggan's *Murphy the Rat: Tales of Tough City* are not for the faint of heart. Murphy the rat has been hardened by his life in Tough City. He "goes looking for fights calling, 'Here Kitty Kitty'." His tangle with the rat catcher results in the a cast on the rat catcher's leg, with "the other leg tied in a knot" along with other gruesome shreddings of clothes and lumps of body parts. Tales of Murphy's toughness line up with rhyming quatrains and couplets about the malicious, the ghostly, the blood-sucking, and the hard put-upon people and animals living in Tough City. Readers who enjoy bathroom humor (a brother who eats pork and one bean "turns into a blast-o-matic") and puns ("never stick your neck out" for a vampire) will find lots to guffaw about in this book. Daniel Sylvestre's expressionist paintings are both comedic and dark.

The Natural World

Nature has long been the source of inspiration for poets. Huck, Hepler, Hickman, and Kiefer (1997: 409) explain that children, like poets "are very attuned to the world around them." The poetry collections featured in this section evoke the sense of wonder and fascination that children and poets share in the living things in our world.

FOR YOUNGER READERS

Quilts representing the four seasons accompany short poems, often with internal or end rhymes in delightfully unexpected places, in Anna Grossnickle Hines's *Pieces: A Year in Poems and Quilts*. The first sign of spring, the return of a crow, is captured in "Ballet." Papa Wren's tasty bits gathered for the brooding Mama Wren are "Takeout." In the poem "Pageantry" Hines venerates the colors of autumn. Hines includes an endnote about making the quilts and about quilting as an American tradition and art form.

Robins, crayfish, fireflies, and spiders; these are some of the 14 winged, hoofed, running, and crawling creatures featured in Marilyn Singer's *Fireflies at Midnight*. The short poems, often rhymed, follow the rhythm of a summer day, starting with the robin, who asserts "Let me be first to greet the light," and ending with the mole at dawn, who advises, "Sleep unhurried/Sleep unworried."

The illustrator, Ken Robbins, has manipulated photographs of the creatures to add texture and dimension to close-up views without losing sight of the creatures' natural surroundings.

Winner of the Lee Bennett Hopkins Award, Douglas Florian's *Beast Feast* is the first of a series of poetry books on living things. Carefree, concrete words and pictures together make it evident that the camel has "features haggard, harsh, and hairy" and that the toad is "squat and plump." Readers young and old delight in Florian's humorous pronouncements on each creature (e.g., "There's moa and moa and moa and moa" of the boa). A more recent collection of Florian's playful and pithy poems is *Mammalabilia*. The paintings that accompany each of the poems, created by Florian himself, follow in the poetry's mischievous shoes; for example, the "aquatic" otter reclines in a bathtub while reading a book titled H_2O.

Readers learn about dog breeds and their personalities in Maya Gottfried's *Good Dog*. Accompanied on the opposite page by a photo gallery of Robert Rahway Zakanitch's paintings on black backgrounds, these poems are told in first person from the dog's perspective. The poems are mostly free verse with requests, memories, admonishments, and apologies, including a memo to the Pekingese's person apologizing for "the stain on the piano bench," and the "hair on that nice wool suit" and ending with a postscript asking where the dog's chew bone is, for "I was sure that I'd left it on your pillow." Lovingly told, the poems are humorous and heartwarming.

FOR OLDER READERS

Barbara Nickel's *From the Top of a Grain Elevator* follows the seasonal rhythms of rural life: the harvest, the town and country fair, and Halloween "inside my snowsuit-tutu." Nature looms large in the poems." Kathy Thiessen's black-and-white etchings provide the texture of the cultivated and harvested fields. Particularly detailed and alive is the "Magpie Quartet," beak to beak hovering over the growing field. A bold, round sun and the distant grain elevator witness every scene. Nickel uses shape poem, tanka, and sonnet forms. She explains how she experimented with the meter and form in particular poems and provides a glossary of prairie terms.

Kristine O'Connell George's *Hummingbird Nest: a Journal of Poems* is a Claudia Lewis Poetry Award winner. The arrival of the "pixie tidbit" that is the hummingbird is announced in the first poem, "Visitor." Human and feline responses to the hummingbird's building of a nest; the hatching, nurturing, and teaching of the chicks; and the empty nest, lead to a "hummer of a summer" in the final poem, "New Visitors." Barry Moser's fresh, delicate watercolors echo the gentle, informative tone of the poetry. As O'Connell explains in a final "Author's Note," the poetry truly is a journal of her family's summer in Claremont, California. Two pages of quick facts about hummingbirds and a bibliography end the book.

Paul Fleischman's *Joyful Noise: Poems for Two Voices*, a Newbery Award winning book, is meant to be read aloud. Fleischman gives voice to a number of insects, such as water boatmen and book lice. The poems are written in two columns (one for each voice), with some text overlapping so the two voices read together. The poems are whimsical and pay tribute to the possibilities of the life of an anthropomorphized insect. Eric Beddows' black-and-white illustrations are realistic enough to distinguish each insect from the other, but many take poses that seem to have human intentions.

Other titles in this series, each recognizing a different realm of the animal kingdom, include *In the Swim, Insectlopedia, Mammalabilia,* and *On the Wing.*

In for Winter, Out for Spring by Arnold Adoff (illustrated by Jerry Pinkney) surveys the natural world over the course of a year. Adoff captures memorable moments that occur across the months: the first flakes of winter, the softened ground of spring, the green grass and dew of summer, and the apple honey buns of autumn. Bringing a human connection to the natural world, Adoff provides readers a family to guide them through the snapshots of each season: "The Winter Season Under Snow/ We Know This House is the Centre." The poems in this book are written in free-verse style, and the white spaces between words and verses are a signature style of this award-winning poet.

Multicultural Poetry

The experiences and perspectives of people who live in countries and communities beyond the immediate experience of many children in our classrooms are celebrated in the poetry featured in this section. On the other hand, for some students, the poetry honors familiar lives that are not often recognized in mainstream poetry for children. Insight and fresh ways of seeing the world abound as you read the following poetry.

FOR YOUNGER READERS

Children learn about the 54 articles of the United Nations Convention on the Rights of the Child in the 15 poems that make up Sheree Fitch's *If You Could Wear my Sneakers*. The poem for which the book is titled, for example, brings to life Article 2: "All rights apply to all children without exception." Speculating what might happen "If you were me and I were you," the poem proposes: "Maybe we could see the us/ We never got to meet." The animal themes and Darcia Labrosse's playful watercolor illustrations bring a lighthearted tone to the serious issue of many children living in countries where governments are not meeting children's essential needs, despite having ratified the Convention. The final pages of the book match the poems to the corresponding Convention articles.

The *Song within my Heart*, written by Lee Bennett Hopkins Award winner David Bouchard, lyricizes the childhood of illustrator Allen Sap, on the Red Pheasant reserve in northern Saskatchewan. The *boom boom* of the pow wow drums repeat across the endpapers and into the narrative poem, told by a Nokum (grandmother) to her beloved grandson in unrhymed quatrains. Readers come to know that "Your stories, songs and beating heart/Are truly yours and yours alone." Allen Sapp's oil color impressionist oil paintings are alive with the people who bring their hearts, songs, and stories to the pow wow.

The poetry of Pulitzer prize winner Gwendolyn Brooks, originally published in 1984, has been reprinted, this time swathed in American Faith Ringgold's colorful, ebullient folk art, in *Bronzeville Boys and Girls*. Readers come to know Bronzeville's children, and their homes, apartments, and parks through the detailed illustrations that fill the page from corner to corner. The voices of Bronzeville children, such as Keziah, Charles, Narcissa, and Eldora, tell of childhood hopes, desires, observations, fears, sadness, and secrets in rhyming verses. Paulette, for example, asks her mother, "What good is sun/If I can't run" when told that being an eight-year-old means that she is ready to be a lady.

Walter Dean Myers and his artist son Christopher Myers pay tribute to jazz, particularly its African-American heritage, through poetry and dynamic illustrations on swirling acrylic backgrounds in *Jazz*. The book, winner of both a Coretta Scott King Award winner and a Lee Bennett Hopkins Poetry Award, begins with an introductory historical overview and ends with a jazz timeline. In between, the pages swing with 15 poems celebrating styles of jazz and the musicians who played them. Some of the illustrations, such as that of pianist "Twenty-finger Jack," rise up from the page to meet the reader, and the lyrical text ensures that the reader's "feet just got to dance."

Remember the Bridge: Poems of a people by Carole Boston Weatherford is a book that honors the heroes from more than 400 years of African-American history. Freedom fighters, singers, and storytellers, as well as anonymous heroes whose labor set the path to freedom, are celebrated in this strong poetry collection.

Jane Yolen's *Sacred Places* is a reverent pilgrimage to sacred sites, such as Itsukushima, a Japanese shrine dedicated to the gods of the sea; Ganga, the Ganges river of Northern India whose waters are considered most sacred by Hindus; the Mayan temple at Copán in Honduras; Christian cathedrals in western Europe; Mecca, the birthplace of Muhammad, the Moslem prophet, in Saudi Arabia; Uluru, also known as Ayers Rock, the map of the myths of the Australian Aboriginal Dreamtime; and the Wailing Wall in Jerusalem, where Jewish pilgrims commemorate the destruction of the First and Second Temples. Free-verse poems highlight the symbolism of each site, as in the poem, "Ganga": "For all life is one life,/and all life ends/here at the river,/and begins." Short descriptions of each sacred place and a map of the world identifying the location of each provide further information.

David Shannon's muted acrylic paintings opposite each poem add to the solemnity of the book.

David Roessel and Arnold Rampersad introduce their collection of Langston Hughes's poetry, needing no title other than Hughes's name, with an authoritative biography of one of the most influential African-American poets. Their anthology of 26 poems includes widely-known works, such as "I, Too," "The Dream Keeper," "Aunt Sue's Stories," and "Mother to Son." The long, dark-skinned figures in Benny Andrews' collage and oil illustrations stretch and bend to poetry influenced by blues, jazz, and Negro spiritual rhythms. The images, like the words, assert and celebrate African American identity amongst the political prejudices of the USA in the early- to mid-20th century: "Tomorrow,/I'll be at the table/When company comes." A short descriptive paragraph provides a context for each poem, and unfamiliar words used in the poem are defined at the bottom of the page.

The 75 poems in Veronique Tadjo's edited collection *Talking Drums: A Selection of Poems from Africa South of the Sahara* take up lofty and difficult themes that have stimulated eloquent and deep thought across continents and time: the universe, love and celebrations, animal kingdom, people, death, pride and defiance, and changing times. Tadjo's pen-and-ink drawings evoke the lines, shapes, and patterns of Senegalese mud paintings. Tadjo has provided a map of Africa and a glossary of African terms encountered in the poems.

Poetry Forms

We have not paid great attention to the structured poetry forms, the haiku, couplets, quatrains, tanka, sonnets, ballads, limericks, etc. that often come to mind when thinking about poetry. Our emphasis has been, instead, on insight, imagination, emotions, images, and sounds, with the intention that the form should support and enhance all of the former. The form should not take over as the primary consideration. In the following poetry collections, form is highlighted, as gifted poets use their eyes, ears, and hearts to create specific types of poetry.

FOR YOUNGER READERS

Seventeen haiku look at everyday animals and birds from new angles in Jack Prelutsky's *If Not for the Cat*. A mouse, for example, certainly would be more content "if not for the cat," and from the mother kangaroo's perspective, the joey in her pouch is certainly "the future of [her] kind." This book brings together the well-regarded poet with master artist Ted Ran, whose illustrations use various media, including sumi brush drawings in India ink, traditional watercolors, chalk, spatter, and printmaking.

Paul Janeczko and J. Patrick Lewis, two masters of word play, together produce a collection of senryu poems (similar to haiku with 17 syllables, but on topics related to human lives rather than nature). The title, *Wing Nuts: Screwy Haiku*, lets readers know that they're in for a frolic with words and ideas: Noah Webster puts "the cart before the horse"—he has no choice, of course! And when the babysitter arrives with her list of "Do Not's" the illustrations show that the children are indeed "tied in *nots*." Throughout the book, Tricia Tusa's cartoon ink-and-watercolor illustrations extend the puns (e.g., grandpa's underwear pulled up under his armpits is clearly "a chest of drawers.")

Poet Joyce Sidman and illustrator Michelle Berg collaborate so successfully on a narrative concrete poem of a dog and a cat, *Meow Ruff*, that it is hard to tell where the poetry ends and the illustrations begin. Trees, clouds, platforms, rain, and the lawn are cleverly formed with words and geometric shapes. Thoughts arc over the endearing protagonists, and over the three crows that monitor both the initial conflict between the hissing ferocious cat and the tree-climbing fearful dog and its friendly resolution.

FOR OLDER READERS

The list of honors and awards for Paul B. Janeczko's *A Poke in the I: A Collection of Concrete Poems* is long and impressive; it includes the Lee Bennett Hopkins Honor Book and the *New York Times* Best Illustrated Children's Book of the Year. Words, clever and playful themselves, at times fly off the page (Robert Froman's "Ky Day Dream"), at other times reflect in the water (John Hollander's "Swan and Shadow"), spin in circles (John Agard's "Skipping Rope Spell"), and merge from two lanes (Allen Jones' "Merging Traffic"). Romping alongside the poems are Chris Raschka's torn origami paper, checkered cloth, watercolor, and ink illustrations.

Paul B. Janeczko's *Kick in the Head* is also an award winner, receiving a Claudia Lewis Award. This collection of 29 poems combines well-known poetry forms—including haiku, concrete poems, couplets, quatrains, acrostics, elegies, ballads, list poems, limericks, sonnets, and cinquains—with forms that are not so widely known, such as senryu, tercet, triolet, villanelle, clerihew, and aubade.

Readers will find a Shakespeare sonnet alongside a Robert W. Service ballad and an ode by Gary Soto. The only shortcoming is that lengthier poems are excerpted, as teaching the forms seems to be the primary purpose of the book. Each poem appears along with a sentence describing the form, and an expressionist-style illustration in watercolor, ink, and torn paper. Janeczko introduces the collection by suggesting how to read the book and encouraging an open mind about poetry forms. He ends the book with explanations of each form.

Teaching with Poetry

The Online Poetry Classroom can be found at **http://www.poets.org/page.php/prmID/6**

The Academy of American Poets website has a page for educators of students in older grades: the Online Poetry Classroom includes a Teacher Forum for sharing ideas and seeking help from colleagues, Teacher Resources with lists of over 300 recommended poems to teach, tips for teaching, and links for resources for teaching poetry. Also helpful to teachers are essays and lessons and units for teaching poetry.

Personal Response

- Students draw/paint pictures or to create sculptures out of clay, toilet paper rolls, craft sticks, and other materials in the classroom. The sculptures could be used as puppets to enact the poetry.
- Students jot down their feelings, thoughts, personal connections, images, and questions as they read poems. Ask students to talk about their responses to the poems with a trusted peer.
- Students dramatize nursery rhymes in small groups as the class sings them.

Reading and Writing Skills

- Write the words of a nursery rhyme or other poetry on cards and place them in a pocket chart. Give the rhyming word cards to individual students. Read the rhymes with children as you sing/chant them, pointing to each word in turn. Ask who has the missing rhyming word and how she/he knows that's the word (highlight beginning and vowel sounds, the length of the word in comparison to how long the word sounds) and ask the rest of the class to confirm. Continue this pattern with other rhyming words in the poems.
- Students create their own versions of rhymes on pages with all but the rhyming words written. Generate other words that could replace the missing words—they could be nonsense rhyming words if you want to emphasize sound (e.g., replacing "dock" with "zock" in "Hickory Dickory Dock"), or words that are of a similar type (e.g., another type of food in "Georgie Porgie" instead of "pie"). The students use their knowledge of letters and sounds and the examples from the class activity to write words in the blanks and then read them to peers.
- To develop phonemic awareness (the ability to hear separate sounds in words), sing the nursery rhymes with your students, inviting them to clap their hands or stand up when they hear certain sounds at the beginnings of words or certain vowel sounds (e.g., when they hear the

"l" sounds while singing "Mary Had a Little Lamb": children stand up for "little," sit down for "lamb," and then stand up again for "little").

- Students read poems as choral speeches: performing some lines or phrases with everyone's voice, some with particular students' voices; using gestures and facial expressions; and playing with volume, speed, etc. While students practice and perform their poems as a choral speech, the repetition and attention to the meaning of the poems will help them develop their fluency as readers.

Literary Elements

- Talk with students about purposes of titles for poems (e.g., to sum up the important ideas or introduce main characters). Invite students to create new titles for familiar nursery rhymes based on their assessment of the main ideas/themes of the rhymes.
- Students think about the line breaks in a poem and how meaning or rhythms are influenced by the line breaks. Georgia Heard (1999) explains that the poem's rhythm is created not only in the accents and syllables of words, but also in the lines and where they are broken on the page. Line breaks can occur where readers would naturally take a breath or where poets want to emphasize certain words or images.
- Students write words and phrases that roll off their tongue in ways they enjoy, or that create vivid pictures for them as they read poems. They then create a collage of these words, phrases, and images (student-drawn or painted).
- Students read through large collections of nursery rhymes in small groups, selecting five to eight of their favorites. Ask students to look for similarities across the selection, based on rhyme schemes, topics, themes, characters, or whatever other criteria seem relevant to students. The small groups' rhymes could then be gathered together into a collection organized with headings that describe the similarities.

Critical Reading and Writing

- Engage students in discussions about the gender of characters in nursery rhymes and what assumptions about being female or male seem to be made in the rhymes. Ask students whether those assumptions hold true today. Have students rewrite the rhymes with characters of a different gender and talk about how well the poems "work" or how they seem to fit with the students' views of what males and females do.
- Students conduct research into the origins of particular nursery rhymes and how they have been adapted over the ages (Iona and Peter Opie's *Oxford Dictionary of Nursery Rhymes* would be a good place to start). They then write a short history of the chosen nursery rhyme and explain why they feel that the rhymes are still relevant or are not relevant in today's world.

Poets might create tension by using a technique called *enjambment*, where the natural rhythm of a line is interrupted by being carried onto the next line.

Poetry Lists

Nursery Rhymes

Ada, Alma Flor & Campoy, Isabel (2003) *!Pio Peep!: Traditional Spanish nursery rhymes.*

Booth, David (1993) *Dr. Knickerbocker and other rhymes.*

Denton, Kady Macdonald (Ed.) (2005) *A child's treasury of nursery rhymes.*

DePaola, Tomie (2001) *Tomie de Paola's Mother Goose.*

Engelbreit, Mary (2008) *Mary Engelbreit's Mother Goose: One hundred best-loved verses.*

Goldstein, Bobbye S. (Ed.) (2003) *Mother Goose on the loose.*

Opie, Iona and Peter (1997) *Oxford dictionary of nursery rhymes.*

Opie, Iona & Wells, Rosemary (1996) *My very first Mother Goose* (Companion: *Here comes Mother Goose*)

Reid, Barbara (2007) *Sing a song of Mother Goose.*

Scheffler, Axel (2006) *Mother Goose's nursery rhymes: And how she came to tell them.*

Classics

Carroll, Lewis (2004: Ill. Stéphane Jorisch; 2007: Ill. Christopher Myers; originally published in *Through the Looking Glass*, 1872) *Jabberwocky.*

Eliot, T.S. (1987, first published 1939) *Old Possum's book of practical cats.*

Hall, Donald (Ed.) (1999) *The Oxford illustrated book of American children's poems.*

Lear, Edward (Vivien Noakes, ed.) (2004, first published 1846) *The complete verse and other nonsense.*

— (2007, first published 1867). *The owl and the pussycat.*

Milne, A.A. (1973, first published 1927) *Now we are six.*

Moore, Clement (1998, 2004, 2006; first published 1823) *Night before Christmas/The night before Christmas/'Twas the night before Christmas; or, account of a visit from St. Nicholas.*

Noyes, Alfred (2005, first published 1913) *The highwayman.*

Service, Robert W. (1986, first published 1907) *The cremation of Sam McGee.* Stevenson, Robert Louis (1985, first published 1885) *A child's garden of verses.*

Tennyson, Alfred, Lord (2005, first published 1832) *The lady of Shalott.*

Thayer, Ernest L. (2006, first published 1888) *Casey at the bat.*

Collections

Booth, David (1989) *Til all the stars have fallen.*

Cullinan, Bernice (Ed.) (1996) *A jar of tiny stars: Poems by NCTE award-winning poets.*

Greenberg, Jan (2001) *Heart to heart: New poems inspired by twentieth-century American art.*

Hopkins, Lee Bennett (1990) *The place my words are looking for.*

— (2002) *Seeing the blue between: Advice and inspiration for young poets.*

— (2005) *Oh no! Where are my pants? and other disasters: Poems.*

Prelutsky, Jack (selected) (1999) *The 20th century children's poetry treasury.*

Janeczko, Paul B. (2007) *Hey you!: Poems to skyscrapers, mosquitoes, and other fun things.*

Rosenberg, Liz (1996) *Invisible ladder: an anthology of contemporary American poems for young readers.*

Humor and Everyday Life

Duggan, Paul (1992) *Murphy the rat: Tales of tough city.*

Fitch, Sheree (2005) *If I had a million onions.*

Florian, Douglas (1994) *Bing Bang Boing*

— (1999) *Laugh-eteria*

Grimes, Nikki (2006) *Thanks a million.*

Heidebreder, Robert (2007) *Lickety-split.*

Lee, Dennis (2001, first published 1974) *Alligator pie.*

— (2002) *Garbage delight another helping.*

— (2000) *Bubblegum delicious.*

Lesynski, Loris (2001) *Nothing beats a pizza.*

— (2003) *Cabbagehead.*

— (2006) *I did it because...*

Little, Jean (1998) *Hey world, here I am!*

McGough, Roger (1983) *Sky in the pie.*

McNaughton, Colin (1987) *There's an awful lot of weirdos in our neighbourhood.*

— (1990) *Who's been sleeping in my porridge?*

— (2000) *Making friends with Frankenstein.*

Mitchell, Steven (2003) *The wishing bone and other poems.*

New, William (2002) *Llamas in the laundry.*

Patten, Brian (1985) *Gargling with jelly.*

Prelutsky, Jack (1984) *The new kid on the block.*

— (1990) *Something big has been here.*

— (1996) *A pizza the size of the sun.*

— (2008) *My dog may be a genius*

Rosen, Michael (1974) *Mind your own business.*

Scieszka, Jon (2004) *Science verse.*

Silverstein, Shel (2004) *Where the sidewalk ends 30th anniversary edition.*

Stevenson, James (1995) *Sweet corn.* (sequels: *Candy Corn; Corn Chowder; Cornflakes; Corn-fed; Popcorn*)

Natural World

Adoff, Arnold (1991) *In for winter, out for spring.*

Fleischman, Paul (1988) *Joyful noise: Poems for two voices.*

Florian, Douglas (1994) *Beast feast.* (sequels: *Bow Wow; Meow Meow; In the Swim; Insectlopedia; On the Wing*)

— (2000) *Mammalabilia: Poems and paintings.*

George, Kristine O'Connell (1997). *The great frog race and other poems.*

— (2004) *Hummingbird nest: A journal of poems.*

Gottfried, Maya (2005) *Good dog.*

Hines, Anna Grossnickle (2001) *Pieces: A year in poems and quilts.*

Levy, Constance (2002) *Splash! Poems of our watery world.*

Nickel, Barbara (1999) *From the top of a grain elevator.*

Sidman, Joyce (2005) *Song of the water boatman and other pond poems.*

Singer, Marilyn (2003) *Fireflies at midnight.*

Multicultural Poetry

Bouchard, David (2002) *The song within my heart.*

Brooks, Gwendolyn (2007) *Bronzeville boys and girls.*

Bryan, A. (1992) *Sing to the sun: Poems and pictures.*

Fitch, Sheree (1997) *If you could wear my sneakers!*

Myers, Walter Dean (2006) *Jazz.*

Rampersad, Arnold & Roessel, David (Eds.) (2006) *Langston Hughes.*

Johnson, Angela (1998) *The other side: Shorter poems.*

Tadjo, Véronique (2000) *Talking drums: A selection of poems from African South of the Sahara.*

Weatherford, Carole Boston (2002) *Remember the bridge: Poems of a people.*

Yolen, Jane (1996) *Sacred places.*

Poetry Forms

Grandits, John (2004) *Technically, it's not my fault.*

Janeczko, Paul B. (Ed.) (2001) *A poke in the I: A collection of concrete poems.*

— (Ed.) (2005) *Kick in the head: An everyday guide to poetic forms.*

Janeczko, Paul B., & Lewis, J. Patick (2006) *Wing nuts: Screwy haiku.*

Prelutsky, Jack (2004) *If not for the cat.*

Sidman, Joyce (2006) *Meow ruff: A story in concrete poetry.*

CHAPTER 3 Fairy Tales and Other Traditional Literature

Folktales are the most gifted travelers, adapting themselves to culture after culture, yet keeping a hard core of individuality, holding to the point of the story. (Johnson, Sickels, Sayers and Horovitz, 1977: 284)

Stith Thompson (1977) tells us that tales of the common folk, or folk tales include all forms of prose narrative that have been handed down through the ages. This includes nursery rhymes and folk tales, including fairy tales, fables, myths, legends, and epics.

Fairy tales and nursery rhymes for children began to appear in chap-books after 1700. Chapbooks were popular works with a few crude woodcut illustrations sold by itinerant peddlers (chapmen) for a few pence.

Traditional literature comes from our need to understand the human and natural worlds and to explore possible ways of living and being within them. In his *Republic*, Plato wrote that traditional stories nurture the imagination that is needed to move beyond the here and now to what could be, that is needed to recreate the world so it is a better place. Reflecting the desires and motivations that are basic to being human, traditional literature has had universal appeal to young and old around the world across the ages. Human nature, from its noblest pinnacle to its most contemptible depth, provides the fibre of the stories. They are flavored by the cultural beliefs, practices, and values that arise when groups of people are living in particular environments. Passed along from generation to generation through oral storytelling, these folktales "become voices for an entire culture." They "take on social and moral significance for a community of listeners who are seeking answers about the best ways to live" (Darling, 1996: 180). Like the cultures in which they are created, these stories are living, breathing, and ever-changing.

In spite of the name, fairy tales generally were rags-to-riches love stories, with very few fairies involved. The forerunners of modern European-based fairy tales were translated from collections by Charles Perrault and his niece, Madame d'Aulnoy, and by the Grimm brothers, Jacob and Wilhelm.

Charles Perrault was born into a distinguished bourgeois family in 1628. His *Histoires ou Contes du Temps Passé* (1697) was translated into English in 1729 as *Tales of Past Times*. His collection was written to entertain fellow aristocrats with lively, fanciful stories that transformed popular folk tales into moralistic tales. Well-known tales from his book included *Sleeping Beauty Little Red Riding Hood, Bluebeard, Cinderella*, and *Puss in Boots*.

Jacob and Wilhelm Grimm were born in the village of Hanau, Germany, in 1785 and 1786 respectively. With the goal of compiling something that would venerate German culture, they collected oral and literary tales, publishing the first of their *Kinder-und Hausmärchen* (translated as *Tales for Children)* in 1812. The Grimm brothers believed that the common folk were the guardians of the folk stories that appeared in their collection and tried to keep the stories as true to the form in which they were told as possible. Their best-known tales include

Snow White and the Seven Dwarfs, Hansel and Gretel, The Elves and the Shoemaker, Rumpelstiltskin, and *The Frog Prince.*

Characteristics of Fairy Tales

Hans Christian Andersen, born in Odense, Denmark, in 1805, is known as the father of the modern fairytale. His stories originated in written, rather than oral, form and thus are considered literary folktales. Among Andersen's best known tales are *The Little Mermaid, The Emperor's New Clothes, Little Ugly Duckling, The Tinderbox, Princess and the Pea, The Snow Queen, The Nightingale,* and *The Steadfast Tin Soldier.* At the time of his death in 1872, he was an internationally renowned and treasured artist.

The stories of the people of particular cultures and countries are often identifiable by their settings and other features. Huck, Hepler, Hickman, and Kiefer (1997) have identified characteristics particular to tales from various countries. Russian fairy tales, for example, often have peasants outwitting tsars, helpful animals, and the youngest child triumphing. In Celia Barker Lottridge's story, *Music for the Tsar of the Sea,* illustrated with Harvey Chan's pastels and occasional monochromes drawn with charcoal, the protagonist, Sadko, earns Russian kopeks for his music. The daughter of the tsar of the sea, who follows him above the water surface, becomes the river Volkov that flows to the Volga River and eventually to the Caspian Sea. In addition, the time and place are established early and briefly in the introduction: "Long ago in the city of Novgorod."

Many African tales are pourquoi stories or talking-beast tales with animal tricksters. In another of Lottridge's books, the highly-awarded *The Name of the Tree,* the protagonists are animals of the savannah—gazelles, elephants, giraffes, monkeys, zebras. The story begins: "Once, long ago in the land of the short grass, there was a great hunger." Illustrated by Ian Wallace with muted shades of the savannah, this Bantu tale makes a hero of the slow-moving tortoise who remembers the name of the tree, Ungalli, where his fellow beasts, the long-remembering elephant and swift gazelle, forget as their preoccupation with their obvious talents leads them to stumble along the way.

There is no rigid formula for identifying the fairy tale genre. As is the case with all genres, elements of fairy tales will vary with the storyteller's purpose and audience.

Opening and Ending Conventions

Folktales take place in the past and often begin with a phrase that indicates the historical nature of the story and introduces the main characters. Ed Young's *Lon Po Po,* a Red Riding Hood variant in which the wolf visits three girls in the guise of their grandmother (Po Po), begins with "Once long ago there was a woman who lived alone in the country with her three children, Shang, Tao and Paotze." Similarly, "The Chestnut Tree," retold in Rina Singh's collection of stories about magical trees *A Forest of Stories: Magical Tree Tales from Around the World,* begins with "In the days when princes ruled the regions of Japan, there lived a poor fisherman named Saburo."

Fairy tales are almost invariably success stories in which the protagonist's wishes and needs are fulfilled. Wickedness and malice are overcome and even punished. Although the antagonists in the story might not agree that the ending was satisfying, the storyteller assures listeners that the protagonists "lived happily ever after." In *Lon Po Po,* the eldest daughter, Shang, tricks the wolf by promising luscious gingko nuts that can only be gathered by climbing the gingko tree. With her sisters safely out of reach of the wolf, Shang lures the villain into a basket that is raised and then dropped, killing the wolf. This phrase closes the story: "On the next day, their mother returned with baskets of food from their real Po Po, and the three sisters told her the story of the Po Po who had come." Rina Singh's "The Chestnut Tree" ends with the betrothal of the poor fisherman's daughter to the prince, because she was the only one who could move the prince's ship, made from a chestnut tree that she had befriended. The story ends, "Her good fortune was indeed a gift of friendship from the chestnut tree."

Characters

Issues for Discussion
Should children be introduced to traditional literature? What does traditional literature offer today's children?

Folktale characters often symbolize good, evil, power, wisdom, kindness, and other human qualities. Little description is needed—storytellers rely on listeners to imagine what characters are like as they follow the characters' actions and to consider what they already know about human nature from previous stories and their lived experience. The story characters end up being fairly stereotypical, although characters from one story often have idiosyncrasies that identify them with that story. In Robin Muller's *Molly Whuppie and the Giant*, the giant is known by all as one who has harmful intentions toward children and for whom we are to feel little sympathy when he is robbed and kills his children and wife, mistakenly believing he is killing Molly and her sisters. Molly Whuppie's giant is quite like the one in *Jack and the Beanstalk*, told by British writer, Alan Garner. This giant's first words to his wife make his intentions clear:

> "Fee! Fi! Fo! Fum!
> I smell the blood of an Englishman!
> Be he alive, or be he dead,
> I'll grind his bones to make my bread!

In this story, however, it is the giant who is killed by Jack while pursuing the protagonist down a beanstalk.

Princes who long for princesses have things in common, as well. There is nothing they will not do to win the princess. Take Pradeep in "Pradeep and the Princess Labam," one of ten fairy tales in Jan Andrews' *Out of the Everywhere: New Tales for Canada*. Pradeep ventures into the forest where his parents have warned him not to go. He feeds hungry ants, pulls a sliver out of a bear's paw, and helps four men who inherit four objects of magic. But when he sees Princess Labam he falls in love and ends up calling on all the resources gathered in his wilderness wanderings in order to win her heart. He is not unlike the prince in Paul Zelinsky's *Rapunzel*, who falls in love with the sequestered girl after hearing her singing. He is willing to climb her tresses to see his true love. Before the two can live together with their two children, the prince endures a fall from the tower in which the wicked sorceress has confined Rapunzel, and the ensuing blindness and years of wandering blindly in the wilderness with nothing but roots and berries to eat. Zelinsky's Renaissance-style oil paintings earned this book a Caldecott Medal.

Plot Structures

To engage readers or listeners from beginning to end, fairy tales jump right into the conflict and stride purposefully from event to event with only enough elaboration to create suspense and capture the audience's attention. In Eric Kimmel's adaptation of a Japanese tale, *Three Samurai Cats*, we are introduced to the nobleman's rat problem immediately. He loses little time in contracting the samurai cats to exterminate the rat. Two of the samurai cats make attempts to use force and might. Unsuccessful, they are replaced by the third samurai, who puts the rat in a position to defeat himself by getting rolled into a sticky rice ball. The pen-and-ink with oil paint illustrations carry much of the action, as they are often in cartoon frames without dialogue or narration.

Similarly, the introduction of the problem is quick and the means for resolving the problem are clear early on in Virginia Hamilton's *The Girl who Spun Gold*. A Rumpelstiltskin-like figure, Lit'mahn Bittyun, saves Quashiba, the newlywed Queen, from being sequestered in a room for a year and a day by her husband. Lit'mahn spins fibre into gold, but the tension builds as Quashiba attempts, in vain, to fulfill her part of the bargain with Lit'mahn—telling him his name. Three times the gold is spun and three times the Queen makes three guesses. Finally, the tension is resolved as the King has unknowingly discovered the little man's name and tells his wife about it. The Queen is saved from having to spend her life in Lit'mahn's shade when he explodes into "a million flecks of gold that flowed into the night and disappear[s]" from her life forever. Award-winning Leo and Diane Dillon's illustrations are of metallic paint on acetate, over-painted with gold paint and gold leaf borders.

Themes

Folktales are told to entertain their audience. At the same time, they communicate the values of the culture through the qualities—love, kindness, inner and physical strength, courage, wisdom—that are rewarded in the stories. In many stories, the small, vulnerable character overcomes a more powerful force, or proves to be emotionally stronger or more virtuous than larger and older characters. One example is the little girl (she is not named) in Michael Lind's *The Bluebonnet Girl*. She throws her beloved doll into the fire when no one else will give up something precious to them, bringing rain to end a devastating drought. With the rains come the bluebonnets, "blue as the feathers that burned on the doll." Sacrifice of self for the good of all is an important theme in this Comanche tale.

Loyalty is the theme of the Hans Christian Andersen story illustrated by Demi in *Nightingale*. It is the story of a bird whose singing brings tears to the Emperor's heart. Captured to live in a cage and sing for the Emperor, the nightingale escapes with the arrival of a wind-up nightingale. When the mechanical singer breaks down, the nightingale returns to sing and revive the Emperor when he becomes very ill.

Honesty and kindness to the vulnerable are the themes of Rafe Martin's *The Language of Birds*, a Russian tale of two brothers. Vasilli lies to get what he wants. Ivan listens to the birds, saving a ship from a storm and pirates, and his brother from being beheaded because he cannot keep the crows away from the king's home. The reward is marriage to the princess, of course.

In Sheldon Oberman's *The Wisdom Bird*, biblical figures King Solomon and Queen Sheba engage in a show of their wisdom. Empathy is an important theme: the king finds in his answers to the hoopoe bird's three questions that breaking his promise to the Queen was more honorable than keeping it. Neil Waldman's acrylic paintings blend the tale's Jewish and African traditions.

Motifs

A motif is "the smallest part of a tale that can exist independently" (Huck, Hepler, Hickman, & Kiefer, 1997: 276). Here are some common motifs and fairy tales in which they are found.

TRANSFORMATIONS

The push in all transformation stories is for characters to resume their original forms, whether they be human or animal. In a number of wonder tales, people are transformed by malevolent magical characters into animals. The best known of the transformed princes is the Frog Prince, who needs a kiss from a princess to bring him back to his original princely form. The common wisdom that a woman must meet a lot of frogs before finding her prince comes from this tale, told by Marilyn Helmer in *Three Royal Tales*. She tells another tale with a transformation motif, "Beauty and the Beast" in *Three Tales of Enchantment*. True love breaks the spell of a fairy that transformed a prince into a beast. Another *Beauty and the Beast* book that is not to be overlooked is written and illustrated by Jan Brett. Her realistic and sumptuous illustrations add a regal flair to the story.

Charlotte Huck retells the Scottish tale *The Black Bull of Norroway*. A prince who has been transformed into a bull by a wicked witch is finally returned to his original form when the youngest of three sisters agrees to marry him. Kindness, resourcefulness, and perseverance lead the heroine to her happiness as she sets different standards from those of her sisters when it comes to finding a husband. Anita Lobel's watercolors are bold and vibrant with the black bull figuring large.

Sometimes, animals transform into people, as in Susan Cooper's *The Selkie Girl*, and Odds Bodkin's *The Crane Wife*. The selkie girl unwillingly becomes the wife of a farmer/fisherman when he steals her seal skin while she and her sisters fulfill their once-a-year land-longing and sunbathe on the rocks of an island. The selkie wife bears five children before discovering where her husband has hidden her seal skin. She leaves her land children to be with her sea children, returning once each year when the land-longing brings her back to the island. Warwick Hutton's watercolors wash across the pages in cool blues and greens. The crane wife is not such an unwilling wife as the selkie wife. She is a crane who can transform into a woman. Repaying the kindness of a lonely sailmaker leads the crane wife to offer her human self as a wife. She also offers to weave a magical sail to help her poverty-stricken husband. Greed overshadows the sailmaker's love for his wife, and he commands her to make more sails in spite of her protests. When he ignores her request not to watch her make the sails, she is freed from her obligations to him and she flies away as a crane, never to be seen in human form again. Award-winner Gennady Spirin does a masterful job of illustrating the story with watercolor and gouache paintings in earthy colors, using an ephemeral white for the cranes and all things natural.

MAGICAL OBJECTS

In fairy tales, magical objects may heighten a protagonist's talents, but they can also bring out the worst in characters. The eponymous dragon's pearl in Julie Lawson's book changes the poverty-stricken dreary lives of a boy and his mother by multiplying whatever it touches—the grasses in the field, the rice in the pot, and the money in the jar. Paul Morin's rich, textured illustrations in golds and reds capture the heat and dryness of drought-stricken China. The boy, Xiao

Sheng, swallows the pearl during a robbery by a jealous neighbor, transforming into a dragon who brings needed rains to the land.

The goose's magic in Barbara Reid's *Golden Goose* lies in its sticking qualities when people try to snatch it from Rupert, the poor woodcutter's widow's boy. The sight of all the people who have stuck to the goose as the boy carries it into town sets the melancholy Gwendolyn to laughing. Rupert wins half the wealth of Gwendolyn's father (the promised reward for such a feat) and Gwendolyn's heart. Reid's detailed clay illustrations add to the lightheartedness of this story, an adaptation of a Grimm brothers' tale.

In Roch Carrier's retelling of a French-Canadian fairy tale, *The Flying Canoe*, the title reveals the magical object. On New Year's Eve 1847, 11-year-old Baptiste and his lumberjack friends working in the woods of the Ottawa Valley grow more and more homesick. Resolved to see their families again before the stroke of midnight, the crew board a magical canoe that lifts them into the air, across villages, and closer to home.

A Caldecott-winning tale, Tomie de Paola's *Strega Nona* is about a woman who owns a magical cooking pot. With the right words, the pot can be coaxed to bubble out pasta. But Big Anthony gets in over his head when he neglects to find out that blowing three kisses will cease the pasta production. DePaola's characteristic cartoon-like illustrations add to the humor and lightheartedness of the story.

WISHES

The values of a culture are apparent in the kinds of things that characters wish for and in the outcomes of their wishes. Margot Zemach's *The Three Wishes: An Old Story* tells the English tale of a woodcutter who saves an imp caught under a fallen tree. The imp repays the kindness by granting the woodcutter three wishes. Of course, there is an admonition to wish wisely! Famous last words they are, as the arguments over what to wish for result in links of sausages dangling from the end of the woodcutter's nose with one wish remaining. Spending life with a husband who sports sausage links is unthinkable, so the wife makes the practical choice in her last wish.

The deft touch of a poet is evident in phrases such as "Red from toes to crown!" in J. Patrick Lewis's *At the Wish of the Fish*. The simpleton/silly goose/pancake (readers are invited to take their pick) Emelya meets an enchanted pike that promises him every wish he makes will come true. Many wishes are silly and in keeping with his indolent personality. The love of the tsar's daughter brings out the best in Emelya, and he uses his wishes to bring together the common folk and royalty for a banquet—there's no sense of entitlement in this Russian hero. Katya Krénina's watercolor and gouache illustrations in earthy colors add a folksy touch.

REPETITION

Storytellers tell fairy tales without the memory aid of written text. Repeated phrases, chants, or poems make a story more storyteller-friendly as they lighten the burden on the memory. The Wolf/Little Pig duet: "Little Pig, Little Pig, let me come in" followed by "Not by the hair on my chinny-chin-chin!" provides one such rhythmic memory aid in Marie Louise Gay's *The 3 Little Pigs*. Colorful pen-and-watercolor drawings whorl the animal characters into action.

Repetition is a feature of folktale plots for the same reason. Marilyn Helmer makes this feature apparent in her book, *Three Tales of Three*. Goldilocks finds the mother and father bears' beds, chairs, and porridge either too much or too little, and the baby bear's just right. The three billy goats Gruff each have an encounter with the troll. Promises of a bigger meal are given by the first two goats and the troll is overcome by the biggest of the three. And in the family of the three little pigs, each with a penchant for different building materials, two pigs have unhappy wolf encounters and the third bests the wolf with his brick house. The repetition of three provides a familiar and satisfying structure for story listeners to follow, as well.

Types of Fairy Tales

Wonder Tales

Well-known wonder tales are "Cinderella," "Snow White and the Seven Dwarfs," "Jack and the Beanstalk," and "Beauty and the Beast."

Stith Thompson (1977: 8) borrows from the Grimm brothers, calling wonder tales *marchen*, stories that "move in an unreal world without definite locality or definite characters and [are] filled with the marvelous." Human desires for love and happiness are fulfilled in these tales of magic and the supernatural. Before those desires can be fulfilled, however, wonder-tale protagonists carry readers/listeners through hair-raising adventures in besting some creative and malevolent magical antagonists.

Robin Muller has written and illustrated a wonder tale, *The Nightwood*, based on the English fairy tale "Tamlane." The malicious Elfin Queen has cast spells on the elfin ball so that "most mortals never return, and those who do pine away, blind to the beauty of their own world." But wonder-tale aficionados know well that true love overpowers evil magic. Elaine holds onto her beloved Tamlynne as he changes from roaring bear to strangling serpent to fiery brand, and they are both saved. American Jane Yolen tells this story beautifully in her collection of 13 stories, *Not a Damsel in Distress*, as well.

Ian Wallace's foreboding, textured illustrations in pastel pencil on black paper set the dark tone for *Hansel and Gretel*. In this wonder tale, parents do the unthinkable: they leave their children in the forest to fend for themselves or die. The wicked witch who lures the children with her house of cake, in hope of cooking and eating Hansel, ends up in the oven herself due to Gretel's quick thinking. With the evil-intentioned mother and wicked witch dead, Hansel and Gretel join their father and enjoy the wealth amassed by the witch.

Robert San Souci's *The Faithful Friend*, illustrated with the unmistakable textured etchings of Brian Pinkney, is both a Caldecott Honor book and a Coretta Scott King Honor book. San Souci uses the Martinique version of a story that can be traced back to the Grimm brothers' story "Faithful Joannes." West Indian zombies, assigned by the quimboiseur (wizard) Monsieur Zabocat, use their magic to evil ends in an attempt to prevent the marriage of Pauline, the wizard's niece, to her beloved Clement. The betrothed couple avoids the poisoned water and mangoes, and a deadly fer de lance snake through the quick, selfless acts of their friend, Hippolyte. Because of the curse of the zombies, Hippolyte "turns to stone from the soles of his feet to the top of his head," but the curse is broken by Clement's willingness to sacrifice his life for his friend. Wonder tales end in satisfying ways, as goodness is rewarded and evil is punished.

Cumulative Tales

Cumulative tales, with repeated details that build to a climax, are well-loved by young children. The story of the *Gingerbread Boy* (Galdone), chased by its creator and a host of others, is one of the best-known cumulative tales. The repeated actions are encouraged by the repeated invitation of the brazen baked good on legs: "Catch me if you can."

A number of Canadian author/illustrators have created books of cumulative tales. Aubrey Davis's *Bone Button Borscht* tells of a beggar who cannot find a source of food in one community. Buttons from his jacket serve as a soup base and members of the community volunteer all the other ingredients. Illustrator Dusan Petricic uses pencil and watercolor illustrations. Particularly noticeable are the bright, warm yellow lights in the windows of the houses after the community has learned about sharing, and a thin line of light that leads the beggar to the warmth of the synagogue fire. Davis and Petricic paired up again to create *The Enormous Potato*, the cumulative tale in which many characters work together to solve a problem too large for one to solve alone. A farmer plants a potato that grows so large he cannot pull it out of the ground by himself. The farmer calls to his wife for help and even with the two of them pulling and pulling, it just will not budge. Their daughter and a host of ever-smaller animals join in until the potato pops out. There is, of course, a feast of the tuber to celebrate.

Phoebe Gilman's *Something from Nothing* and Sims Taback's *Joseph Had a Little Overcoat* tell a well-loved tale of a grandfather's gift of a precious blanket/overcoat to his grandson, Joseph. As Joseph grows older, the blanket becomes tattered and torn and has to be made into smaller and smaller pieces of clothing: a jacket, then a vest, a handkerchief, and a button. When it appears that nothing remains of the blanket, Joseph finds one last thing he can make from it—a story! In Gilman's illustrations is an underground story featuring mice who take the pieces of the blanket that fall through the floorboards and create clothing for their family. In Taback's illustrations are cut-outs that foreshadow what the overcoat will become.

Jan Thornhill's *The Rumour: A Jataka tale from India* is a Buddhist moral tale about a worrywart young hare who fears the world is breaking up. Evidence: a mango breaks from a branch and falls with an explosive sound close to her while she sleeps. Boars, deer, tigers, and rhinoceroses join in the flight through the forest. Finally, a sensible lion asks the right questions to determine that the world truly is intact, and all animals return to their forest homes. Thornhill illustrates with vibrant colors, using patterned borders of mangoes and flowers on every page. More information about the animals, all endangered species, is provided at the end of the book.

Pourquoi Tales

Why?—the question that many three-year-olds ask about their world—is answered in pourquoi tales. They could also be called "Comment" tales because they also answer the question *How?* These stories often tackle questions that science has not touched: *Why Mosquitoes Buzz in People's Ears* (Aardema), and how the bear ended up with such a short, stubby tail (in Jan Thornill's *Crow and Fox and other Animal Legends*). In the latter, we find that Bear's tail had frozen into the ice at the suggestion of Fox, who claimed the tail method to be the secret to his fishing success. Bear's desperate pulling on his tail to get it out of the ice snapped it off. And bears to this day have short tails. This is one of eight tales about animal duos that Thornhill gathered from every continent. Borders for the illustrations are based on textiles from the tales' countries of origin. American Aardema's Caldecott award-winning book about mosquitoes is also a cumulative tale. The iguana, distracted by the mosquitoes buzzing in his ears, does not hear the python's greeting. This unintentional snub leads to Mother Owl's inability to "wake the sun so that the day can come." Finally, the King finds out the source of the problem, but the mosquitoes continue to buzz in peoples' ears because of their guilty conscience. They are saying, "Zeee! Is everyone still angry at me?"

A northern tale in Bob Barton's *The Bear Says North,* "The Reindeer Herder and the Moon" tells of a lovelorn Moon who comes down to earth to woo a young girl. She is not interested in his advances and depends on the magic of her trusty reindeer to hide her from Moon. Finally, captured by the girl and in a weakened state while on earth, Moon agrees never again to return to earth. He also agrees to become the people's calendar, measuring the year for them. This tale tells of how the cycles of the moon came to be.

A book of Ojibway tales collected by Herbert T. Schwarz and illustrated by renowned artist Norval Morrisseau, *Windigo and other Tales of the Ojibways* includes "The Silver Curse." This story explains how the sleeping giant "mountain" came to rest in Lake Superior at Thunder Bay, Ontario. Another pourquoi tale of note, Toye's *The Loon's Necklace,* has endured as a Canadian classic, perhaps because of Elizabeth Cleaver's collage illustrations. Made with torn paper, paper cut-outs, and linocuts, the illustrations have been recognized with an Amelia Frances Howard-Gibbon Award. In this story of how the loon got its white markings, an old man is given sight by a loon who brings him under water. In return, the old man gives the loon a necklace of white shells that leave the markings we see today on the loon's black neck and feathers.

Beast Tales

Animals talk and act like humans in beast tales. Unlike fables, beast stories are not told with a didactic purpose, but rather to entertain. The animals of the countryside appear in the tales of each culture. European tales often have animals of the barnyard in their cast. A rooster plays the leading role in Celia Barker Lottridge's retelling of the Hungarian folktale of *The Little Rooster and the Diamond Button.* This is a "swallowing" tale in which the less powerful find ways to get their due. A plucky rooster finds a diamond button and is about to take it home to his poor old mistress, but a rich, greedy sultan seizes the button from under the rooster's beak. The rooster's attempt to recover it are met with violence—being thrown into wells, fires, and bee hives—but the rooster's multi-purpose stomach swallows the water and then uses it to quench the fire. He swallows the bees and then releases them to torment the sultan. Joanne Fitzgerald's watercolor illustrations with decorative borders add to this story of the little guy with goodness and generosity in his heart overcoming the powerful and mean-spirited.

Award-winning author Virginia Hamilton teams up with award-winning illustrator James E. Ransome in *Bruh Wolf and the Tar Baby Girl.* Bruh Wolf, frustrated by Bruh Rabbit's insistence on raiding his peanut patch, makes a tar baby scarecrow. Rabbit, the clever trickster, evades capture and being served up for Bruh Wolf's supper by begging Bruh Wolf not to throw him the briar patch outside the garden fence. The story is told in Gullah, the speech of the Sea Islands of South Carolina. Another beast/trickster tale, *Mrs. Chicken and the Hungry Crocodile*, is from Liberia. Won-Idy Paye and Margaret H. Lippert tell of the vain but clever Mrs. Chicken. Captured by a crocodile, Mrs. Chicken plays the trickster role and saves her life by convincing the crocodile that they are sisters. Julie Paschkis's gouache paintings add to the humor of this tale.

Realistic Tales

Realistic tales are quite rare in traditional literature. Many of these are humorous with foolish characters. One of the best-known tellers of humorous realistic tales is Isaac Bashevis Singer. The title story in a collection of Jewish tales, *Zlateh the Goat and Other Stories*, is about a poor peasant boy on the way to the butcher to sell Zlateh, the family goat. A fierce three-day snowstorm forces boy and goat to take refuge in a haystack where Zlateh provides warmth and milk as she feasts on the hay. The grateful family decides that Zlateh is more valuable to them alive and they never talk again of selling her. Debby Waldman retells another Jewish folktale of a boy named Yankel who repeats others' stories and gets them into trouble in *A Sack Full of Feathers*. He learns an important lesson after the rabbi asks him to place a feather on every doorstep in the village. Cindy Revell's cartoon illustrations are in bold primary colors, and a colorful scarf creates a unique border for many pages.

Richardo Keens-Douglas's *The Trial of the Stone* takes place in a rural setting where hippopotamuses loll about and people walk from village to village to visit relatives. While one such traveler, Matt, is on his way to visit his grandfather, he takes a nap in the forest, placing three coins (all the money he has) under a stone for safety. A thief steals the coins, and, in the absence of evidence incriminating anyone else, Matt charges the stone with the theft. All the commotion at the trial of the stone results in the judge ordering each spectator to pay a fine of one penny for disturbing the proceedings—money that is turned over to Matt. The green of the rural setting, the humor of the story (even the hippos have grins on their faces) and many of the events are conveyed in Stéphane Jorisch's watercolor, gouache, and pen-and-ink illustrations.

Peter Eyvindson teams up with Craig Terlson to tell an Icelandic tale, *The Backward Brothers See the Light*, of three brothers that "seemed to have only one brain between them for they often acted in a strange and backward manner." The humorous cartoon watercolors are appropriate as characters bring light into their newly-built house by carrying it from the outside in their cups.

Award-winning illustrator Demi has created a sumptuous version of Hans Christian Andersen's *The Emperor's New Clothes*. She explains that gold is the color of purity and that the Chinese symbols she uses also remind readers of aspects of purity in life. The Emperor allows his vanity to overtake his better judgment and ends up parading in front of his people in his underclothes. An innocent child is the only one to say with honesty what he sees.

Author/illustrator Jon Muth brings together his love of Zen Buddhism and Eastern culture in *Stone Soup*, a story of three monks who decide that a village that closes its doors against them must learn generosity. They trick the villagers into contributing to a community soup that feeds everyone. Dreamy watercolors and ink drawings illustrate this story.

Marcia Brown's *Dick Whittington and His Cat* is a realistic tale of a poor boy who seeks his fortune in London. Giving his cat, the only thing in his possession, to the merchant as a good to trade, Dick is rewarded handsomely when the king of the Moors offers half of his treasure to be rid of the rats and mice that overrun his palace. The cat and the king fulfill their obligations and Dick becomes a wealthy boy, generous in giving to those in need and growing to be a gentleman who catches the eye of the rich merchant's daughter and ends up being happily married to her. Lino cuts in black, white, and yellowish-brown illustrate the story.

Trickster Tales

Tricksters are often small, mischievous, rule-breaking or subverting characters. Their trickery often puts more powerful or larger characters in difficult and/or embarrassing situations—something that children and many others seem to delight in!

African trickster tales are often of Anansi the spider. In Canadian Adwoa Badoe's collection of 10 Ghanaian Ananse stories, *The Pot of Wisdom: Ananse Stories*, each trickster tale is illustrated by Baba Wagué Diakité's glaze on ceramic tile with rich, deep colors and spider borders. The story for which the book is titled places Ananse in a foolish light, as he waves all eight of his arms in victory after successfully bringing the pot of all wisdom up to the Sky God's home in the skies. The Sky God points out that the pot would not have dropped and broken, scattering wisdom to "the very ends of the earth" if Ananse had not found it necessary to wave all eight of his arms.

Raven is the trickster of many west-coast tales of Canada and the US. Gerald McDermott's Caldecott Honor book *Raven* uses sparse narrative and gouache, colored pencil, and pastel on cold-press watercolor paper to show how Raven, reborn as the grandchild of the Sky Chief, opens the box containing the sun and brings it to the sky so that the earth could have light.

Two favorite African American trickster tales are in Virginia Hamilton's collection, *A Ring of Tricksters: Animal Tales from America, the West Indies, and Africa*. In "Bruh Wolf and Bruh Rabbit Join Together," Bruh Rabbit convinces Bruh Wolf to enter into an agricultural commercial arrangement where Bruh Rabbit always gets the edible part of the plant to sell and Bruh Wolf always gets the wrong end. Bruh Wolf's only compensation for his troubles is "maybe Bruh Wolf learned something about a rabbit: Bruh Flop-ears is always asking for help. Then, he helps himself!" Being clever again has its rewards in the story "Buzzard and Wren have a Race." Bruh Buzzard challenges Bruh Wren to a race to the highest heights, expecting that his massive wings will help him win the day. Bruh Wren agrees to the race, hopping onto Bruh Buzzard's back as he takes flight. Bruh Buzzard can hear Bruh Wren talking above him but can never see him because his wings are in the way. Bruh Buzzard wonders about it all, but keeps his beak shut and never again asks why Bruh Wren flies so low when he is capable of flying higher than Bruh Buzzard flies. Barry Moser's transparent watercolors have drawn delighted chuckles from many a reader. They make it clear that these tales are not to be taken too seriously.

Variants

Variants of fairy tales come from every corner of the globe. No one can confidently explain the presence of these similar tales. Perhaps they come from a common language where human civilizations began (probably India) and then

In the picture book *Glass Slipper, Gold Sandal,* author Paul Fleischman braids many versions of the Cinderella tale into one world-spanning adventure. The story is set in Mexico, Iran, Korea, and Russia, and weaves together a variety of folk traditions while paying homage to our enduring cultures. An additional source is Judy Sierra's book *Cinderella,* with 25 variants.

spread around the world with human exploration and travel. As the stories spread, there were variations with each telling and each storyteller. A second hypothesis is that the existence of variations on similar themes, motifs, and plots is a natural outcome of the shared humanity among all peoples of the world.

Cinderella variants are some of the most widely-known and extensively-studied of fairy tale variants. Charles Perrault's *Cinderella, or the Little Glass Slipper* is the best-known tale in Canada and the United States, possibly because Walt Disney based an animated film on it. However, the first known Cinderella story to be written down is likely to have been the Chinese story *Yeh-hsien,* written in the ninth century.

CINDERELLA VARIANTS

Africa

Climo, Shirley (1989) *The Egyptian Cinderella.*

Steptoe, John (1987) *Mufaro's beautiful daughters: An African Tale.*

Asia

Climo, Shirley (1993) *The Korean Cinderella.*

Coburn, Jewll Rinehart (1998) *Angkat: The Cambodian Cinderella.*

Coburn, Jewell Rinehart with Tzexa, Cherta Lee (1996) *Jouanah: A Hmong Cinderella.*

Han, Oki S. & Plunkett, Stephanie Haboush (1996) *Plunkett Kongi and Potgi: A Cinderella story from Korea.*

Ai-Ling, Louie (1988) *Yeh-Shen: A Cinderella story from China.*

Middle East

Climo, Shirley (1999) *The Persian Cinderella.*

Jaffe, Nina (1998) *The way meat loves salt: A Cinderella tale from the Jewish tradition.*

Silverman, Erica (1999) *Raisel's riddle.*

Europe

Climo, Shirley (1996) *The Irish cinderlad.*

Daly, Jude (2000) *Brown and trembling: An Irish Cinderella story.*

Grimes, N. (2002) *Walt Disney's Cinderella.*

Huck, Charlotte (1989) *Princess Furball.*

Jacobs, Joseph (1989) *Tattercoats.*

Mayer, Marianna (1994) *Baba Yaga and Vasilisa the brave.*

McClintock, Barbara (2005) *Cinderella.*

Perrault, Charles (Trans. A.E. Johnson) (2000) *Cinderella, Puss in Boots and other favorite tales.*

The Americas

dePaola, Tomie (2002) *Adelita: A Mexican Cinderella story.*

Hooks, William H. (1987) *Moss gown.*

Pollock, Penny (1995) *The Turkey girl: A Zuni Cinderella story.*

Martin, Rafe (1992) *The Rough-face Girl.*

San Souci, Robert D. (1998) *Cendrillon: A Caribbean Cinderella.*
— (2000) *Little Gold Star: A Spanish American Cinderella tale.*
— (1994) *Sootface: An Ojibwa Cinderella story.*
— (1989) *The talking eggs: A folktale from the American South.*
Schroeder, Alan (1997) *Smoky Mountain Rose: An Appalachian Cinderella.*

Modern Fairy Tales

Many modern fairy tales are delightfully humorous and entertaining, as they take new perspectives on familiar stories and characters. Examples are Jon Scieszka's *The True Story of the 3 Little Pigs!* in which A. Wolf tells the story through his eyes, and British Roald Dahl's *Roald Dahl's Revolting Rhymes*, which takes a satirical look at six fairy tales.

In other cases, the modern fairy tales are adapted to a contemporary setting. In Babette Cole's *Prince Cinders*, Cinderella is a "fella" who attends the "rock'n' Royal Bash." Michael Emberley sets his book, *Ruby*, about a mouse that plays Red Riding Hood's role, in urban America.

Modern tales often have the same motifs as traditional ones, but there is a contemporary twist to them. In Philemon Sturges' *The Little Red Hen (Makes a Pizza)*, the title character makes pizza instead of bread, and in British Raymond Briggs's *Jim and the Beanstalk*, Jim helps an old giant who needs false teeth and a wig. In other cases, the gender of the protagonists is reversed, as in Helen Ketteman's *Bubba the Cowboy Prince: A Fractured Texas Tale* and Tony Johnston's *The Cowboy and the Black-eyed Pea*. In the latter, the wealthy daughter of a Texas rancher devises a plan to find a real cowboy, someone whom she would love for herself and not just for the longhorn herd that her deceased father had left her. She knows that real cowboys are sensitive—"at the least touch he'll bruise like the petals of a desert rose"—and ends up rescuing the one real cowboy who is so afflicted by the black-eyed pea she places under his saddle that he cannot prevent the longhorns from stampeding. Helaine Becker's *Mother Goose Unplucked* is a collection of games, puzzles, quizzes, recipes, riddles, jokes, scavenger hunts, tongue-twisters, and other madcap activities that spring from nursery-rhyme and folktale characters and plots. Claudia Davila's cartoon illustrations and zany fonts add to the fun of this "seriously cracked" book.

Teaching with Fairy Tales

Personal Response

- Invite students to create an illustration to depict what they think might happen to a character or characters after the story ends.
- Older students learn a favorite fairy tale well enough to be able to tell it to a peer or younger audience. They may use the template on page 65 to help them prepare for the storytelling. The idea is for students to tell the story in their own way, rather than to memorize the story word for word.

Reading and Writing Skills

- To help students recognize that reading involves predicting using the available information, create an overhead transparency of a cloze of two or three paragraphs of one fairy tale (the cloze is made by replacing every fifth or sixth meaningful word with a blank). Do a think-aloud to show students how they can use meaning cues and syntax cues to figure out what words would work in each of the blanks.
- To help students in punctuating dialogue, ask them to read through a number of fairy tales, noting how the dialogue is punctuated. Have them write down examples of dialogue and then look for patterns that they can follow when they write stories with dialogue.

Literary Elements

- Students compare and contrast the morals and lessons in a number of trickster tales. What do they tell us about human qualities that the cultures the tales come from value and the ones they discourage?
- Students analyze Cinderella variants using the chart on page 66.

Critical Reading and Writing

- Students compare and contrast what female and male fairy-tale characters do to solve problems, determining if there are gender patterns. Consider who works independently and who enlists the help of others. Also consider what kind of help the characters ask for. Then think about other ways in which male and female fairy-tale characters might solve their problems, and write alternative endings to favorite fairy tales.
- Students analyze social and cultural stereotypes in fairy tales using the chart on page 67. Ask the questions: What impression do you get of these types of characters from the fairy tales you're reading? Do you think all people who are poor or rich (for example) are like this? How would the story change if the character was not stereotyped in this way?

Fables

Fables are brief moralistic tales meant to instruct. They centre on a single event involving animal characters. The animals are not named, as each represents basic qualities of human nature. The moral that one is to learn from the story appears at the end.

The first print versions of fables were written in Greek, translated into Latin and then into English by William Caxton in 1484. Aesop, a Greek slave thought to have been born in Asia Minor around 600 BC, is the source of the best-known fables in the English-speaking world. La Fontaine, a French poet, drew on the written collections of Aesop's fables that were available in the 17th century, writing the stories in verse. From India, the Jataka tales were also moralistic animal stories. They were much longer than Greek fables, intended to instruct young princes on appropriate behavior.

Some scholars believe that several storytellers initially told fables. They question the existence of Aesop, the Greek slave.

Three award-winning illustrators have created visually stunning books of fables. In Jerry Pinkney's *Aesop's Fables*, pencil, colored pencil, and watercolors portray the animals and multi-ethnic people realistically with remarkable texture and detail. Pinkney's collection is extensive, containing 60 fables. The illustrations steal the show in Helen Ward's *Unwitting Wisdom: An Anthology of Aesop's Fables*. Ward introduces each of her 12 favorite fables with arresting watercolor title pages and pithy statements summing up the fable (e.g., "A Time to Dance – in which a cricket learns about work—THE HARD WAY"). In *Mice, Morals & Monkey Business* Christopher Wormell brings life to the crafty animals of Aesop's fables with exquisite linoleum-block prints.

Award-winning writers have created books of fables, as well. In *Birds of a Feather and Other Aesop's Fables*, folksinger and writer Tom Paxton retells ten of Aesop's fables in verses with join-along rhythms, accompanied by Robert Rayevsky's grainy, textured, surrealistic illustrations. If Jane Yolen's name appears on a book, it's worth taking a second look. She does not disappoint in *A Sip of Aesop*, using rhymes to write modern retellings of 13 fables, including "The Dog in the Manger" and "Counting Your Chickens." In *Aesop & Company*, Barbara Bader introduces the origins of the stories and retells the legends surrounding Aesop's life. Detailed etchings by award-winning Arthur Geisert add visual complexity to the 19 fables.

Other retellings of Aesop's fables include Native American versions in *Doctor Coyote* by John Bierhorst, *no's Aesop* by Japanese artist Mitsumasa Anno, and the humorous twist of *The Exploding Frog*, with tales retold by John McFarland and illustrated by James Marshall. *Disabled Fables*, illustrated by artists with development disabilities, is a special rendition of the familiar fables.

Teaching with Fables

Personal Response

- Invite younger students to draw a picture with a caption of a fable character they would like to be, a character they feel sorry for, or a character that they feel deserved what happened to her or him.
- Older students talk with a partner and then write three morals from favorite fables that make sense to the students and that they might take to heart. Ask students why these lessons work for them.

Reading and Writing Skills

- Students rewrite a favorite fable as a free-verse poem that can be read as a choral speech. Print the fable onto an overhead to demonstrate how to create line breaks for a poem. Do a think-aloud to explain where you might cut and change words to make a poem from the prose form, and how meaning and rhythm change depending on where the line breaks are.
- While students practice and perform their fable poems as a choral speech, the repetition and attention to the meaning of the fables will help students to develop their fluency as readers.

Literary Elements

- To raise students' awareness of character development, ask them to work with a partner to perform an interview of one of the animals in a favorite fable for their class or a small group of peers. Students should consider probing into the animal's motivations for her/his actions and

Preparing to Tell a Story

Title _____

Events

Introduction

Conclusion

Phrases/Rhymes to memorize

Comparing and Contrasting Variants

Titles of Variants and Countries of Origin			
Opening Conventions			
Ending Conventions			
Clues to the Country of Origin			
Characters' Talents			
Tasks to be Done			
Verses/Refrains/Chants			
Themes			
Motifs			

Analyzing Characters in Fairy Tales

Write the titles of three fairy tales you have read in the top row. Using their actions, other characters' responses to them, or the rewards or punishments that they receive in the story, what impressions do you have of characters who are of these types? Write your impressions in the spaces under each title.

Titles of Fairy Tales			
Rich characters			
Poor characters			
Small characters			
Big characters			
Young characters			
Old characters			
Urban characters			
Rural characters			

what might have happened to the character in the past to cause her/him to act as she/he has.

- The purpose of fables is to instruct. Invite students to consider how the story would change if its purpose were to entertain. How would the plot change? Would new characters be introduced? Would more information about characters be needed? Students could then rewrite the stories with the new purpose of entertaining an audience.

Critical Reading and Writing

- Students assess the outcomes of selected fables in terms of their sense of justice. Were the consequences of characters' actions fair? A debate on the topic could ensue.
- Students infer how appropriate the advice in selected fables is for today's world. What has changed since the time of Aesop, and what has remained the same, to render the advice useful or not?

Legends and Epics

Legends and epics are stories passed by word of mouth and popularly accepted as having some historical accuracy (Saxby, 1996). Through the passage of time, the protagonist's deeds have been glorified and the protagonist has been made into a hero figure. Greek legends stem from Homer's epic poems, the *Iliad* and the *Odyssey* (c. 850 BC), telling of the Trojan War and its aftermath. Jason, Odysseus, and Theseus are the best known Greek heroes. Norse myths stem from the 13th-century Icelandic sagas, the *Elder Edda*, a collection of 34 poems sometimes referred to as the Iliad of the North. Moses and Samson are epic heroes from the Hebrew Old Testament. Beowulf and Arthur are ancient Britain's best-known heroes. William Caxton's printing of Mallory's *Morte d'Arthur* in 1485 sparked many written retellings and chapbook versions. Other legendary and epic heroes include Roland from France, El Cid of Spain, and Siddharta from India. These larger-than-life characters stir the imagination and keep alive the belief that humans can rise above their foibles and pettiness to do great things.

> The hero's journey is one of going out into the world, battling the forces that would hinder all things good, and finally triumphing to save themselves and the world.

Inscribed onto clay tablets more than 5000 years ago in Mesopotamia (present day Iraq and Syria), the epic of Gilgamesh, king of the city of Uruk, is one of the oldest stories in the world. Ludmila Zeman conducted research in leading museums around the world to recreate the world of Gilgamesh's time. In *Gilgamesh the King*, a god-man is sent by the Sun God to rule the people of Uruk. In *The Last Quest of Gilgamesh*, Gilgamesh seeks the secret of everlasting life following the death of his friend Enkidu. The first hero of Western literature, Gilgamesh embodies the qualities we associate with heroes today: courage, perseverance in the face of hardship, willingness to sacrifice for a lofty goal, and compassion.

> Zeman also retells one of the epic tales of the thousand-and-one nights in *Sindbad's Secret*. Her signature pencil, colored pencil, and watercolor illustrations and textured borders sweep along this grand tale of the hero surviving a shipwreck, overcoming sea and island monsters, threatened with death-by- elephant, and despairing at seeing his beloved on a funeral pyre with her Maharajah.

The epic story of *The Iliad and the Odyssey* is retold and illustrated in cartoon style by Marcia Williams. Each page tells of a single event and is given a title as a chapter in a chapter book would have. Master British storyteller Rosemary Sutcliff and illustrator Alan Lee team up on two books about Odysseus: *Black Ships Before Troy* and *The Wanderings of Odysseus*. The perils met by Odysseus and his men as they fight the Trojan War and then encounter the flesh-eating

Cyclopes, the enchantress Circe, and the Land of the Dead, among others, are told in Sutcliff's masterful style. Lee's realistic watercolor illustrations make the heroic Odysseus seem real, and the malevolent monsters and sorceresses more menacing. Warwick Hutton has retold and illustrated a book about one of Odysseus's adventures in *Odysseus and the Cyclops*. Odysseus's clever trickery of the one-eyed Cyclopes, which allows his crew and himself to escape, is illustrated with cartoon-like watercolor, muting the danger of the situation.

In *The Wolf of Gubbio*, Michael Bedard retells one of the legends of St. Francis of Assisi, the son of a wealthy Italian cloth merchant who embraced a life dedicated to serving others and God. In this story, St. Francis tames a wolf that had terrorized the people of Gubbio, killing humans and livestock.

Rosemary Sutcliff tells 13 stories from the Arthurian cycle in *The Sword and the Circle*. She explains in an author's note that, if King Arthur had lived, it was during the Dark Ages following the withdrawal of Roman legions from Britain and the occupation by the Saxons, a period from which there is little recorded history. Her book begins with the legend of King Arthur's accession to the throne after removing the sword set in stone by Merlin the Magician. She weaves stories of King Arthur's knights—Sir Gawain, Lancelot, and Percival being the best-known—with the stories of King Arthur's epic life. American Margaret Hodges and illustrator Trina Schart Hyman collaborated on an illustrated collection of three Arthurian legends. Their book, like Sutcliff's, is adapted from Sir Thomas Malory's *Le Morte d'Arthur*, one of the first books printed in England. Hyman's illustrations, painted with india ink and acrylic, were inspired by two 14th- and 16th-century paintings.

Veronika Martenova Charles adapted the Iroquois legend, *The Maiden of the Mist*, telling a version in which the Seneca girl elects to take her canoe over the edge of Niagara Falls in an effort to save her people from a sickness thought to be sent by the thunder god. She makes a deal with the god's son to marry him if he will help her people. Both carry out their end of the bargain and the real cause of the sickness, a malicious serpent, is eradicated. The maid's voice is heard calling to her children to this day.

James Houston wrote an Inuit legend that he heard while living in the Canadian North. His story is of *Tikta'Liktak*, an Inuit hunter who sets out to find food for his hungry family. After many adventures, Tikta'Liktak feels the end is near, as the ice floe he is on floats out to sea, and he builds a stone grave for himself. The sea spirit saves him by sending seals and a polar bear, which he kills to make a boat from the bladders. He eventually makes his way back to his people.

The legend of *Golem*, a human figure created by a Jewish righteous man, a *tzaddik* to protect the Jews living in a walled Prague ghetto in 1580, is written and illustrated by Caldecott-award winning David Wisniewski. His cut-paper collages tell the story as powerfully as the words: earthy colors and wispy cuttings of illustrations show how Golem was created. Fiery reds and oranges depict the mob rioting at the gates of the ghetto and the desperation of Golem, who wants to hold on to his life after the danger to the Jews has passed.

In *John Henry: An American legend*, Caldecott Medal winner Ezra Jack Keats has written and illustrated a tale of a man born with a hammer in his hand and big enough to help around the house within a short time of his birth. Turning broken paddlewheels to rescue ships and pounding out dynamite fuses to rescue underground mine workers in a cave-in are the legacy of this legendary hero. The vital force of a man who wins a rock-drilling contest against a steam drill pulsates throughout this story.

Myths

Myths are stories that grow out of a need to explain why things are as they are and how they came to be. Awe and wonder about the unknown and the unknowable have led to the creation of myths. Joseph Campbell (1988: 4) tells us that

> myths are stories of our search through the ages for truth, for meaning, for significance. We all need to tell our story and to understand our story. We all need to understand death and to cope with death, and we all need help in our passages from birth to life and then to death. We need for life to signify, to touch the eternal, to understand the mysterious, to find out who we are.

Sheldon Oberman has artfully woven 12 myths of the Minoan Civilization into a captivating story in *Island of the Minotaur: Greek Myths of Ancient Crete*. A fast-paced narrative style, together with Blair Drawson's bold cartoon-like drawings, engage young readers, though the gravity of the mythic stories is diminished somewhat by the style of the illustrations.

Priscilla Galloway retells two Greek myths: *Atalanta: The fastest runner in the world* and *Daedalus and the Minotaur*. She teams up with illustrator Normand Cousineau, whose ink-and-gouache illustrations have a stained-glass feeling to them, often with colorful borders. Atalanta is a huntress who is distracted by golden apples in a collaborative effort by Aphrodite and prince Melanion so the young man can win her love. The second book is about Daedalus, an inventor who fled Athens with his son Icarus when accused of murder. At the royal court of Crete, King Minos commands Daedalus to build a labyrinth to hide the Minotaur, a royal child rumored to be half-bull and half-man. Once the labyrinth is built and father and son have seen the Minotaur, their lives are in danger—to escape, Daedalus makes wings for himself and his son.

In Demi's *King Midas*, a Greek king with questionable taste in music ends up with donkey's ears, courtesy of Apollo, the sore loser of a music competition. Returning Dionysis's satyr leads to the granting of a wish. It seems like a good idea at the time, but King Midas grows to rue his choice: it is hard to get a decent meal when everything he touches turns to gold. Demi's sumptuous gold-leaf illustrations gild this story, which ends with a happy King Midas, whose swim in the River Pactolus helps him lose his golden touch.

Poet Kate Hovey wrote *Arachne Speaks,* the story of a weaving contest between the girl Arachne and the goddess Athena. Both weavers tell the story in turn. Canadian illustrator Blair Dawson uses acrylics to give close-ups of the two protagonists. But even though Arachne outweaves the goddess, she can never best her. Ready to hang herself after Athena destroys her shuttle and her woven masterpiece, Arachne instead becomes immortal as her spider

> . . . descendants thrive,
> Weaving [their] story again and again,
> to the planet's end—
> even then, [they] will survive.

Writer and illustrator Christina Balit retells the myth of the island of Atlantis in *Atlantis, the Legend of a Lost City*. Greek god Poseidon transforms the barren island on which his human wife lived into a paradise island. As long as Poseidon stays with them, the people of Atlantis live in peace and are wise and great-spirited. When Poseidon moves back to his underwater kingdom, human nature takes hold and human weaknesses prevail. Poseidon, forced to carry out his curse, stirs the seas into swallowing the island where it is "waiting to be discovered…" Gold and orange, and the cool colors of the seas wash over entire pages, adding a Mediterranean feel to the book.

Notable collections of Norse myths have been put together by Padraic Colum in *The Children of Odin* and Mary Pope Osborne in *Favorite Norse Myths*. The latter is powerfully illustrated by Troy Howell, whose acrylic with oil washes were inspired by the images carved in stone, bone, and wood left behind by the Vikings throughout Scandinavia and other regions of the Viking world. American author Marianna Mayer teams up with Canadian illustrator Laszlo Gal to retell one Norse myth, *Iduna and the Magic Apples*. Iduna, the renewing one, ensures that the gods are eternally young with her ever-renewable supply of magic apples. When Loki gives in to the evil Thiassi, and allows him to carry off Iduna to his ice castle, the gods become ever weaker and the heaviness of winter descends on Asgard, home of the gods. Only Loki can rescue Iduna. He turns her into a bird so she can escape Thiassi's prison. Iduna and her life-giving apples return to Asgard. Gal's resin-color wash with egg tempera illustrations are richly textured and mystical.

Questions of how the earth was created and how living things came to inhabit it have been asked by peoples around the world. Virginia Hamilton gathered from every continent 25 creation myths that attempt to answer such questions in her book, *In the Beginning*. At the end of each myth, Hamilton comments on its origins and elaborates on the gods of the cultures from which the stories come. Barry Moser's watercolor illustrations are somber interpretations of the creators and the created in the myths. One of the tales in the book, an Iroquois myth, is retold by American John Bierhorst in a book illustrated by Robert Andrew Parker: *The Woman who Fell from the Sky*. The creator is a sky woman who had been living on a floating island in the air. Pushed out of the sky by her husband, who is angry at finding out she is to give birth, the sky woman's fall is cushioned by sky people who turn into birds and animals. She gives birth to "Sapling, born to be gentle, and … to Flint, whose mind was hard as stone." The two continue to create the living things and seasons and heavens; always with two paths, one sapling-like and the other flint-like. The woman disappears in smoke and her two children leave the earth as two paths in the universe when their creation work is finished. Parker uses luminous gouache and pen-and-ink sketch-like illustrations to add to the sense of something being created.

Teaching with Legends, Epics, and Myths

Personal Response

- Students discuss and write in response journals who their personal hero is and what it means to them to be a hero.
- Students discuss and write about which epic/legend/myth figures they would like to meet and what questions they would like to ask the story characters.

Reading and Writing Skills

- Demonstrate reading comprehension strategies by reading the first paragraph of one or two epics, myths, or legends; explain how you use the clues in the paragraph to predict what will happen next and to infer characters' motivations for subsequent actions.
- Writing endings to epics, legends, and myths is difficult for student writers. Invite students to analyze how selected stories end, to assess the degree of satisfaction that the students feel with the endings, and to consider what the creators of the stories did to bring the story to a satisfying close. Students consider how they can use what they have learned from the stories in their own writing.

Literary Elements

- Students create cartoons of the main events in a favorite epic, myth, or legend.
- Students consider the themes of selected myths, epics, or legends. Then they create newspaper headlines and photographs (they could incorporate Internet images, if they choose) showing the stories' themes.

Critical Reading and Writing

- Students compare and contrast heroes and heroines from myths, epics, and legends with popular culture heroes of today. How has the image of a hero changed and how has it remained the same?
- Students work in small groups to create scripts for plays that draw on the characters and plots of a favorite epic, myth, or legend, but bend the gender stereotypes.

Traditional Literature Lists

Fairy Tales

Andersen, Hans Christian (1985: Ill. Demi) *The nightingale.*

Andrews, Jan. (2000) *Out of the everywhere: New tales for Canada.*

Aardema, Vera (1975) *Why mosquitoes buzz in people's ears.*

Badoe, Adwoa (2001) *The pot of wisdom: Ananse stories.*

Barton, Bob (2003). *The bear says north: Tales from northern lands.*

Becker, Hélaine (2007) *Mother Goose unplucked.*

Bodkin, Odds (1998) *The crane wife.*

Brett, Jan (1989) *Beauty and the Beast.*

Briggs, Raymond (1997) *Jim and the beanstalk.*

Brown, Marcia (1985) *Dick Whittington and his cat.*

Carrier, Roch (2004) *Flying canoe.*

Cooper, Susan (1986) *The selkie girl.*

Dahl, Roald (2002) *Roald Dahl's revolting rhymes.*

Davis, Aubrey (1995) *Bone button borscht.*

— (1998) *The enormous potato.*

dePaola, Tomie (1975) *Strega Nona.*

Demi (2000) *The emperor's new clothes.*

Emberley, Michael (1990) *Ruby.*

Eyvindson, Peter (1991) *The backward brothers see the light.*

Gal, Laszlo & Gal, Rafaella (1997) *The parrot.*

Galdone, Paul (1983) *The gingerbread boy.*

Garner, Alan (1992) *Jack and the beanstalk.*

Gay, Marie Louise (1994) *The three little pigs.*

Gilman, Phoebe (1992) *Something from nothing.*

Hamilton, Virginia (1997) *A ring of trickster tales: Animal tales from America, the West Indies, and Africa.*

— (2000) *The girl who spun gold.*

— (2003) *Bruh Rabbit and the tar baby girl.*

Helmer, Marilyn (2000) *Three tales of three.*

— (2001) *Three tales of enchantment.*

— (2003) *Three royal tales.*

Huck, Charlotte (2001) *The black bull of Norroway.*

Johnston, Tony (1996) *The cowboy and the black-eyed pea.*

Keens-Douglas, Richardo (2000) *The trial of the stone.*

Ketteman, Helen (1997) *Bubba the cowboy prince: A fractured Texas tale.*

Kimmel, Eric A. (2003) *Three samurai cats: A story from Japan.*

Lawson, Julie (1992) *The dragon's pearl.*

Lewis J. Patrick (1999) *At the wish of the fish.*

Lind, Michael (2003). *The bluebonnet girl.*

Lottridge, Celia Barker (1989) *The name of the tree.*

— (1998) *Music for the tsar of the sea.*

— (2001) *The little rooster and the diamond button: A Hungarian folktale.*

Martin, Rafe (2000) *The language of birds.*

McDermott, Gerald (1993) *Raven: A trickster tale from the Pacific Northwest.*

Muller, Robin (1991) *The nightwood.*

— (1993) *Molly Whuppie and the giant.*

Muth, Jon J. (2003) *Stone soup.*

Oberman, Sheldon (2000) *Wisdom bird.*

Park, Janie Jaehyune (2002) *Tiger and the dried persimmon.*

Paye, Won-Idy & Lippert, Margaret H. (2003) *Mrs. Chicken and the hungry crocodile.*

Reid, Barbara (2000) *The golden goose.*

San Souci, Robert D. (1995) *The faithful friend.*

Schwarz, Herbert T. (1969) *Windigo and other tales of the Ojibways.*

Scieszka, Jon (1989) *The true story of the 3 little pigs!*

Singer, Isaac Bashevis (1984). *Zlateh the goat and other stories.*

Singh, Rina (2003) *A forest of stories: Magical tree tales from around the world.*

Sturges, Philemon (1999) *The little red hen (makes a pizza).*

Taback, Sims (1999) *Joseph had a little overcoat.*

Thornhill, Jan (1993) *Crow and Fox and other animal legends.*

— (2002) *The rumor: A Jataka tale from India.*

Toye, William (1977) *The loon's necklace.*

Trottier, Maxine (1998) *The walking stick.*

— (2001) *There have always been foxes.*

Waldman, Debby (2006) *A sack full of feathers.*

Wallace, Ian (1994) *Hansel and Gretel.*

Yee, Paul (1989) *Tales from Gold Mountain: Stories of the Chinese in the New World.*

Yolen, Jane (2000) *Not one damsel in distress: World folktales for strong girls.*

— (2003) *Mightier than the sword: World folktales for strong boys.*

Young, Ed (1989) *Lon Po Po: A red riding hood story from China.*

Zelinsky, Paul (1997) *Rapunzel.*

Zemach, Margot (1986) *The three wishes: An old story.*

Fables

Anno, Mitsumasa (1987) *Anno's Aesop.*

Bader, Barbara (1999) *Aesop & Company.*

Bierhorst, John (1987) *Doctor Coyote: A Native American Aesop's fables.*

Goal, L.A. (Ed.) (2004) *Disabled fables.*

McFarland, John (1981) *The exploding frog: and other fables from Aesop.*

Morpurgo, Michael (2005) *The McElderry book of Aesop's fables.*

Paxton, Tom (1993) *Birds of a feather and other Aesop's fables.*

Pinkney, Jerry (2000) *Aesop's fables.*

Ward, Helen (2004) *Unwitting wisdom: An anthology of Aesop's fables.*

Wormell, Christopher (2005) *Mice, morals & monkey business: Lively lessons from Aesop's fables.*

Yolen, Jane (2000) *A sip of Aesop.*

Legends and Epics

Balit, Christina (1999) *Atlantis: The legend of a lost city.*

Bedard, Michael (2000) *The wolf of Gubbio.*

Charles, Veronika Martenova (2001) *Maiden of the mist: A legend of Niagara Falls.*

Hodges, Margaret (2004) *Merlin and the making of the king.*

Houston, John (1965) *Tikta'Liktak: An Eskimo legend.*

Hutton, Warwick (1995) *Odysseus and the Cyclops.*

Keats, Ezra Jack (1965) *John Henry: An American legend.*

Sutcliff, Rosemary (1981) *The sword and the circle: King Arthur and the knights of the round table.*

— (1995) *The wanderings of Odysseus: The story of The Odyssey.*

Williams, Marcia (1996) *The Iliad and the Odyssey.*

Wisniewski, David (1996) *Golem.*

Zeman, Ludmila (1992) *Gilgamesh the king.*

— (1995) *The last quest of Gilgamesh.*

— (2003) *Sindbad's secret: From the tales of the thousand and one nights.*

Myths

Bierhost, John (1993) *The woman who fell from the sky: The Iroquois story of creation.*

Colum, Padraic (2004) *The children of Odin.*

Demi (2002) *King Midas.*

Galloway, Priscilla (1995) *Atalanta: The fastest runner in the world.*

— (1997) *Daedalus and the Minotaur.*

— (1999) *My hero Hercules.*

Hamilton, Virginia (1988) *In the beginning: Creation stories from around the world.*

Hovey, Kate (2000) *Arachne speaks.*

Mayer, Marianna (1988) *Iduna and the magic apples.*

Oberman, Sheldon (2003) *Island of the minotaur: Greek myths of Ancient Crete.*

Osborne, Mary Pope (1996) *Favorite Norse myths.*

CHAPTER 4: Picture Books

Years ago, Arabic books welcomed their readers. The first page that the reader saw would say, "Welcome! Thank you for honoring this book by reading it. Your eyes warm my heart. The book is illuminated by your gaze." (Ellabbad, 2006: 25)

Every reader can remember a special picture book or two from her or his early years—the one that was shared on a parent's lap, read under bedcovers, or listened to on the classroom rug. Adults who enjoy books can likely recall a received-as-a-gift picture book, their first-book-taken-from-the-library picture book, or their favorite "Read it again, please!" picture book. The picture book, along with the experience of listening to it being read or reading it ourselves, is often one of the strongest childhood memories we carry with us. As we grow up, picture books are as vital as the foods that nourish us.

The picture book is a vibrant art form in which words and illustrations synthesize a new creation that can entertain or inform readers. Picture books have a strong attraction for readers young and old, but are especially appealing to today's visually-oriented children. The illustrations are as important as—or more important than—the text in conveying the message. They illuminate the text, extend the words into possibilities of meaning, and surprise the reader/listener with new interpretations. While the illustrations are the core of the book, the text is still essential. After all, it inspired the pictures.

Quality picture books seamlessly meld print and illustrated components, forming a rich and rewarding reading experience. The question, "What age is that book suitable for?" seems almost irrelevant. The well-chosen picture book embodies those qualities of word and picture that draw the reader's own experience to the page and let the child see and hear new meanings, a transaction between the child's own world and that of the author/illustrator. There are picture books of every type that will meet the needs and interests of particular children, that will comfort, entertain, inform, stimulate, and challenge young readers at various stages of development. As David Booth and Bob Barton (2000: 21) remind us: "The picture book speaks to most children; it speaks to the child in all of us."

Most picture books are written with vocabulary a child can understand but not necessarily read. For this reason, picture books tend to have two essential functions in the lives of young readers: they are first read to young children by adults, and then children read them themselves once they begin to learn to read. Some picture books are also written with older children in mind, developing themes or topics that are appropriate for children even into early adolescence. In our classrooms, students can participated in a shared reading/listening with a picture book and subsequently make connections or clarify meanings as they

The utter simplicity of children's book may make it difficult for adults to appreciate the complexity in thought and preparation their creations requires. Many people try to produce books for children, but the percentage of picture book manuscripts that are actually published each year is unbelievably small. Still, today's picture book industry is a vibrant one, and is evolving to meet the needs of 21st-century readers.

explore and exchange ideas with others through discussion or drama. The picture book can support or extend a curricular theme; can serve as a model for writing; can be the well from which personal stories are drawn; can inspire talk, writing, visual expression. Moreover, picture books can serve young people in their own reading development, helping them come to understand the joy of words, the power of story, and the wonder of illustration.

The Picture Book as a Format

We need to keep in mind that a picture book is a format. Picture books can be found in all genres of children's literature: informational texts, traditional tales, poetry, and all kinds of fiction.

Picture books convey their message through a series of visual images with a limited amount of text (or none at all); both text and illustration are necessary to construct meaning. Picture books with plot, in which the written and visual text equally convey the story line, are considered to be *picture storybooks*. An *illustrated book* is different from a picture book in that it is dominated by the text; the illustrations may extend the text and add to the story, but are not necessary to convey its meanings.

- Usually picture books follow a 32-page format with word count less than 500 words. In exceptional cases they could contain 24 to 48 pages and 2000 words, but without exception they incorporate illustrations that provide visual input, even for non-readers.
- Picture books run the gamut of media, including watercolors, woodcuts, lithography, photography, or collage.
- A number of picture books are written and illustrated by the same person (e.g., John Burningham, Lois Ehlert, Chris Van Allsburg), but just as often the author and the illustrator are different individuals.
- Some picture books, especially the ones for very young children, may contain no or very small number of words.
- Picture books have a range of purposes, from introducing rhymes and serving as manipulative toys to helping children learn concepts. They tell stories or impart information, thus providing an enriching source to young readers as they learn about themselves and others.

A Timeline of Picture Books That Mattered

1658 Comenius, Johannes Amos. *Orbis Sensualitium Pictus* (The Visible World in Pictures). Comenius added illustrations to informational text to increase children's understanding.

1886 Greenaway, Kate. *A – Apple Pie*. Greenaway's Victorian images of an idealized childhood of gardens and fancy-dressed children fill this old-fashioned alphabet book.

1899 Bannerman, Helen. *The Story Little Black Sambo*. This book is significant and controversial for its original illustrations depicting an iconic racist stereotype.

1926 Milne, A.A., Ill. E.H. Sheperd. *Winnie-the-Pooh* The adventures of a fictional bear named after a teddy bear belonging to the author's son, Chrisopher Robin.

1926 Gag, Wanda. *Millions of Cats*. This tale, about an old man who sets off to find the prettiest cat in the world, is often regarded as the first modern picture book.

1939 Bemelmans, Ludwig. *Madeline*. The adventures of a young girl who shows bravery and kindness in the face of adversity.

1947 Brown, Marcia. *Stone Soup: An Old tale*. This retelling of the traditional folktale was the winner of the first Caldecott Honor award.

1947 Brown, Margaret Wise; Ill. Clement Hurd. *Goodnight Moon.* Set in a single room, the text is a poem that has become a classic for parents to read to—and along with—children.

1954 Dr. Seuss. *The Cat in the Hat.* This book uses a vocabulary of only 223 distinct words, of which 54 occur once and 33 twice. Its success spawned the Beginner Books and the growth of elementary literacy learning in classrooms in the US.

1962 Keats, Ezra Jack. *The Snowy Day.* The first picture book with African-American protagonist. After seeing a *Life* magazine photo, Keats was determined to create stories with minority children as central characters.

1963 Sendak, Maurice. *Where the Wild Things Are.* "One of the very few picture books to make an entirely deliberate and beautiful use of the psychoanalytic story of anger." (Spufford, 2002: 49)

1967 Martin, Bill Jr.; Ill Eric Carle. *Brown Bear, Brown Bear, What Do You See?* Millions of children have answered the questions in this rhymed book, which introduces them to a parade of brightly-colored animals.

1969 Carle, Eric. *The Very Hungry Caterpillar.* A book that helps children learn about different foods, the days of the week, counting, and the life cycle of butterflies. This book has been translated into more than 50 languages (George W. Bush named this his favorite childhood book).

1977 Toye, William; Ill. Elizabeth Cleaver. *The Loon's Necklace.* Cleaver's collages illustrate a favorite West Coast Aboriginal legend. Horn Book claimed this book to be a touchstone for picture book art in Canada.

1978 Briggs, Raymond. *The Snowman.* This story, about a boy's magical adventures with his snowman, is told entirely in comic-book format, and can be considered the grandfather of the wordless graphic picture book.

1985 Van Allsburg, Chris. *The Polar Express.* A magical Christmas tale, weaving together reality and fantasy, this story appeals to children in its conveyance of the world of magic, and to adults who can recollect (consciously or not) their own childhood imaginings.

1986 Bourgeois, Paulette; Ill. Brenda Clark. *Franklin in the Dark.* Childhood emotions dealt with in a safe gentle story; first in a series.

1986 Munsch, Robert; Ill. Sheila McGraw. *Love You Forever.* One of the all-time best-selling picture books, this story about the evolving relationship between a boy and his mother is considered part of the children's literature genre, although it is mostly popular as a picture book for adults (i.e., mothers).

1989 Martin, Jr., Bill and John Archambault; Ill. Lois Ehlert *Chick Chicka Boom Boom.* The leader of the pack in alphabet books, not only for the author's genius for rhythm in rhyme, but for introducing the Matisse-like art of Lois Ehlert to the world of children's books.

1993 Raschka, Chris. *Yo! Yes?* Readers eavesdrop on a playground conversation in this book with highly verbal and visual language.

2007 Selznick, Brian. *The Invention of Hugo Cabret.* The winner of the Caldecott medal, this illustrated book is 523 pages long.

Issues for Discussion
- Which picture book titles do you think should be included in this timeline?
- Choose one of the titles from this timeline to investigate. Why do you think this book is significant? What would you tell others about this book?

Classification of Picture Books

There are more than 50,000 English-language children's titles in print, with 5,000 new titles published every year in the United States alone, to help parents, teachers, or librarians bring the right book to children at the right moment.

There are books to be shared with infants sitting on a parent's lap or books that can be read within a classroom community with children gathered together sitting on a rug. There are books that children choose for themselves in the classroom library and books that a teacher chooses to support a theme, introduce an issue, or entertain the class.

Picture books have been written featuring characters that appear in popular television shows (e.g., *The Backyardigans, Teenage Mutant Ninja Turtles, Dora the Explorer*); other recognizable names have become beloved series characters in the kingdom of picture books (e.g., *Clifford, Curious George, Peter Rabbit*). There are picture books with only one word on each page (*In My World* by Lois Ehlert) and others with powerful narratives (*The Ghost-Eye Tree* by Bill Martin Jr.). There are books written to appeal to boys (*Smash! Crash!* by Jon Scieska) and others written mainly for girl audiences (*Fancy Nancy!* by Jane O'Connor) There are picture books to be given as gifts to newborn babies (*On the Day You Were Born* by Debra Frasier) and titles that still sit on adult bookshelves (*The Giving Tree* by Shel Silverstein). There are "Wow!" picture books, such as Robert Sabuda's striking pop-ups in *Encyclopedia Prehistorica Dinosaurus* or David Carter's knockout *600 Black Dots*. Many young children have a favorite off-to-bed book; e.g., *Time for Bed* by Mem Fox or *Night Cars* by Teddy Jam. To provide a balance for books about a farting dog (*Walter, The Farting Dog* by William Kotzwinkle and Glen Murray), there are rich stories presented in such books as *Zen Ties* written by Jon J. Muth or the prequel premise to fairy-tale stories in Allan Ahlberg's book *Previously*. There are books that explode with color (*And to Name but Just a Few: Red Yellow Green and Blue* by Laurie Rosenwald) and others that have been illustrated in black and white (*Round Trip* by Ann Jonas), white on white (*Trail* by David Pelham), and even black on black—deciphered by touch (*The Black Book of Colors* by Menana Cottin and Rosana Faria).

There are picture books that are considered nonfiction, titles that can fit into a multicultural literature category, others that feature poetry and rhyme, and many that are considered to be traditional folk tales. Although picture book references appear in each chapter of *Good Books Matter*, this chapter gives focused attention to the world of picture books which can be enjoyed by both emergent and older readers.

More Than 100 Picture Book Author/Illustrators

Jon Agee: *The Incredible Painting of Felix Clousseau*

Allan and Janet Ahlberg: *Each Peach Pear Plum*

Aliki: *A Medieval Feast*

Mitsumasa Anno: *Anno's Journey*

Ludwig Bemelmans: *Madeline*

Sandra Boynton: *Barnyard Dance!*

Jan Brett: *The Hat*

Marc Brown: Arthur (series)

Anthony Browne: *Voices in the Park*

John Burningham: *Would You Rather…*

Eric Carle: *The Grouchy Ladybug*

Peter Catalanotto: *A Song for Solomon Singer*

Lauren Child: *I Am Too Absolutely Small for School* (series)

Barbara Cooney: *Miss Rumphius*

Lucy Cousins: Maisy (series)

Donald Crews: *Ten Black Dots*

Tomie de Paola: *Strega Nona*

Kady MacDonald Denton: *Would They Love a Lion?*

Leo and Dianne Dillon: *To Every Thing There Is a Season*

Lois Ehlert: *Red Leaf, Yellow Leaf*

Ten Picture Book Authors

Eve Bunting
Doreen Cronin
Mem Fox
Robert Krauss
Robert Munsch
Laura Numeroff
Hyawin Oram
Jon Scieszka
Jane Yolen
Charlotte Zolotow

Ten Picture Book Illustrators

Jose Aruego
Quentin Blake
Richard Egielski
Stephen Gammell
Ted Lewin
Michael Martchenko
Barry Moser
Jerry Pinkney
Lane Smith
Julie Vivas

Lisa Campbell Ernst: *The Gingerbread Girl*
Ann Dewdney: *Llama Llama Red Pajama*
Ian Falconer: Olivia (series)
Sarah Fanelli: *My Map Book*
Jules Feiffer: *Meanwhile*
Denise Fleming: *The Everything Book*
Michael Foreman: *War Game*
Fiona French: *Snow White in New York*
Paul Galdone: *The Three Billy Goats Gruff*
Marie Louise Gay: *Caramba*
Mordecai Gerstein: *The Mountains of Tibet*
Emily Gravett: *Spells*
Susanna Gretz: *Riley and Rose in the Picture*
Phoebe Gillman: *Something from Nothing*
Paul Goble: *The Girl Who Loved Wild Horses*
M.B. Goffstein: *An Artist*
Colin and Jacqui Hawkins: *Whose House?*
Kevin Henkes: *Chrysanthemum*
Eric Hill: Spot (series)
Tana Hoban: *I Read Signs*
Shirley Hughes: Alfie's World (series)
Satomi Ichikawa: *La La Rose*
Roberto Innocenti: *Rose Blanche*
Alison Jay: *Picture This…*
Oliver Jeffers: *How To Catch a Star*
Steve Jenkins: *Actual Size*
Ann Jonas: *The 13th Clue*
William Joyce: *George Shrinks*
Ezra Jack Keats: *Hi, Cat*
Charles Keeping: *Through the Window*
Steven Kellogg: Pinkerton (series)
Maryann Kovalski: *The Wheels on the Bus*
Leo Lionni: *Frederick*
Anita Lobel: *Potatoes, Potatoes*
Thomas Locker: *Water Dance*
James Marshall: George and Martha (series)
Mercer Mayer: Little Critter (series)
Robert McCloskey: *Make Way for Ducklings*

David McPhail: *Pigs Aplenty, Pigs Galore*
Bernard Most: *The Cow That Went Oink*
Jon J. Muth: *The Three Questions*
Christopher Myers: *Wings*
Jan Ormerod: *Sunshine*
Todd Parr: *It's Okay to Be Different*
Antoinette Portis: *Not A Box*
Jan Pienkowski: *Little Monsters*
Dav Pilkey: The Dumb Bunnies (series)
Daniel Pinkwater: *At the Hotel Larry*
Patricia Polacco: *Thank You, Mr, Falker*
Stephane Poulin: *Have You Seen Josephine?*
Chris Raschka: *Yo! Yes?*
Peggy Rathmann: *Officer Buckle and Gloria*
Barbara Reid: *The Subway Mouse*
Peter H. Reynolds: *The Dot*
Anne Rockwell: *Welcome to Kindergarten*
Tony Ross: *Dr. Xargles' Book of Earthlets*
Robert Sabuda: *Winter's Tale: An Original Pop-up Journey*
Allan Say: *Grandfather's Journey*
Laura Vaccaro Seeger: *Walter Was Worried*
Maurice Sendak: *Where the Wild Things Are*
Dr. Seuss: *Green Eggs and Ham*
David Shannon: No, David! (series)
Peter Spier: *People*
William Steig: *Sylvester and the Magic Pebble*
Janet Stevens: *Tops & Bottoms*
James Stevenson: *July*
Simms Taback: *Joseph Had an Overcoat*
Nancy Tafuri: *Have You Seen My Duckling?*
Shaun Tan: *The Red Tree*
Chris Van Allsburg: *The Polar Express*
Ian Wallace: *Boy of the Deeps*
Melanie Watt: *Scaredy Squirrel*
Rosemary Wells: Max and Ruby (series)

David Wiesner: *Flotsam*
Brian Wildsmith: *Squirrels*
Mo Willems: *Don't Let the Pigeon Drive the Bus*

Audrey Wood: *Silly Sally*
Arthur Yorinks: *What a Trip!*
Ed Young: *Lon Po Po*

Picture Books for All Ages

Picture books can be classified by theme, by topic, by genre, by author, by art style, by country of origin. To better support parents, teachers, and librarians, we have chosen to look at the various stages of development where readers encounter picture books. A further challenge is the variety of ways a picture book is experienced by a child—read to, read with, read alone, read together. Picture books are introduced to infants to help them engage with language and story; they are introduced to primary students to support them with their reading; they are used with students in the middle years and older to read independently. As we consider the literary journey a child takes as he or she learns (and has learned) to read, it is important to recognize that some books that have been listened to at an earlier age prepare readers to read independently as they crack the print code. Books that may seem young because of a limited amount print or written text can perhaps delight older readers when they revisit the books and share them with the children in their lives.

An Overview of Picture Books for Preschool Children (Age 0–4)

We have classified the books into types or themes that appear under the following four reading-level categories:

- Picture Books for Preschool and Early Childhood (Age 0–4)
- Picture Books for the Primary Years (Age 4–8)
- Picture Books for the Middle Years (Age 8–11)
- Picture Books for Older Readers (Age 12+)

It is important to introduce young children to books as early as possible in their lives, and the earlier the better. We admire when babies and young infants engage with a book by pointing to familiar objects, patting the pictures, exclaiming, laughing, and babbling away as each page is turned. Psychologists tell us that the greatest part of our intellectual development takes place before the age of five. The child's preschool years are therefore the most critical ones developmentally. It follows that this period of a child's life requires the richest of educational events. Teacher, bookseller, and writer Dorothy Butler (1998: 7) suggested that books "can be bridges between children and parents, and children and the world." For parents and other caregivers, this last point should be compelling enough reason for sharing books with children. The books young children meet, the event of sitting alongside an adult reading to and with them, and the words and stories that they experience prior to entering the classroom prepare children for the banquet of books in their schoolday journeys.

BOARD BOOKS

- Made of sturdy cardboard, highly visual
- Essentially a look and say themed list of people, animals objects
- Many titles have been published in both regular and board-book format

Barnyard Dances by Sandra Boynton (series)
The Runaway Bunny, Margaret Wise Brown
Counting Kisses: A Kiss and Read Book, Karen Katz

Bright Baby's First Words, Roger Priddy (series)
Max's First Words, Rosemary Wells (series)

PARTICIPATION BOOKS

- Provide concrete tactile materials for young children to explore
- Strong visual appeal, promoting curiosity and discovery
- Pop-up books and lift the flaps are variations of three-dimensional "surprises"

Dear Zoo: A lift-the flap book, Rod Campbell
Spot the Dog, Eric Hill (series)
Pat the Bunny, Dorothy Kunhardt

Gallop, Rufus Butler Seder
Dog, Matthew Van Fleet

CONCEPT BOOKS

- Simple nonfiction books that convey information young children can learn
- Explore a range of topics such as numbers, colors, shapes, etc.
- Abstract and concrete ideas are made accessible to young readers

Color Farm, Lois Ehlert (also: *Color Zoo*)
Go Away, Big Green Monster, Ed Emberley

Where Is the Green Sheep?, Mem Fox; Ill. Judy Horacek
Mouse Paint, Ellen Stoll Walsh

COUNTING BOOKS

- Help young children learn numbers and numerical sense
- Often identify a number of objects to count
- Mostly focus on numbers one to ten, but many titles go further

See also books on Mathematics in Chapter 7: Nonfiction on pages 158–160.

Ten Little Rubber Ducks, Eric Carle
Ten Black Dots, Donald Cres
Count, Deniese Flemeing

One Some Many, Marthe Jocelyn, Ill. Tom Slaughter
One Duck Stuck, Phyllis Root

Picture Books for the Primary Years (Age 4–8)

Cullinan and Galda (2002: 110) appreciate that "children forge connections between the books they read and the life they live because literature reflects every aspects of their expanding world." They identify six categories of such forging of connections:

- The inner world
- The world around family
- The social world
- The natural world
- The aesthetic world
- The imaginary world

How children feel about books alters in the primary years because they begin the process of learning to read. The fact that their ability to understand and their need for complex meaningful stories don't match their reading skills may lead to frustration, or eventually to abandoning books altogether. Since the task of learning to read can be a difficult one for many children, it is important for adults to continue to read aloud to them from as rich a selection of books as possible. Children must be encouraged to see in books a world of excitement and satisfaction. As they listen to powerful stories, look and listen to wonderful picture books, join in with songs and poems, and discover information within nonfiction, they will be building necessary vocabulary, story systems, and experiences that will serve them well as they become independent readers. The initial enthusisasm that beginning readers feel about reading must be supported by high-quality easy readers, and balanced by stories and books rich in language and image. Adults who understand the reading process will continue to share good books with children, extending their young worlds, modeling a love of books, developing language strengths, and building an atmosphere of trust and appreciation.

The primary years cover a wide range of interests and abilities. Some books are shared by adults children, some the children begin to read on their own. Adults must be cautious about matching children with books that they want to read and they can also handle—a difficult task but a vital one. Interaction with such picture books can help children develop from five- and six-year-old beginning readers into strong, independent eight- and nine-year-old readers.

A child's reading strength is dependent on his or her experiences both in life and in print. By sharing a picture book with a child on the lap or with a group, an adult can bring the words alive. At the same time the child can make sense of the pictures or illustrations, as word and image blend to make meaning. The sharing between child and adult as they experience a book also builds a special bond that will strengthen the reading process. Generally, picture books are not read by young children without adult intervention, but they provide the print experiences that will lead to independent reading.

As children mature, their taste for books develops, as do their cognitive and linguistic capabilities and needs. Learning to read and being able to unlock the secrets printed on a page marks an important step toward intellectual growth.

WORDLESS BOOKS

In wordless picture books, the story is revealed through a sequence of illustrations with no—or very limited—print text. Young children who have not yet learned to read can tell a story from examining the illustrations. Many beginning readers, using their developing concept of story, are able to narrate the story with character and narrator voices. Struggling readers can grasp the story elements in wordless books. Wordless books prepare young children to see books as a source of pleasure; children develop a reading readiness, for instance, through handling a book, turning the pages, following sequence left to right; and they develop an interpretation of and response to the story told by the pictures. Wordless books give children the opportunity to be flexible in their interpretation of the story.

Some wordless books offer readers a somewhat simple storyline. In the book *Good Dog, Carl*, first in a series by Alexander Day, a lovable rottweiler is instructed to look after the family baby; when left on their own, dog and infant become playmates. Similarly, we see dog as "man's best friend" in Mercer Mayer's wordless stories, beginning with *A Boy, A Dog and A Frog*. Several wordless picture books are like walking through the rooms of an art gallery. For example, *Yellow Umbrella* by South Korean artist Jae-Soo Lin depicts a high-rise view of colorful umbrellas carried by children walking in the rain: a bonus is a CD of rhythmic songs performed by Don Il Sheen to accompany the text. In Australian Jeannie Baker's *Window*, a mother and son gaze out at an environment that stretches before their household window. The scene changes on each page as the boy grows, helping readers to consider how growth affects the world as they examine Baker's masterly textured collage illustrations.

Many pictures in wordless books are filled with detailed images that suggest a narrative, often of an adventurous journey. These books demand close inspection of the pictures and invite readers to go back and forth between pages to synthesize story elements. Artist Istvan Banyai creates the effect of a camera lens zooming out in the book *Zoom*, which begins with a close-up of a rooster's comb and ends up in outer space. While visiting an art gallery, a young boy's imagination takes flight in the book *Picturescape* by Elisa Gutiérrez, and he is transported into some of the landscape paintings of some of Canada's best-known artists. Japanese Artist Mitsumasa Anno cleverly shows minute details of citizens working and playing in a busy countryside in *Anno's Journey*. In *The Red Book* by Barbara Lehman, a youngster literally gets lost inside a book, and in *Tuesday* by Davie Wiesner, a group of frogs are taken on a surreal journey. Wiesner recently won the Caldecott Award for the wordless book *Flotsam*, in which a beachcomer discovers an underwater camera which had been deposited on a beach. The artist cleverly plays with time, and shifts perspectives with close-up and landscape views, transforming everyday reality into magical possibilities.

ALPHABET BOOKS

Books organized in ABC order—alphabet books—are a special category of books that focus on a concept or a theme. Alphabet books serve many useful purposes, only one of which is related to learning the alphabet. Children from tweo to four years of age point to pictures and label objects on the page; five-year-olds may say the letter names and words that start with each letter; six-year-olds may read the letters, words, or story to confirm their knowledge of letter and sound correspondences. However they are read, alphabet books help children to develop an awareness of words on the page; they increase language learning; and they can serve as a pleasurable activity for children who can feel successful in recognizing alphabet letters.

Some alphabet books have only a single word on the page accompanied by a picture that matches the word (*The Hidden Alphabet* by Laura Vaccaro Seeger). Alphabet books are indeed an art form and provide artists with an opportunity to stretch their graphic talents, as Lisa Campbell Ernst does in *The Turn-Around, Upside-Down Alphabet Book*, and David McLimans in *Gone Wild: An Endangered Animal Alphabet*. *M is for Music* by Kathleen Krull is an example of a picture book that focuses on a topic: in this book a number of words about music match the different alphabet letters (e.g., *echo, elevator music, Elvis*). Another favorite is *Read Anything Good Lately?* by Susan Allen and Jane Lindaman. This book uses a noun–verb phrase pattern while listing all kinds of things we read (e.g., an atlas at the airport). Rhyming couplets are another popular way to share the letters of the alphabet sequentially, such as in Wallace Edwards's *Alphabeasts*. The book *M is for Maple: A Canadian Alphabet* by Mike Ulmer is an example of how the alphabet provides a structural format to give information about a certain topic. This book provides information about 26 people or places in Canada (e.g., *Q is for Quebec, R is for Rocket Richard*). This series includes more than 100 books (e.g., *L is for Lobster, T is for Teacher, Z is for Zamboni*) that give readers information connected to a variety of topics and places.

AN ALPHABETICAL LIST OF ALPHABET BOOKS

Animalia, Graeme Base
Bad Kitty, Nicky Bruel
Chicka Chicka Boom, Bill Martin Jr. and John Archambault; Ill. Lois Ehlert
David McPhail's Animals A–Z, David McPhail
Eating the Alphabet: Fruits and Vegetables from A to Z, Lois Ehlert

From Acorn to Zoo: and Everything in Between in Alphabetical Order, Satoshi Kitamura
The Graphic Alphabet, David Pelletier
The Handmade Alphabet, Laura Rankin
Illuminations, Jonathan Hunt
Jeremy Kooloo, Tim Mahurin
The Kitty Cat Alphabet Book, Andrea Burris & Anna Schad

Today there are a number of sophisticated picture books in which visual images have more significance than letters and words. Hence, alphabet books are suitable for readers of all ages to promote visual literacy, imaginative thought, and word power.

Look Once, Look Twice, Janet Marshall
Matthew ABC, Peter Catalanatto
A *Northern Alphabet*, Ted Harrison
On Market Street, Anita Lobel
Paddington's ABC, Michael Bond
Q is for Duck, Mary Elting & Michael Folsom: Ill. by Jack Kent
R is for Rhyme: A Poetry Alphabet, Judy Young
Superhero ABC, Bob McLeod
Tomorrow's Alphabet, George Shannon
Used Any Good Numbers Lately?, Susan Allen & Jane Lindaman; Ill. Vicky Enright

V is for Vanishing: An Alphabet of Endangered Animals, Patricia Mullins
Whatley's Quest: An Alphabet Adventure, Bruce Whatley & Rose Smith
The Extinct Alphabet Book, Jerry Pallotta
The Yucky Alphabet Book, Jerry Pallotta
The Z was Zapped, Chris Van Allsburg

BOOKS WITH MINIMAL TEXT

Many children need easy books to enable and empower as they learn to crack the reading code. Illustrations are particularly significant in these books, because they serve as cues to help young readers as they work through the print. To further assist children, the font may be larger in these books; the vocabulary may be limited; and there are often repeated words, phrases, and syntactic sentence patterns to carry readers along. Although they are limited in sentence length and text length, these books must an appealing story or interesting concept. Books with minimal text foster a sense of accomplishment by encouraging emergent readers to read independently. The success that children feel with these books moves them forward along the literacy path.

Parents who have shared picture books with children in their infancy will have likely introduced them to books in which objects are labeled (e.g., *Maisy's Amazing Big Book of Words* by Lucy Cousins); however, as they grow older, children need books that are easy for them to read on their own. Some books, such as *Eats* by Marthe Jocelyn, in which readers match creatures with their favorite food, have only one word on each page so children can better pay attention the illustrations as they identify objects and "read" the words. Books may have repeated phrases (*Not a Box* by Antoinette Portis). Others feature a single repeated sentence to accompany a full-page illustration: (*No, David!* by David Shannon repeats a mother's warnings to her mischievous son; *Hello World!* by Manya Stojic is a portrait gallery of children's faces each saying hello in different languages.

Careful decisions are made by publishers of children's books to format words and pictures on the page to guide children through the reading process. A sentence may be unbroken (*Reading Makes You Feel Good* and other books by Todd Parr) or chunked (i.e., broken in a suitable place). The beginning of a sentence may carry over to the next page (William Steig's *Pete's A Pizza*: "He thinks it might cheer Pete up/ to be made into a pizza"). In *Willie the Dreamer* by Anthony Browne, the gorilla hero dreams about his future life: "Willy dreams that he's a movie star/or a singer…" Readers who have had success with these simpler texts can explore books that bridge children to another level of reading texts; e.g., *The Dot* by Peter H. Reynolds has one or two sentences per page.

Even though he failed art in high school, **Todd Parr** went on to become one of the most prolific authors of children's books. Parr's work is recognizable for its bright flat colors, with each figure outlined in black, almost as in a coloring book. In each of his books, a sentence is repeated connected to a theme or topic. The patterned text and visual cues make Parr's books ideal for assisting young readers to read (and write) sentences. Some Todd Parr titles include *The Feelings Book*, *The Peace Book*, *The Family Book*.

Children who have just become independent readers can enjoy beginning-to-read books on their own; they combine controlled vocabulary with creative storytelling. Beginning-to-read books that have the most appeal have strong characterization, engaging plots, and themes that help to provide an understanding of relationships in a child's life. Though some have only one sentence of text per page, the sentences are generally simple, with few clauses.

Because these titles are often the first books children read independently, they are often classified as Easy Reader titles. Beginning readers are a type of picture storybook in which text and illustration can be enjoyed independent of each other. There is often a generous amount of illustration throughout the book; however, beginning readers might not be as reliant on the pictures for making meaning. Beginning books can be considered transition books for children moving from picture books to chapter books. They are designed to be read with minimal or no assistance from an adult.

Many books for beginning readers feature animal characters, covering a wide spectrum of the animal kingdom, and of themes and genres. There are animal characters who have found a place on bookshelves around the world for more than fifty years (*Caps for Sale* by Esphyr Slobodkina, *Corduroy* by Don Freeman, *The Story About Ping* by Marjorie Flack). There are stories with an aardvark (*Arthur* series by Marc Brown), two frogs (*Two Frogs* by Chris Wormell and *Fine As We Are* by Algy Craig Hall) and colored mice (*Seven Blind Mice* by Ed Young). There are books about a baby tiger (*Leo, The Late Bloomer* by Robert Kraus), a baby monkey (*Goodnight, Me* by Andrew Daddo), and a baby koala (*Koala Lou* by Mem Fox). There are books about animals in different environments, including the farm (*Farmer Duck* by Martin Waddell), the jungle (*Jazzy in the Jungle* by Lucy Cousins, the sea (*Swimmy* by Leo Lionni), and the forest (*The Mitten* by Jan Brett). There are information books about animals (*Waiting for Wings* by Lois Ehlert, *Surprising Sharks* by Nicola Davies, *Dogs and Cats* by Steve Jenkins). There are stories about sly animals (*Doctor De Soto* by William Steig), curious animals (*The Sweetest One of All* by Jean Little), and loyal animals (*John Brown, Rose and the Midnight Cat* by Jenny Wagner). There are books about toy animals (*Knuffle Bunny* by Mo Willems and *Monkey and Me* by Emily Gravett) and even books featuring invented animals (*The Gruffalo* by Julia Donaldson and *The Bunyip of Berkeley's Creek* by Jenny Wagner).

Showing how a connection to animals is a great way to involve children in reading, *Wolves* by Emily Gravett is an ideal picture book. Tension is built within the sequence of pictures as a wolf is about to attack an innocent rabbit (who is reading a book called *Wolves*). The text is an informational account, listing a number of facts about wolves. Animals are featured in the titles of other cleverly designed books by Emily Gravett: *Meerkat Mail*, *Little Mouse's Big Book of Fears*, and *Orange Pear Apple Bear*. Children can also learn facts about animals in a series of books written by Doris Cronin, told from the animal's point of view in diary format. In *Diary of a Worm*, we learn about the good news and bad news of being an underground creature as told (with great humor) as a series of diary entries. Sequels include *Diary of a Fly, Diary of a Spider*. Doris Cronin's first claim to fame was her widely popular *Click, Clack, Moo: Cows That Type*. Canada has its own animal hero in Mélanie Watt's *Scaredy Squirrel* trilogy. In the first book, we meet a timid squirrel who is afraid to leave his nut tree and venture into the unknown. Watt includes a variety of writing genres—including

A menagerie of animal characters are born from the paint brush of **Kevin Henkes**. He has told the Caldecott-winning story of *Kitten's First Full Moon* in shades of black and white; *A Good Day* using a palette of vivid pastels. But it's mice that Henkes must think are really nice—they are the heroes and heroines of many of his books: *Julius,the Baby of the World*; *Owen*; *Sheila Rae; The Brave*. Henkes claims that he likes to use animals to represent human characters because he can add more humor to his stories—and it works!

list, timetable, label, and instructions—to entertain the reader. Children can continue to laugh along with this neurotic, but wise, bushy-tailed creature. Watt has also introduced young readers to a very funny, very chunky, and rather rude cat named Chester who is determined to upstage the writer of the book, rewriting her story with annoying red markers. And, of course, the cat comes back in a sequel entitled *Chester's Back*.

Dogs are every popular characters in children's books. In *The Very Kind Rich Lady and Her One Hundred Dogs* by Chinlun Lee, a kind woman feeds and plays with her pets; in this story we learn the names of 100 names for dogs, some plain (Max, Candy), some fancy (Queenie, Silk), and some silly (Pretzel, Zaba), with only a handful of names with more than two syllables. *Bark, George!* by Jules Feiffer is a funny book about a dog who swallows a cat, a duck, and a cow, which forces his mom to take him to the vet to help George with his problem. The repeated syntactic structure, along with Feiffer's simple cartoon drawings, add to the hilarity of this picture book gem. Peggy Rathmann won a Caldecott Medal for her book *Officer Buckle and Gloria*, the story of a dog who literally steals the show from the the policeman who has come to teach the children of Napville some safety rules. Stanley is another dog character who likes to steal the show by causing mischief in the books *Stanley's Party* and *Stanley's Wild Ride* by Linda Bailey. The warm connections we can have with owning and caring for a pet dog be found in such stories as *Courtney* by John Burningham, *How Smudge Came* by Nan Gregory, and *I Want a Dog* by Dayal Kaur Khalsa.

Human characters, of course, appear in picture books for beginning readers, mostly featuring children of this age group. Children can recognize themselves in the family situations portrayed in picture books such as *Knuffle Bunny* by Mo Willems (father and daughter), *Come Away from the Water, Shirley* (mother, father, and daughter), *Big Ben* by Sarah Ellis (brother and sister), *The Hello, Goodbye Window* by Norton Juster (grandparents), and *Oonga Boonga* by Frieda Wishinsky (family). The community and school are popular settings for depicting friendships. *Eddy's Dream* by Miriam Cohen takes us into Miss Cordelia's classroom to meet Eddy, who refuses to join in and pretend play because he thinks "Dreams are stupid!" Through this picture book, illustrated with black-and-white photographs, children can experience a group of inner-city children demonstrating their care for one another and exploring their feelings though play. *Amazing Grace*, the story of an African-American girl who, despite her gender and race, is determined to play the starrring role the class presentation of *Peter Pan*, and *The Colours of Home*, the story of a Somalian refugee child who represents the images of war that he experienced, are two books by author Mary Hoffman that mirror children's feelings about fitting in. In recent years, a number of picture books have been released to help children consider a sense of belonging and building caring communities. *Say Something* by Peggy Moss, *The Recess Queen* by Alexis O'Neill, and *My Secret Bully* by Trudy Ludwig are some worthwhile reads to help young children consider the challenges of confronting bullies, targets, and bystanders.

A child's bonding with a senior citizen not only offers readers the opportunity to think about their own grandmas, grandpas, aunts, and uncles, but also helps to bring focus to elders in our homes and neighborhoods. *Wilfred Gordon McDonald Partridge* by Mem Fox is a must-read treasure that scratches the hearts of readers of all ages. In this story, a small boy tries to discover the meaning of memory so he can restore that of his elderly friend. It is often children like Wilfred Gordon who provide comfort and spirit for seniors: in *The Teddy Bear* by David McPhail, a little boy's stuffed bear gives hope to a homeless man; *Edward the Crazy Man* in Marie Day's book is given attention by a boy named Charlie. Three books about adult literacy in which young children connect with seniors are *Jeremiah Learns to Read* by Jo Ellen Bogart, *The Wednesday Surprise* by Eve Bunting, and *Mr. George Baker* by Amy Hest.

Stories set in fanciful worlds and imaginary kingdoms have a strong attraction for young readers. Phoebe Gilman's *The Balloon Tree* is noteworthy, not only for its exquisite jewel-colored paintings, but also for its engaging story about a brave princess who is left in charge of her kingdom and must save the day with one last balloon. In *The Saddest King* by Chris Wormell, when a small boy breaks the law (i.e., he cries) in a country where everybody is always happy, he is sent to the King who is supposedly the happiest person in the land. As the boy tries to convince the king that it is sometimes okay to be sad, children can think about the different emotions that make up our day-to-day lives. In *Cloudland* by John Burningham, a young boy goes hiking with his parents until he trips and falls off a cliff. He lands in Cloudland, where he frolics with other children until he finds that he is homesick and longs to return to his mother and father. A different kind of other-worldiness is presented in *The Flower*, in which we meet Brigg, who lives in a small gray room in a large gray city. In John Light's story, Brigg finds a book in a library. The book is labeled *Do Not Read,* but Brigg can't resist taking it. This sets off a chain of events involving a packet of seeds and a wildly blooming plant.

SERIES PICTURE BOOKS

As children begin to develop their interests and tastes they often enjoy reading books with familiar characters and recognizable formats. Many of these are can be enjoyed as read-alouds, but as students develop as readers it is these books that move them into independent reading. Recurring characters, such as Beatrix Potter's Peter Rabbit by Beatrix Potter and Ludwig Bemelmans's Madeline, appeared in multiple volumes written long ago. A majority of series picture books have anthropomorphic animal heroes: an aardvark (*Arthur* by Mark Brown), a monkey (*Curious George* by Margret and H.A. Rey), a pig *(Olivia* by Ian Falconer), and a gorilla *(Willy the Champ* by Anthony Browne). Sometimes characters come in pairs *(George and Martha* by James Marshall, *Frog and Toad* by Arnold Lobel, *Henry and Mudge* by Cynthia Rylant). Popular fictional characters that appear in a whole collection of books almost become friends to children, as young readers spend time reading about their adventures, their dilemmas and how they solve them. Series picture books for this age are useful for promoting quantity book-reading and significantly building young children's reading power. When a young child delights in reading more and more books about a single character, it can serve as a barometer for their future lives as readers of fiction.

Picture Books for the Middle Years (Age 8–11)

At one time, most picture books were published for students in the primary grades, but today publishers offer a variety of picture books that appeal to older students. Reasons for the change come from both sides of supply-and-demand: teachers and librarians want books that appeal to visually sophisticated students. Teachers want picture books to use with struggling readers who learn more easily using books with more pictures and fewer pages of dense text than traditional

Predictable or patterned books have strong rhythmic language patterns that help children predict what will be written, providing motivation and satisfaction for young readers. Because they are predictable, their vocabulary is limited, and illustrations are included to reinforce the text, patterned books are important for shared reading and initial reading instruction. Once children are familiar with the syntactic structure, they can replace words to create their own sentences, hitchhiking on the author's language pattern or story structure. For more than 40 years, teachers have invited children to write their own versions of *The Most Important Book* by Margaret Wise and *Brown, Brown Bear, Brown Bear, What Do You See?* by Bill Martin Jr.

textbooks. Second-language learners learn more readily using heavily illustrated texts and picture books instead of text-laden books.

Like many films, a picture book can provide pleasure for an audience spanning a wide age group. Just as *E.T.*, *Finding Nemo*, or *The Chronicles of Narnia* or can be viewed by the whole family, children in the middle years still can share in the delight of the picture book. The medium of literature allows them to experience stories, memoirs, concepts, and dreams as interpreted by authors and artists using photography, collage, etches, and digital images. The text within a picture book needs to be written concisely, and with the art in mind, so children gain a particular and effective communication package. Most of the books for this age group would fall under the category of picture storybook, in which the text and illustrations works together to amplify each other. In all picture books, the art enhances the verbal text; however, in picture storybooks, part of the story is told through the illustrations and part is told through the text. Text and illustrations do not merely reflect each other; combined, they tell a story that goes beyond what each one tells alone.

Since picture books are designed to be read aloud, children can experience literature through the ear and the eye, and perhaps be touched by the emotional quality inherent in this art form. Sometimes adults forget that students in the middle years are especially needful of hearing stories read aloud. Through modeling, the adult demonstrates the importance of reading, their attitude toward print, and the satisfaction of a story. They can share literacy selections, styles, and vocabulary that may be absorbed by the child. By choosing books that children themselves may not, or by selection picture books from other countries and cultures, the adult brings a sophisticated, multi-levelled approach to the process of finding out.

HUMOROUS BOOKS

Books that "make 'em laugh" appeal to students of this age, as their sense of humor is evolving. They still enjoy the world of silly and often get the humor found in the illustrations as well as the language of a number of wacky adventures. In David Shannon's *The Bad Case of the Stripes*, Camilla Cream is so worried about what others think of her eating lima beans that she wakes up on the first day of school to discover that her skin has been transformed into a striped rainbow. Speaking of health: *Dr. Dog*, created by the hilarious Babette Cole, comes to the rescue of the Gumboyle family and supplies cures for headlice, pinworms, and other ailments. *Cloudy With a Chance of Meatballs* by Judi Barrett offers the absurd premise of food falling from the sky in the town of Chewandswallow. One day it snows mashed potatoes and green peas, and on another day low clouds of sunny-side eggs move in followed by pieces of toast. Life is delicious for all the townsfolk—until the weather takes a turn for the worse.

Stories that mix the absurd with the gross are often enjoyed by students of this age. *Parts* by Todd Arnold is the first book in a trilogy in rhyme about a young boy who thinks his body is falling apart when he discovers that he has lost a few hairs. Something gray and wet from his nose turns out to be a piece of his brain! When Dav Pilkey's *Dumb Bunnies* books first came out, they featured a gold sticker that announced the books were "Too dumb to win an award." The author for these books is identified as Sue Denim (i.e. Pseudonym). These books are sure-fire winners for young readers, whether they immediately "get" all the twisted meanings ("Once upon a time there were three dumb bunnies who lived in a log cabin made out of bricks") or not. If students don't smile when they read each of Pilkey's sentences, seeing pictures of Baby Bunny pouring porridge down his pants or putting ketchup on his watermelon might make them laugh out loud. Other Dav Pilkey titles, such as *Dog Breath*, *Kat Kong*, and *Halloweiner*, are sure to delight middle-years readers and can be served as an appetizer to the hilarity of the Captain Underpants series.

BOOKS ABOUT ANIMALS

Animals are central to a number of story picture books that present relevant issues about nature and the environment through intriguing narratives. In *Tiger* by Judy Allen, a secret is held between a young boy and a hunter who comes to a village to shoot a tiger. This is no ordinary hunter and his way of shooting (photographs) is not as threatening as the villagers (and readers) think. The message in this book, and others with animal characters (e.g., *Whale*, *Eagle*), reach beyond a simple story to have students contemplate the plight of endangered species. Ecological awareness and an explanation of the food chain is presented in *Wolf Island* by Celia Godkin. The story follows the changes that occur when a pack of wolves leave a Northern Ontario island for the mainland. At first the wolves' absence goes unnoticed, but over months the mice, the rabbits, the squirrels, and even the owls fight for survival. Jackie Morris's lyrical words in *The Snow Leopard* weave a myth-like tale of the rarely-seen creature, suggesting hope in a time when the world's wild places are being torn away. *Stellaluna* by Janell Cannon is a survival story about a baby bat who is raised like a bird after falling headfirst into a nest. Readers learn not only about the habits of fruit bats, but learn about friendship and acceptance through Cannon's text and glorious full-page paintings.

Animals are also significant to human relationships in a number of picture books. *Waiting for the Whales* by Sheryl McFarlane, for example, illuminates the story of a grandparent and child, and helps readers consider the cycle of death and continuity through the annual appearance of the West Coast whales that come to keep an old man company. The poetic story in *Owl Moon* by Jane Yolen conveys not only the loving companionship between a father and daughter, but also humankind's relationship with the natural world. Set in a silent winter woodland, parent and child patiently await the arrival of the Great Horned Owl. Though readers may have encountered this book in earlier years, it is a story that draws on readers' personal memories of special times spent with special people.

BOOKS ABOUT RELATIONSHIPS

There are all kinds of families. Picture books can hold up a mirror to the family relationships that the students of this age experience. Anthony Browne has written a trilogy of books about family members in *My Mum*, *My Dad*, and *My Brother*. The one-per-page list of tributes for each family member can serve as an inspiration for young readers to write about their own relatives. *The Relatives Came* by Cynthia Rylant will likely prompt readers to think and talk about their own family gatherings, as they read about the car trips, the spread of food on the table, and the bulging household described in this picture book. *Mom and Mum Are Getting Married* is Ken Setterington's celebration of modern-day marriages in a story about two women who choose to have a wedding, much to the joy of their two children, Jack and Rosie.

Life isn't rosy for all families, and a number of stories for this age group depict families challenged by difficulties. David Booth captures the determined spirit of prairie farmers faced with the hardships of drought, dust storms, heat, and locusts in in the book *The Dust Bowl*. Karen Reczuch's realistic illustrations capture the vastness of the land and the intimacy of a family surviving life in "the dirty Thirties." *A Chair for My Mother,* written and illustrated more than 25 years ago by Vera B. Williams, tells the story of a young girl who, along with her waitress mother and grandmother, saves coins in hope of buying a new comfortable chair one day. The hardworking family in DyAnne DiSalvo's *A Castle on Viola Street* strive to get their own house by joining a community program to restore old houses. *Fly Away Home* by Eve Bunting offer readers insight into homelessness in a story about a father and son who are forced to live in an airport and move from terminal to terminal so that they won't be noticed. Hope comes to the boy when a trapped bird finds its way to freedom. Other books that deal with family poverty include *A Shelter in Our Car* by Monica Gunning, *The Magic Beads* by Susin Nielsen-Fernlund, *Uncle Willie and the Soup Kitchen* by DyAnne DiSalvo-Ryan, and *Those Shoes* by Maribeth Buelts.

Several stories recognize the special relationships we have with our teachers. Some humorous titles include *I Know an Old Teacher* by Anne Bowen, *Miss Malarkey Doesn't Live in Room 10* by Judy Finchler, *First Day Jitters* by Julie Danneberg, and a celebration in rhyme, *Hooray for Diffendoofer Day!* by Dr. Seuss and Jack Prelutsky. As well as writing novels and picture books for younger readers, Kevin Henkes has written some quality selections that help readers understand the ups and downs of all children who want feel safe in their classrooms. Lilly, the title character in *Lilly's Purple Plastic Purse*, loves everything about school, especially her teacher Mr. Slinger. When he asks her to be patient about showing her new purse, Lilly can't wait to show off. Mr. Slinger eventually takes away her purse and Lilly sips an angry note into his book bag. The young mouse comes to regret her actions, and an apology and some tasty snacks help to rebuild their caring relationship. In *Wemberly Worried* a young boy has a whole list of things to worry about on the first day of school, and in *Chrysanthemum* a young mouse girl's esteem is shattered when she arrives at school and discovers her classmates making fun of her name. Set in the Blue Ridge Mountains, *My Great-Aunt Arizona* by Gloria Houston tells the story of a woman who returns to teach at the one-room schoolhouse that she herself had learned in. Patricia Polacco draws on real-life incidents to create the stories and art for her picture books. Of particular note is the tribute to her relationship with a special teacher who helped her learn to read and love books in *Thank You, Mr. Falker*. Another teacher became the model for her character Aunt Chip in the book *Aunt Chip and the Great Triple Creek Dam Affair.*

BOOKS ABOUT IDENTITY

A sense of identity is central to a number of books featuring protagonists who are newcomers to North America, as the following four examples (each with "Name" in the title) show. In *My Name is Yoon* by Helen Recorvits, a young Korean girl named Yoon (which means Shining Wisdom) dislikes her English name and tries out new names (e.g., Cat, Cupcake) to make her feel more comfortable when she arrives in her school in the United States. In *My Name is Bilal* by Asma Movin-Uddin, a brother and sister arrive in a new school where they are the only Muslims. Hanging on to their beliefs and heritage, the two students encounter bullying and racism, until one teacher helps them to respect his identity. Though not set in America, names are central to *My Name Was Hussein* by Hristo Kyuchukov, which deals with prejudice and racism. The name Hussein means "handsome" in Arabic, and a young Muslim boy is proud that his name has been handed down in his family for generations. When an army invades Hussein's small Bulgarian town, his family is forced to give up its identiy and choose Christian names. Other stories about immigrant children who struggle with the new language and new school culture are *In English, of Course* by Josephine Nobisso, *I Hate English* by Ellen Levine, and *Josepha: A Prairie Boy's Story* by Jim McGugan.

TRUE STORIES

Picture book stories based on true events introduce young readers to the world of biography and autobiography. *Owen and Mzee* is subtitled *The True Story of a Remarkable Friendship*. This book by Isabella Hatkoff, Craig Hatkoff, and Dr. Paula Kahumbu outlines the astonishing friendship between a baby hippo named Owen and a 130-year-old giant tortoise named Mzee. Separated from his family, Owen is "adopted" by Mzee, and the two animals become inseparable. This book is filled with full-color photographs and will help young readers understand how friendship can endure even in the face of tragedy. Also based on a true story is *Mr. Gaugin's Heart*, originally written in French by Marie-Danielle Croteau. This biography tells how the young Paul Gaugin's grief at his father's death eventually led him to create his first painting.

Several picture books give readers information about the Underground Railroad. *Henry's Freedom Box* by Ellen Levine and *Moses: When Harriet Tubman Let her People to Freedom* by Carole Boston Weatherford are two recent examples. Two picture books were released in 2005 to honour the 50th anniversary of Rosa Parks's heroic action for civil rights when she refused to give up her seat on a bus to a white passenger. Both *Rosa* by Nikki Giovanni and *The Bus Ride That Changed History* by Pamela Duncan Edwards describe the significant event that changed American history. Similarly, *Martin's Big Words* by Doreen Rappaport offers a mini-biography of the life of Dr. Martin Luther King Jr.

Some author/illustrators have taken the initiative to celebrate their own pasts by telling stories about themselves or family members. Allen Say won the Caldecott Medal for *Grandfather's Journey*, his tribute to his grandfather. The artist's paintings weave together to create a family album memoir in Say's story about immigration and acculturation. Peter Sis's *The Wall* won the Caldecott Honour Medal for the recount of his life growing up in Czechoslovakia behind the Iron Curtain.

FANTASY ADVENTURES

The work of two picture book artists, Chris Van Allsburg and Anthony Browne, have a surreal style that particularly appeals to readers in the middle years. Browne's *Voices in the Park* looks quite simple at first glance, but attention needs to be paid to the colorful paintings with many layers that invite up-close inspection and many revisits. A bossy woman, a sad man, a lonely boy, and a young girl enter a park and, through their eyes, we see four different visions. As the story moves from one voice to another, the different perspectives are reflected in the shifting landscape and the seasons. Although the text is limited, readers will be surprised and delighted with the interwoven images presented by the author. In *Into the Forest,* a young boy sets off to visit his ill grandmother, despite his mother's warnings not to go into the forest. Reminiscent of the Red Riding Hood story, this imaginative and psychological exploration of a child's anxiety invites readers to keep the young boy company as he travels deeper and deeper

Patricia Polacco is an author/illustrator who grew up in California and today lives within blocks of her childhood home. Her Irish and Russian Jewish heritage are reflected in many of her stories. In all cases, Polacco's work is drawn from fact and true-to-life incidents. As a young person, Polacco had difficulty reading due to dyslexia, and turned to drawing to gain respect. Relationships with adults (*Chicken Sunday*), friendships (*Rotten Richie and the Ultimate Dare*), or family traditions (*The Keeping Quilt*) set the foundation of Polacco's work. *Pink and Say*, *Mr. Lincoln's Way*, and *The Bee Tree* are other favorites.

into the forest. Anthony Browne's work is recognizable from his iconic gorillas and dreamlike fantasy images that carry forward the style of master of surrealism Rene Magritte. Other titles for this age group include *Into the Forest*, *Changes*, and *King Kong*.

Jumanji by Chris Van Allsburg serves as an example of the author's style. Two bored children are left on their own for an afternoon—and more excitement and danger than they bargained for—when they discover a mysterious board game that brings a rhinoceros stampede, a slithering python, and an erupting volcano into the household. Full-page black-and-white illustrations sit alongside the story on the facing page. Van Allsburg's storytelling is ideal in its setting, tension, and resolution, and his artwork can best be described as extraordinary. Many readers will encounter Chris Van Allsburg's most famous book, *The Polar Express*, at some time in their life, and can learn how the author blends the reality of everyday events with the world of the impossible. Van Allsburg is an ideal picture book artist for readers in the middle years who are developing their tastes as readers, many who come to enjoy the world of fantasy. Between the ages of nine and twelve, students can readily suspend disbelief as they engage with Van Allsburg's curious storylines and hyper-realistic artwork. Other suggested titles include *The Garden of Abdul Gasazi*, *Just a Dream*, and *The Stranger*.

Picture Books for Older Readers (Age 12+)

Picture books are no longer the domain of the very young. The explosion of published works in this format in the past several decades attests to the growing number of picture books that are targeted at an older—and even adult—audience. Not only have the design and formatting become more sophisticated, but strong controversial themes and complex issues relevant to mature readers are found within many powerful examples. Though students from Grade 7 and up may not think it "cool" to choose a picture book to read independently, the special art form allows a shared reading experience by groups, as the words can be read and the pictures viewed at the same time. When a picture book is read aloud by the teacher, students of different ages can consider the central themes; however, with older readers it is important that the book engage them not only with powerful visuals, but also with a story that has universal, archetypal, or strong emotional appeal.

In the classroom, picture books are especially useful to promote core values that underpin the curriculum and generate thoughtful response on a range of issues. They also provide ideal material to enrich students' visual literacy. From early adolescence onward, students are offered texts of increasing depth and are encouraged to actively learn and view with more critical lens. Older readers can also experience picture books by preparing them for reading to young audiences, reliving their own experiences and reflecting on the books that they once loved.

Many older readers enjoy books that take them into fantastical worlds, and several fantasy books for this age have a strong appeal since they are primarily visual. *The Mysteries of Harris Burdick* by Chris Van Allsburg offers the premise that a children's book author/illustrator has disappeared, leaving behind a series of black-and-white drawings, each accompanied by a title and a caption (e.g., "It all began when someone left the window open.") In the introduction to the book, Van Allsburg asks, "What were the stories that went with these drawings?" and it is up each reader to answer this question, either alone or with others, by sharing assumptions and stories out loud or in writing. The central puzzle set up by the author allows students to question, to hypothesize, and to invent narratives that draw on their own experiences and understanding of story schema. The colorful paintings that appear in Rob Gonsalves *Imagine a Night* ask readers to consider a number of dream-like scenarios that take them beyond the boundaries of everyday life. A short piece of text accompanies each of the full-page paintings (e.g., "Imagine a night/when candlelight rises on butterfly wings to greet the lonely stars"). Like Chris Van Allsburg and M.C. Escher, Gonsalves depicts ordinary objects in magical settings, allowing readers to imagine the impossible. Companion books, *Imagine A Day* and *Imagine a Place* offer further visual explorations of fantasy settings, in which readers can swim up to the sun or find themselves in a labryinth of books.

Australian artist Shaun Tan captivates older readers with the wonderfully strange hyper-realistic visuals in his own books, *The Lost Thing* and *The Red Tree*, as well as in his illustrations for John Marsden's *The Rabbits*. *The Arrival* is a 128-page wordless book with hundreds of sepia-toned paintings, some of which appear as full pages and some presented in as many as 12 small squares filling a single page. The story of one man's arrival into a strange futuristic world has no linear narrative links, but conveys personal longing, political suppression, and dehumanized industry. Readers cannot help but move backward and forward as they "read" the real and surreal pictures of this graphic text. Depth of meaning can be gained as readers pore of the illustrations over and over again.

Some picture books seem simple in their presentation, but help readers contemplate philosophical questions or consider world events. Author/illustrator Jon J. Muth built on his studies of Zen to write *The Three Questions*, based on a story by Leo Tolstoy. Young adolescents, seeking answers to their own place in the world, can accompany Nikolai on his journey to find answers to three questions set by the wise old turtle who lives in the mountains: *When is the best time to do things? Who is the most important one?* and *What is the right thing to do?* Rhyming couplets, along with the powerful blend of photographs and paintings, in Australian John Marsden's *Prayer for the Twenty-first Century* express hopes and fears that older readers can recognize (e.g., "May the bombs rust away in the bunkers, And the doomsday clock not be rewound..."). Another Australian author, Margaret Wild, has written the beautiful but challenging book *Woolvs in the Sitee* that takes readers to a sinister and strange world of an abandoned city where a young man named Ben is hiding in a musty basement. Terrified of the "woolvs" that dwell in the shadows of his neighborhood, Ben finds an ally in Missus Radinski, who doesn't believe that the woolvs exist. Invented spellings (e.g., "luvlee wyld crèches") and shadowy sketches work together to make a haunting book that can work on many levels. Margaret Wild is also the author of the picture book *Fox*, which is a compelling read about friendship, loyalty, and abandonment. Dog, who is blind in one eye, and Magpie, who cannot fly, form a friendship that is challenged with the arrival of Fox, who attempts to lure the bird to abandon his friend. This award-winning book is a perfect example of picture book creation, where text and illustrations work alone and together to engage the mind and touch the heart. Although this book can engage readers of all ages, it might help young adolescents consider their own social relationships, risk-takings, and quest for independence.

Many picture books set in times of war help older readers begin to understand the complexity and horror of historical events. *Rose Blanche* tells the story of a young German girl whose curiosity leads her to discover a world beyond the everyday hardships and privations that she and her neighbors have experienced. Rose Blanche follows a group of soldiers after they come to arrest a young boy and eventually discovers a concentration camp in the woods. She takes food to the prisoners until the day the town is liberated, but it is on that day that she is shot by the soldiers. The paintings in Roberto Innocenti's book take up more space than the verbal text, and transport readers into the innocence and horror of a small town in World War II Germany. In *The Always Prayer Shawl* by Sheldon Oberman, a young Jewish boy's family decides to set up a new life in order to escape the revolution engulfing his village in Czarist Russia. The black-and-white art by Ted Lewin takes readers into the past, while the colored paintings that complete the book tell the story of a prayer shawl handed down from grandfather to grandson. Eve Bunting also recounts the story of a family forced pack up their belongings to flee their home as war approaches. *Gleam and Glow* is inspired by real events describing how a young boy finds hope in the survival of two special fish. *The Composition* by Antonio Skarmeta is a picture book originally published in Spanish in Venezuela. This book is about children living under an unspecified dictatorship. On the day after one of the fathers is taken away by soldier, a military officer enters the school classroom and demands that the children enter a writing contest using the title "What My Family Does at Night." The pressure of the children to betray their parents is central to this political story. Other titles with war settings include *Memorial* by Gary Crew, *Sami and the Time of the Troubles* by Florence Parry Heide and Judith Heide Gilliland, *Potatoes, Potatoes* by Anita Lobel, *The Conquerers* by David McKee, and *Faithful Elephants* by Yukio Tsuchiya.

Graphic Picture Books: Spanning the Continuum

Comics have always been popular; however, in recent years, more and more artists have been using the graphic format to tell a story. Emergent readers have always relied on visual cues to make meaning, but the pictures used in graphic texts are designed specifically to give information. Most significant is the use of speech bubbles as a way of representing conversation. Very young children are exposed to this text feature in such books as Jez Alborough's books *Hug* and *Yes!*, and Jeanette Winter's *Mama*, which is a simplified telling of the story of Owen the hippo and Mzee the tortoise. Peggy Rathmann uses repeated dialogue in her board book *Goodnight Gorilla* ("Good night, Gorilla"; "Good night, Elephant.") and countdown book *Ten Minutes To Bedtime.* Young readers who are learning how text and pictures work together to make meaning can have success "reading" the pictures only, or reading the narration or dialogue that accompanies the text.

When Mo Willems's book *Don't Let The Pigeon Drive the Bus!* was first published, the author was offering many young readers a first introduction to the speech-bubble convention for presenting dialogue. With minimal text, this book is a about a persistant bird; when he ends up throwing a tantrum, young children might recognize their own behaviors. Other pigeon adventures include *Don't Let the Pigeon Stay Up Late, The Pigeon Finds a Hot Dog,* and *The Pigeon Wants a Puppy.* Because of its repeated syntactic pattern ("Wolf, are you there?") and pictures that match the text ("I am putting on my jacket"), *Let's Play in the Forest* by Claudia Ruela is a graphic story suitable for beginning readers. Over the years, the picture books by the author/ illustrator Aliki have featured illustrations filled with characters who speak with speech bubbles. Several of her

Eve Bunting, who grew up in Ireland with a world of storytelling, is the author of more than 200 books for children. *Smoky Night*, a story set in the Los Angeles riots, was the winner of the Caldecott Medal in 1995. *Riding the Tiger*, with distinct woodcut illustrations by David Frampton, is an allegorical fantasy that invites older readers to consider the power of temptation and the loss of control that comes when you riding a tiger. Although many of the protagonists in Eve Bunting's picture books are younger than ten years old, her work helps older readers consider sensitive issues such as homelessness (*December*), racism (*One Green Apple*), and gangs (*Your Move*.)

A culture of technology and media exposure enriches visual literacy for today's children. As they learn to read, the graphic picture book offers an appealing format for cueing meaning. A growing number of 21st-century picture books use the comic-book format with increasing complexity.

titles are laid out in comic-strip format—panels, cartoon-like drawings, and speech bubble conversation help young readers to read words and pictures separately or alone. In *The Play's The Thing*, a teacher invites her class to put on a dramatization of the song "Mary Had A Little Lamb," which brings much tension and excitement as the children work together to rehearse and present the play. In *Communication*, Aliki offers different kinds of communications and the functions they serve. The format of these books offer appropriate resources for readers theater, with students reading aloud the text by taking on the character's parts.

Superhero: The Adventures of Max and Pinky by Maxwell Eaton III shows the adventures of Max and his pet pig, Pinky, when they decide to play superheroes. As sidekick, the pig gets stuck with a number of unappealing duties and, when he quits playing, Max finds himself in real trouble. Each page features one sentence of narration and an illustration in which the characters' conversations appear in speech bubbles. A larger number of comic frames are found *When Randolph Turned Rotten* by Charise Mericle Harper. The story about a beaver and a goose who are friends will likely entertain young readers as much as the appearance of a number of talking characters. In *Pssst!* a little girl's walk through the zoo is interrupted by a sequence of strange requests from each of the caged animals (e.g. "Can you get us bicycle helmets?" ask the Sloths. This picture book delights not only because of the six panel comic frames that appear throughout, but also because of line drawings and environmental print filled with puns and jokes. For *Sticky Burr* by John Lechner, there is very little narration, but the book is filled frames where mostly one or two characters speak.

Several picture books in graphic format are available for students ages 9 - 12 who enjoy the comic strip format. Author/ illustrator Marcia Williams has written a series of books that retell familiar and traditional tales. *The Illiad and the Odyssey, Tales from Shakespeare*, and *Oliver Twist, and other great Dickens Stories* have vivid storyboard formats with an abundance of text, each accompanied by short narrative paragraphs.

Teaching With Picture Books

Personal Response

- Invite students to isolate a sentence (or two) from the text, then have them create an illustration to accompany the snippet. Invite students to create an illustration that might have been included in the book, perhaps imitating the book's illustration style.
- Students work with friends to dramatize a story or part of a story. Have them plan their dramatization: what characters might be needed in their dramatization; if there will be a narrator; what dialogue from the picture book will be included in their dramatization. Students should also give careful attention to the sequence of events outlined in the picture book.
- Students complete the Tic Tac Tell chart (page 97) to record their personal responses to a picture book. Students can meet in groups to share their opinions with others.

Reading and Writing Skills

- Invite students to hitchhike on the pattern of a picture book. To prepare students for this activity, isolate the pattern by focusing on the syntactic structure, the rhyme scheme, and the format used to present ideas. Choosing a topic of their own, students imitate the model used in the chosen book. Useful pattern books for this activity: *The Important Book* by Margaret Wise Brown; *Somewhere Today* by Shelley Moore Thomas; *What Does Peace Feel Like?* by V. Radunsky; *Jack's Talent* by Maryann Cocca-Leffler.
- Tell students to imagine that they are a character in the picture book they read, and have them write a letter from the point of view of this character. Writing in role, students can consider who the charater might write to; what information to include in the letter; what problem the character would write about; what feelings the character might talk about; etc/ Students can exchange letters with a partner and write a letter in response to ask questions, give advice, or tell what the letter made them think about.

Literary Elements

- Organize an author study. Display a number of titles by a single author. You might read aloud a single title each day over a period of time, and invite children to choose books by the author to read independently. Students work together to brainstorm a list to help them identify the style and literary elements used by the author: *How to recognize a book by…*
- Picture book illustration is a unique form of artistry. Have students consider the medium used and how effectively the illustrations convey meaning: How does the artist's choice of color help to convey certain feelings? Do the illustrations give as much (or more) information than the text? Does the illustration match the text? Is each illustration in the book necessary, or might some have been eliminated? Is there an illustration you wanted to see included that wasn't? Is the illustration chosen for the cover the best choice?

Critical Reading and Writing

- Conduct a picture book contest. Each student can contribute one title they think might be worthy of an award. You may wish to consider books by a single author, information books, or books on a theme, such as humorous books or books about animals. To prepare for the contest, students brainstorm a list of criteria that they think should be considered to make a picture book "the best." Students can work in small groups and then as a whole class to determine Gold, Silver, and Bronze medal-winning picture books.

Tic Tac Tell

Complete this graphic organizer by writing words to describe a picture book you've enjoyed reading. Use the chart to tell others about this book. Start your book talk by choosing three items in a row.

Title of book	First sentence of book	Author's name
		Illustrator's name
A sentence I liked	**A sketch that could be considered for the book**	**Three interesting words** _____ _____ _____
My opinion of this book	**I learned about…**	**I wondered about…**

Picture Book Lists

Classifying Picture Books

Ahlberg, Allan; Ill. Bruce Ingman (2007) *Previously.*

Burton, Virginia Lee (1939) *Mike Mulligan and his steam shovel.*

Carter, David (2008) 600 *Black dots.*

Cottin, Menena & Rosana Faria (2008) *The black book of colours.*

Ehlert, Lois (2002) *In my world.*

Fox, Mem (1994) *Time for bed.*

Frasier, Debra (1991) *On the day you were born.*

Jam, Teddy; Ill. Eric Beddows (1988) *Night cars.*

Jonas, Ann (1983) *Round trip.*

Johnston, Crockett (1953) *Harold and the purple crayon.*

Kotzwinkle, William & Glen Murray; Ill. Audrey Colman (2001) *Walter the farting dog* (series)

Pelham, David (2007) *Trail.*

Martin, Jr., Bill & John Archambault; Ill. Ted Rand (1985) *The ghost-eye tree.*

Munsch, Robert; Ill. Michael Martchenko (1986) *The Paper Bag Princess.*

Muth, Jon J. (2008) *Zen ties.*

O'Connor, Jane; Ill. Robin Preiss Glasser (2005) *Fancy Nancy*

Rosenwald, Laurie (2007*) And to name but just a few: red yellow green blue.*

Sabuda, Robert & Matthew Reinhart (2005) *Encyclopedia Prehistorica Dinosaurus: The definitive pop-up.*

Scieszka, Jon; Ill. David Shannon (2008) *Smash! Crash!*

Silverstein, Shel (1964) *The giving tree.*

Picture Books for the Primary Years

Aliki (1993) *Communication.*

— (2005) *The play's the thing.*

Allen, Susan & Jane Lindamen; Ill.Vicky Enright (2005) *Read anything good lately?* (sequel: *Written anything good lately?)*

Alborough, Jez (2001) *Hug* (also: *Yes)*

Anno, Mitsumasa (1977) *Anno's journey* (sequels: *Anno's Italy, Anno's Britain)*

Bailey, Linda; Ill. Bill Slavin (2003) *Stanley's party* (sequel: *Stanley's wild ride)*

Baker, Jeannie (1991) *Window.*

Banyai, Istvan (1995) *Zoom* (sequel: Re-Zoom)

Brett, Jan (1989) *The mitten.*

Brown, Margaret Wise; Ill. Leonard Wiseguard (1949) *The important book.*

Browne, Anthony (1997) *Willy the dreamer* (sequel: *Willy's pictures)*

Burningham, John (1996) *Cloudland.*

— (1983) *Come away from the water, Shirley.*

— (1994) *Courtney.*

Bunting, Eve; Ill. Donald Carrick (1989) *The Wednesday surprise.*

Cohen, Miriam; Ill. Adam Cohen (2000) *Eddy's dream.*

Cousins, Lucy (2002) *Jazzy in the jungle.*

—(2007) *Maisy's amazing big book of words.*

Cronin, Doreen; Ill. Betsy Lewin (2000) *Click, clack, moo: cows that type!*

Cronin, Doreen; Ill. Harry Bliss (2003) *Diary of a worm* (sequels: *Diary of a fly; Diary of a spider)*

Daddo, Andrew: Ill. Emma Quay (2005) *Goodnight, Me.*

Davies, Nicola; Ill. James Croft (2003) *Surprising sharks.*

Day, Alexandra (1987*) Good dog, Carl* (series)

Day, Marie (2002) *Edward the "Crazy Man".*

Donaldson, Julia; Ill. Axel Scheffler (1999) *The Gruffalo.*

Eaton, Maxwell III (2007) *Superheroes: The adventures of Max and Pinky.*

Edwards, Wallace (2002) *Alphabeasts.*

Ehlert, Lois (2001) *Waiting for wings.*

Ellis, Sarah; Ill. Kim LaFave (2001) *Big Ben.*

Ernst, Lisa Campbell (2004) *The turn-around, upside-down alphabet book.*

Feiffer, Jules (1999) *Bark, George!*

Flack, Marjorie (1933) *The story about Ping.*

Fox, Mem; Ill. Julie Vivas (1985) *Wilfred Gordon McDonald Partridge.*

—; Ill. Pamela Lofts (1988) *Koala Lou.*

Freeman, Don (1968) *Corduroy.*

Gravett, Emily (2005) *Wolves* (also: *Little Mouse's book of fears; Meerkat mail; Orange pear apple bear*).

— (2007) *Monkey and me.*

Gregory, Nan; Ill. Ron Lightburn (1995) *How Smudge came.*

Gulierrez, Elisa (2005) *Picturescape.*

Hall, Algy Craig (2008) *Fine as we are.*

Harper, Charise Mericle (2007) *When Randolph turned rotten.*

Henkes, Kevin (2007) *A good day.*

Hest, Amy; Ill. Jon J. Muth (2004) *Mr. George Baker.*

Hoffman, Mary; Ill. Caroline Binch (1991) *Amazing Grace.*

— ; Ill. Karin Littlewood (2002) *The colour of home.*

Houston, Gloria; Ill. Susan Condie Lamb (1992) *My great-aunt Arizona.*

Jenkins, Steve (2007) *Dogs and cats.*

Jocelyn, Marthe; Ill. Tom Slaugher (2007) *Eats.*

Juster, Norton; Ill. Chris Raschka (2005) *The hello, goodbye window.*

Khalsa, Dayal Kaur (1987) *I want a dog.*

Kraus, Robert; Ill. Jose Aruego (1971) *Leo the late bloomer*

Krull, Kathleen; illus. Stacy Innerst (2003) *M is for music.*

Lechner, John (2007) *Sticky Burr.*

Lee, Chunlun (2001) *The very kind rich lady and her one hundred dogs.*

Light, John; Ill. Lisa Evans (2006) *The flower.*

Lionni, Leo (1963) *swimmy.*

Little, Jean; Ill. Marisol Sarrazin (2008) *The sweetest one of all.*

Liu, Jae-Soo and Dong Ill Sheen (2002) *Yellow umbrella.*

Ludwig, Trudy; Ill. Abigail Marble (2005). *My secret bully* (also: *Just Kidding*)

Martin, Jr. Bill: Ill. Eric Carle (1967) *Brown Bear, Brown Bear, what do you see?* (series)

Mayer, Mercer (1967) *A boy, a dog and a frog* (series)

McLimans, David (2006) *Gone wild: An endangered animal alphabet.*

McPhail, David (2002) *The teddy bear.*

Moss, Peggy; Ill. Lea Lyon (2004) *Say something.*

O'Neill, Alexis; Ill. Laura Huliska-Beith (2002) *The Recess Queen.*

Parr, Todd (2005) *Reading makes you feel good*

Portis, Antoinette (2007) *Not a box* (sequel: *Not a stick*)

Rathmann, Peggy (1996) *Good night, Gorilla.*

— (1995) *Officer Buckle and Gloria.*

— (2004) *Ten minutes to bedtime.*

Rex, Adam (2007) *Pssst!*

Reynolds, Peter H. (2003) *The dot* (also: *Ish*)

Rueda, Claudi (2006) *Let's play in the forest.*

Seeger, Laura Vaccaro (2003) *The hidden alphabet.*

Shannon, David (1998) *No, David!* (series)

Steig, William (1982) *Doctor de Soto.*

— (1998) *Pete's a pizza.*

Stobodkina, Esphyr (1938) *Caps for sale.*

Stojic, Manya (2002) *Hello world!*

Ulmer, Mike; Ill. Melanie Rose (2001) *M is for maple: a Canadian alphabet.*

Waddell, Martin: Ill. Helen Oxenbury (1996) *Farmer Duck.*

Wagner, Jenny; Ill. Ron Brooks (1973) *The bunyip of Berkeley's Creek.*

—; Ill. Ron Brooks (1977) *John Brown, Rose and the midnight cat.*

Watt, Mélanie (2006) *Scaredy Squirrel* (sequels: *Scaredy Squirrel makes a friend, Scaredy Squirrel at the beach*).

— (2007) *Chester* (sequel: *Chester's back*)

Wiesner, David (1997) *Tuesday.*

— (2006) *Flotsam.*

Willems, Mo (2003) *Don't let the pigeon drive the bus* (sequels: *Don't let the pigeon stay up late; The pigeon finds a hot dog; The pigeon wants a puppy*).

— (2004) *Knuffle Bunny: a cautionary tale.* (sequel: *Knuffle Bunny, too: a case of mistaken identity*).

Wishinsky, Frieda; Ill. Michael Marchenko (1998) *Oonga boonga*

— ; Ill. Dean Griffiths (2002) *Give Maggie a chance.*

Wormell, Chris (2003) *Two frogs.*

— (2007) *The saddest king.*

Young, Ed (1992) *Seven blind mice.*

SERIES

Allard, Harry G.; Ill. James Marshall: Miss Nelson.

Bemelmans, Ludwig: Madeline.

Birdwell, Norman: Clifford, the Big Red Dog.

Bourgeois, Paulette; Ill. Brenda Clark: Franklin.

Brown, Marc: Arthur.

Browne, Anthony: Willy the Champ.

De Brunhoff, Jean: Babar

Falconer, Ian: Olivia.

Lobel, Arnold: Frog and Toad.

Marshall, James: George and Martha.

Milne, A.A.: Winnie-the-Pooh.

O'Connor, Jane; Ill. Robin Preiss-Glasser: Fancy Nancy

Parish, Peggy; Ill. Lynn Sweat: Amelia Bedelia

Potter, Beatrix: Peter Rabbit.

Rey, Margret & H.A.: Curious George.

Various authors: Caillou.

Wells, Rosemary: Max.

Zion, Gene; Ill. Margaret Bloy Graham: Harry, the Dirty Dog.

Picture Books for the Middle Years

Allen, Judy; Ill. Tudor Humphries (1992) *Tiger* (also: *Whale; Eagle*)

Arnold, Todd (2000) *Parts* (trilogy)

Barrett, Judi; Ill. Ron Barett (1984) *Cloudy with a chance of meatballs.*

Bogart, Jo Ellen; Ill. Laura Fernandez & Rick Jacobson (1999) *Jeremiah learns to read.*

Booth, David; Ill. Karen Reczuch (1996) *The dust bowl.*

Bowen, Anne: Ill, Stephen Gammell (2008) *I know an old teacher.*

Browne, Anthony (1998) *Voices in the park.*

— (2004) *Into the forest* (also: *Changes; King Kong; Piggybook*)

— (2007) *My brother* (also: *My dad; My mum*)

Buelts, Maribeth; Ill. Noah Z. Jones (2007) *Those shoes.*

Bunting, Eve; Ill. Ronald Himler (1991) *Fly away home.*

Cannon, Janell (1993) *Stellaluna.*

Cole, Babette (1994) *Dr. Dog.*

Croteau, Marie-Danielle; Ill. Isabelle Arsenault; Trans. Susan Ouriou (2007) *Mr. Gaugin's heart.*

Danneberg, Julie; Ill. Judith Dufour Love (2000) *First day jitters.*

DiSalvo, DyAnne (2001) *A castle on Viola Street.*

DiSalvo-Ryan, DyAnne (1991) *Uncle Willie and the soup kitchen.*

Denim, Sue; Ill. Dav Pilkey (1994) *The dumb bunnies* (series) (also: *Dog breath; Hallo-Weiner; Kat Kong).*

Dr. Seuss & Jack Prelutsky; Ill. Lane Smith (1998) *Hooray for Diffendoofer Day!*

Edwards, Pamela Duncan; Ill. Danny Shanahan (2005) *The bus ride that changed history: the story of Rosa Parks.*

Finchler, Judy; Ill. Kevin O'Malley (1995) *Miss Malarkey doesn't live in room 10* (series).

Giovanni, Nikki; Ill. Bryan Collier (2005) *Rosa.*

Godkin, Celia (1993/2006) *Wolf Island.*

Gunning, Monica; Ill. Elaine Pedlar (2004) *A shelter in our car.*

Henkes, Kevin (1991) *Chrysanthemum.*

— (1995) *Lilly's purple plastic purse*

— (2000) *Wemberly worried.*

Kyuchukov, Hristo; Ill. Allan Eitzen (2004) *My name was Hussein.*

Levine, Ellen; Ill. Steve Bjorkman (1995) *I hate English.*

— ; Ill. Kadir Nelson (2007) *Henry's freedom box: A true story from the Underground Railroad.*

McFarlane, Sheryl; Ill. Ron Lightburn (1991) *Waiting for the whales.*

McGugin, Jim; Ill. Murray Kimber (1994) *Josepha: A prairie boy's story.*

Mobin-Uddin, Asma; Ill. Barbara Kiwak (2005) *My name is Bilal.*

Morris, Jackie (2007) *The snow leopard.*

Nielsen-Fernlund, Susin; Ill. Genevieve Cote (2007) *The magic beads.*

Nobisso, Josephine; Ill. Dasah Ziborova (2002) *In English, of course.*

Rappaport, Doreen; Ill. Bryan Collier (2001) *Martin's big words.*

Recorvits, Helen; Ill. Gabi Swiatkowska (2003) *My name is Yoon.*

Polacco, Patricia (1996) *Aunt Chip and the great triple creek dam affair.*

— (1998) *Thank you, Mr. Falker.*

Say, Allen (1993) *Grandfather's journey.*

Rylant, Cynthia; Ill. Stephen Gammell (1993) *The relatives came.*

Setterington, Ken; Ill. Alice Priestly (2004) *Mom and Mum are getting married.*

Sis, Peter (2007) *The wall: growing up behind the Iron Curtain.*

Shannon, David (1998) *A bad case of stripes.*

Van Allsburg, Chris (1981).*Jumanji.*(also: *The garden of Abdul Gasazi; Just a dream; The stranger)*

— (1985) *The Polar Express.*

Weatherford, Carole Boston; Ill. Kadir Nelson (2006) *Moses: when Harriet Tubman led her people to freedom.*

Yolen, Jane; Ill. John Schoenherr (1987) *Owl moon.*

Picture Books for Older Readers

Eve Bunting; Ill. David Diaz (1995) *Smoky night*

— ; Ill. David Diaz (2000) *December.*

— ; Ill. David Frampton (2001) *Riding the tiger.*

— ; Ill. Peter Sylvada (2001) *Gleam and Glow.*

— ; Ill. Ted Lewin (2006) *One green apple.*

Crew, Gary; Ill. Shaun Tan. (2004) *Memorial.*

Gonsalves, Rob (2003) *Imagine a night* (sequels: *Imagine a day; Imagine a place)*

Heide, Florence Parry & Judy Heide Gilliland; Ill. Ted Lewin (1992) *Sami and the time of troubles.*

Innocenti, Roberto (1985) *Rose Blanche.*

Lobel, Anita (1967/2004) *Potatoes, potatoes.*

Marsden, John (1997) *Prayer for the twenty-first century.*

Marsden, John; Ill. Shaun Tan (2003) *The rabbits.*

Mckee, David (2004) *The conquerors.*

Muth, Jon J. (2002) *The three questions.*

Oberman, Sheldon; Ill. Ted Lewin (1994) *The always prayer shawl.*

Skarmeta, Antonio; Ill. Alfonso Ruano (2003) *The composition.*

Tan, Shaun (2002) *The lost thing.*

— (2003) *The red tree.*

— (2007) *The arrival.*

Tsuchiya, Yukio; Ill. Ted Lewin (1951/1988) *Faithful elephants.*

Van Allsburg, Chris (1984) *The mysteries of Harris Burdick.*

Wild, Margaret; Ill. Ron Brooks (2000) *Fox*

—; Ill. Anne Spudvilas (2006) *Woolvs in the sitee.*

Williams, Marcia (2005) *The lliad and the Odyssey* (also: *Oliver Twist and other great Dickens stories; Tales from Shakespeare*).

CHAPTER 5 Novels

Among the encompassing definitions we could give "the novel" ("a mirror walking down a road," "a narrative of certain size with something wrong with it," is this: a novel is a vast heap of sentences, like stones, arranged on a beach of time. (Jonathan Lethem, *New York Times Review*, June 3, 2007)

Reading novels provides young people with an opportunity to reflect on human behaviors, emotions, values, relationships, and conflicts. When young people read a novel, they are invited to step outside their own lives and to become spectators observing imaginary events that might or might not occur in real life. At the same time, they become participants in these events as they are drawn into the story and share the feelings and experiences of the characters.

As young people develop their lives as readers—and this is a lifelong process —they come to appreciate a story not only by identifying with the characters but also by seeing through the eyes of the author. In reading and responding to novels, children become aware of how an author uses his or her talents and skills to create stories. They learn to note the author's choices in terms of style, language, action, and characters. As they read, they can rewrite the novel in their minds. They can reflect on their interaction with the text and make connections to their personal library of literary experiences.

In the classroom, we can explore novels that have been read as a class or by a group, that investigate a theme, or that have been read aloud by the teacher. As well, we can introduce and explore response activities that prepare readers for the novel, that accompany the reading of a novel, or that help readers reflect on the novel. Novels contain a wealth of stories; response activities will lead to dozens more.

Young people can increase their reading power through intensive and extensive experiences with novels. Readers can choose from a vast range of novels written by many fine authors. They can take countless imaginary journeys involving characters and situations that may be familiar or completely new. Novels can also provide road maps to help readers cope with life's difficulties.

Selecting Novels

As teachers—working with librarians, bookstore owners, parents, relatives, and friends—we can bring books to the attention of readers. To help match students with a suitable novel

- give students several books from which to choose
- have available novels that vary by topic, author, and level of difficulty
- be aware of the students' interests and needs
- consider the cultural identity of the character(s) in the book
- read aloud part or all of a novel, and recommend other books on the same theme or by the same author

- encourage the use of the library
- talk with students about their reading
- survey students to find current favorites
- share opinions of peers, librarians, and reviewers

A Continuum of Novels for Young Readers

Chapter Books

Chapter books are the stepping stones for young readers (ages seven to nine) into the world of novels. The distinguishing features of chapter books are the short chapter format (often with a title for each chapter), the inclusion of a number of illustrations throughout the book, and somewhat larger print than the books these readers will later meet.

As children learn to read a series of sequential chapters that create a complete story, they are given a chance to anticipate and predict—the major thinking operations in reading. When seven- to nine-year-olds choose chapter books, it marks a reading plateau for these readers, because they are now able to sustain their interest over several chapters, making sense of plot and characters as the information builds up. As the incidents and images in the books grow one upon the other, the children build a larger framework for understanding, and may come to realize the pleasure and satisfaction that comes from "a longer read."

Most significantly, the chapter books that young readers encounter usually belong to a series by one author. Many children at this young age like to collect things, and series books are another way for children to build collections. Because they take the guesswork out of choosing something to read, books in a series are easily accessible to young readers. The familiarity of the characters, the comfort of a recognizable author's style, and the enjoyment of a theme, such as mystery or humor, combine to form a strong appeal for these young readers.

Many characters in chapter books experience similar school lives to the children who read them. Readers can connect to these characters at the same time as they are amused by the cartoon-like fictional behaviors. Young girls in particular are enraptured reading about Barbara Park's feisty *Junie B. Jones* and her adventures in Kindergarten and Grade 1. Boys, more than girls, enjoy reading the witty tales of *Marvin Redpost* by Louis Sachar or *Jake Drake* by Andrew Clements. The popular aardvark characters in the Arthur picture book series by Marc Brown have moved on to appear in Arthur chapter books, which are enjoyed equally enjoyed by both boys and girls. Similarly, *The Kids from Polk Street School* and *The New Kids from Polk Street School* by Patricia Reilly Giff, *The Pee Wee Scouts* by Judy Delton, and *The Adventures of the Bailey School Kids* by Debbie Dadey and Marcia Thornton Jones allow readers to enter the neighborhoods and join the clubs of these popular story characters.

Many adults enjoy getting wrapped up in a good mystery book that challenges them to follow the clues and diversions laid out by the author as they seek solutions along with the story characters. Not only can children enjoy mystery stories for the same reasons, but this genre provides an authentic context for looking for meaning and synthesizing information. Children who enjoy reading *Nate the Great* by Marjorie Wienman Sharmat might move on to meet the girl with a photographic memory in the Cam Jansen series by David Adler, and then read about Donald Sobol's mastermind *Encyclopedia Brown* in stories that challenge readers to get involved in solving cases along with the son of a police

Peer acceptance is important to children at this age, so often children like to do what their friends are doing and read what their friends are reading. Reading the same chapter books can be a way to belong.

Some parents and teachers, who hope to stretch children's appreciation and awareness of the world of literature, may be concerned about the sameness of series books. However, being hooked on a series can lead these young readers to move beyond chapter book series to "real" novels. It is important that children not be pushed into reading novels that are not interesting to them or too difficult for them, for success in this phase in their reading growth may determine their futures as readers.

chief. Like the popular adult series by Sue Grafton, Ron Roy's *The A–Z Mysteries* is a collection of mystery stories each with an alphabetically sequential alliterative title (e.g., *The Absent Author, The Bald Bandit*) for young readers.

Both *The Magic Tree House* by Mary Pope Osbourne by and *The Time Warp Trio* series by Jon Scieszka invite children to hop aboard the pages of a book and travel to another time, another place. The dozens of titles in these two adventure series have helped activate children's prior knowledge of the world and learn new information about history and geography. At the same time, young readers come to learn how the world of fiction relies on the suspension of disbelief as the imagination is ignited. Children can choose to read these books sequentially in the order they were written, or select particular topics and settings that appeal to them. Both these adventure series are episodic, and usually involve the protagonists work toward solving problems in the world they are trapped in. For example in *Mummies in the Morning: Magic Tree House #3*, Jack and his sister are whisked off to Ancient Egypt where they encounter a long-dead queen who needs their help. In *Tut Tut*, the Time Warp Trio travel back in time and find themselves in a weird predicament involving a young Pharaoh named Thutmose and his evil minister, Hatsnat.

Another fictional trip to Egypt occurs in the book *The Mummy with No Name*, a title in the best-selling *Gironomo* series of 30+ titles. Geronimo is an Italian-speaking mouse who works for a fictional newspaper and goes around the world getting in trouble and solving problems. The books, authored by Geronimo Stilton, are written as though they are autobiographical adventure stories—by Geronimo Stilton. Some titles include *The Phantom of the Subway, the Mona Mousa Code*, and *Field Trip to Niagara Falls*. Frieda Wishinsky's Canadian Flyer Adventures describe the time-travel trips of characters Emily and Matt: *Crazy for Gold, Danger, Dinosaurs* and *Yikes, Vikings* are some sample titles in this series.

Fiction for Developing Readers

The middle years are the quantity years, when children gain reading power through in-depth experiences with novels. Many fine books have been written with this in mind. Children enjoy reading several books by a favored author or in a popular genre. Common themes link the most widely-read books—humor, school friends, mystery, fantasy—and children should be given as many opportunities as possible for choosing the books they wish to read on their own. Boys and girls may prefer different types of books; however, there are fine novels, if brought to their attention, that will fill their interest needs and present non-sexist portrayals of characters.

Children in the middle years represent a great range of reading abilities. Yet their common need is to read widely and often. A large selection of books is necessary for children who are moving into independent reading, but who may not have much security with print, and who need high motivation accompanied by material that is accessible. A child in Grade 3, 4, or 5 requires books that are of interest and that are also written at a level that the child can handle. Children at this age often want books that are short, so that they can read them over a short period of time, yet they also want the status of reading "thicker" books. Children need a book with a story in which they can become immersed, so that they want to read it completely to feel the satisfaction and pleasure that a good book gives. Books that are written with a controlled vocabulary but little art will seldom make a child want to continue reading.

Barbara Park says that being the mother of two sons has influenced her writing and helped her to tune into situations that children find to be funny. She likes to write about kids who are neither popular nor in control of life's events. One of Park's earliest novels, *Skinnybones*, gives us the character of Alex Frankovitch, whose Little League exploits have amused children since its publication in 1982. Barbara Park's series on Junie B. Jones is one of the most popular series for young girls who read chapter books.

Reading a series of books continues to be a draw for many readers who are eager to discover more about familiar characters. There is a transition from chapter books to easy-to-read novels that can be identified by several features

- the print size gets smaller
- the number of illustrations diminishes
- the length of the book increases

Some easy-to-read novels are still divided into chapters, but there is a noted reduction in pictures to accompany the text.

Over the years, such books as *The Hardy Boys* and *Nancy Drew* have maintained their enormous popularity with students. Similarly, young readers enjoy the familiar plot structures and take comfort in the heroes of series such as *Ramona, Boots & Bruno, Amber Brown, Aldo Applesauce, Abby Hayes* and *The Babysitters Club*. Popular authors at this level include Judy Blume, Beverly Cleary, Andrew Clements, Roald Dahl, Gordon Korman, Dav Pilkey, Lemony Snicket, R.L. Stein, and Eric Wilson. Once students have read and enjoyed one or two books by a popular author, they tend to want to read other books by that author. Young readers will likely continue this pattern until they are tired of the formula, or they experience a change in reading tastes.

Although not technically a series, it is common for many authors to write one or more sequels to engage young readers. Gordon Korman has a number of survival trilogies that are episodic and filled with suspense: *Dive, Everest, Island,* and *Kidnapped.* Many books feature animals with anthropomorphic characteristics —children who enjoyed reading about *The Mouse and the Motorcycle* by Beverly Cleary usually go on to read *Runaway Ralph* and *Ralph S. Mouse.* The animal characters in *The Cricket in Time Square* by George Selden reappear in *Tucker's Countryside* and *Harry Kitten and Tucker Mouse*; and the same vampire rabbit and his friends have nocturnal adventures in *Bunnicula, The Celery Stalks at Midnight, Howliday Inn,* and *Nighty Nightmare* by James Howe. Other collections feature characters that are the same age, in similar family situations, as the children who read the books, but with humorous out-of-the-ordinary adventure that is the stuff of fiction. Mordecai Richler's fictional hero *Jacob Two Two* appears in *Jacob Two Two Meets the Hooded Fang* and *Jacob-Two Two and the Dinosaur.* For more than 30 years, children have fallen in love with Judy Blume's Peter and his bothersome brother in *Tales of a Fourth Grade Nothing, Superfudge, Fudge-a-mania,* and *Double Fudge.*

Many novels continue to tickle the funny bone of young readers because of the extraordinary events depicted in them. The adventures of the wacky characters we meet in each chapter of *Sideways Stories from a Wayside School* by Louis Sachar are a perfect example of exaggerated humor. Who wouldn't laugh at Mrs. Gorf, with her long tongue and pointed ears; Dana, who was covered from head to foot with mosquito bites; or John, who could read words when standing upside-down? Similarly, the characters in *The Fabled Fourth Grades of Aesop Elementary* provide some rambunctious fun in modern-day fables, complete with morals by Candace Fleming. Some other examples of laugh-out loud out-of-the-ordinary adventures: *Chocolate Fever* by Robert Kimmel Smith is the story of a boy breaking out in brown bumps with the world's first case of chocolate fever; because of a bet with his friends, a young boy must eat fifteen worms in fifteen days *How to Eat Fried Worms* by Thomas Rockwell; in *The Nose from Jupiter*, the first book in a series of four by Richard Scrimger, a young boy discovers an alien living inside his nose.

Novels with dog characters seem to automatically attract young readers. There are funny novels about dogs, (*Dog Friday* by Hilary McKay, *Daggie Dogfoot* by Dick King-Smith, *The Meanwhile Adventures* by Roddy Doyle) and sad novels about dogs (*Where the Red Fern Grows* by Wilson Rawls and *Stone Fox* by John Reynolds Gardner). There are novels in which dogs behave like humans (*Dominic* by William Steig) and humans behave like dogs (*Barry, Boyhound* by Andy Spearman). There is even a novel about dog novels (*No More Dead Dogs* by Gordon Korman).

Other books for this age group have a strong appeal because the humor becomes just a bit darker or a bit ruder. Leading the parade are the books by Roald Dahl. Most children (and adults) can recall a favorite Dahl book they've enjoyed—*James and the Giant Peach, Charley and the Chocolate Factory, The Twits*—because of the sinister characters, fantastic settings, and remarkable adventure described within. In recent years, *A Series of Unfortunate Events* by Lemony Snicket (aka Daniel Handler) and the heroic adventures of Dav Pilkey's *The Adventures of Captain Underpants* books (with bizarre titles like *Captain Underpants and the Attack of the Talking Toilets*) have helped the children's book industry explode. These are books that children devour and want to own for themselves.

Many novels for ages 8 to 11 begin to engage children with real-life problems, bringing strong emotional connections to the stories being told. Many of these stories describe strong relationships with pets or animals in the community. Jean Little addresses the concerns of young children by writing about problems with peers, making friends, and overcoming fears. In *Different Dragons*, a Labrador retriever named Gully helps a young boy overcome his fears of dogs and of sleeping alone in the dark; nervous about making friends in her new neighborhood, a young girl becomes enamored with a stray Maltese terrier in *Lost and Found*. *Stone Fox* by John Reynolds Gardiner is the story of a race between a boy and his sled dog, and an Aboriginal man named Stone Fox. *In the Year of the Panda* by Miriam Schlein, a young Chinese a farm boy finds a baby panda near his mountainside home. Knowing that he can't keep the animal, he begins to nurture and care for the cuddly creature in the wild. A flock of wild geese help a young boy deal with his problems in *Jacob's Little Giant* by Barbara Smucker; similarly, swans help a mentally challenged young boy learn to cope in *Summer of the Swans*, and a fox helps a lonely boy grow stronger in *The Midnight Fox*, both by Betsy Byars.

It is at this age that realistic fiction begins to represent the world the children live in at home and at school, and authors begin to help developing readers contemplate the complexities of building friendships and finding their place in the family. Set in the past, Newbery Award-winning *Sarah Plain and Tall* and its sequels, *Skylark, Caleb's Story* and *More Perfect than the Moon*, invite young readers to cheer for children their age who have experienced loss and learn to adjust to having a new parent. In *Edward's Eyes*, Patricia MacLachlan creates a stirring portrait of a boy who loves music, books, and baseball. When Edward unexpectedly dies, his parents donate his eyes so they can give sight to another boy. *The Jacket* by Andrew Clements depicts a school incident involving a hand-me-down jacket that forces a white boy to become aware of racial discrimination and prejudice when he looks to his father for advice. Coping with death is a central theme in *A Taste of Blackberries* by Doris Buchanan Smith and *Mick Harte Was Here* by Barbara Park, *Sun & Spoon* by Kevin Henkes and *Missing May* by Cynthia Rylant.

Fiction for Independent Readers

For children who have developed into mature, independent readers, there are many novels available at an appropriate print and emotional level, that will also challenge their concepts and ideas. Rather than moving to more difficult or more adult fiction, these children need to deepen their reading experiences by moving into quality alongside quantity. Novels from other countries, other

On his website, **Andrew Clements** writes, "I don't know a single writer who wasn't a reader first." He published his first novel, *Frindle*, about a boy who makes up a new word, in 1990. He has since gone on to write a range of fictional material including picture books, chapter books, and young adult novels. Titles by Andrew Clements include *The Janitor's Boy, The School Story, The Landry News, The Report Card*, and *No Talking*.

The power of the peer group often determines what young people want to read; we must recognize this if we hope to influence reading materials selected by middle-years and young adolescent readers. By providing books of a similar theme to those they have read, but that are stronger in artistic merit, we can make the reader aware of other appropriate novels, thereby helping to build the literary foundation of future readers.

Boy/girl friendships are at the heart of *Skellig* by David Almond, *The Penderwicks* by Jeanne Birdsall, *Words of Stone* by Kevin Henkes, and *Belle Prater's Boy* by Ruth White.

cultures, or other contexts can present these young readers with problems and situations of greater complexity, subtle characterization, and multifaceted plot structures. These children can read the novels that represent the best of fiction for children.

Fiction for middle-years readers continues to revolve around several recurring themes—friends, family, fantasy, humor, sports, mystery, adventure, nature, and contemporary issues. These universals represent the interests and concerns of pre-adolescents: peer groups, their place in the social system, and the complexity of growing up. Even the most fantastical of novels reveals an underpinning of real situations and problems.

For many children in Grades 4 to 6, novels provide road maps for the challenges of contemporary life. They can identify with and live through the exploits of the fictional characters, and learn about many aspects of life vicariously through books, all while having enriching literary experiences. Since good books are forms of art, the perceptions and views built up through novels can give children a strong affective and cognitive basis for life, as well as a secure grounding in literacy.

Bridge to Terabithia by Katherine Paterson broke ground in highlighting a special friendship between a boy and a girl, and many novels have since featured strong male and female protagonists who grow and learn from each other. *If a Tree Falls at Lunch Period* by Gennifer Choldenko alternates between the viewpoints of Kirsten and Walk, seventh-graders at an elite private school. These two friends help readers to consider how race, wealth, weight, and other issues have an impact on friendships when they are faced with a mean but influential classmate. A troubled boy and his mother, and a man and his lonely daughter, come together in a run-down motel in *Greetings from Nowhere* by Barbara O'Connor. As the characters in this novel try to help the widow who must sell her home, they hope to create a brand new life for themselves. In Jerry Spinelli's *Eggs*, nine-year-old David forms a friendship with a quirky, independent 13-year-old girl named Primrose. Despite their differences, David and Primrose form a tight friendship as they help each other deal with coming from broken homes. In Spinelli's *Smiles to Go*, Will Tuppence's understanding of friendship is tested when he is caught in a love triangle with Mi-Su and his friend BT.

At this age, boys and girls can make strong emotional connections to the books they read, particularly with characters with special needs. *The Thing About Georgie* is that he is small—a dwarf, in fact—and, in this novel by Lisa Graff, the hero needs to overcome his small stature and his fears of becoming a not-so-big older brother. Although she wants a "normal" life, in the novel *Rules* by Cynthia Lord, 12-year-old Catherine learns to cope with a brother with autism and a family that revolves around his disability. The "rules" that introduce each chapter give Catherine strength as she comes to understand the answer to the question, "What is normal?" A funny and heartwarming character named Joey Pigza gives readers a compassionate understanding of what it's like to be a special needs learner, in *Joey Pigza Swallowed the Key*, the first book in the series by Jack Gantos. Sequels include *Joey Pigza Loses Control, What Would Joey Do?* and *I Am Not Joey Pigza*.

Just as students of this age group reflect on their relationships in school and community, they also give careful thought to their own families and their places in them. A wide range of family situations are portrayed in novels for independent readers in Grades 4 to 6. Deirdre Baker's *Becca at Sea* describes the adventures of a young girl who visits her grandmother's cottage while her parents prepare for the arrival of a new baby. Georgina, the heroine in *How to Steal a Dog* by Barbara O'Connor, lives with her overworked mother and younger brother in the family car in a small town in North Carolina. Desperate to help her mother improve the family situation, she solicits the help of her brother to get money by stealing a dog and then claiming the reward that she thinks the owners are bound to offer. In *Jakeman* by Deborah Ellis, the bus to Wikham Prison carries Jake and his older sister Shoshona, along with a group of other unhappy kids, all anxious to see their mothers. Tired of being bossed around and following orders, Jake hatches a plan to find the Governor and plead with him to pardon their moms. Ten-year old Lucky Trimble is determined to run away when she finds about that her legal guardian might abandon her, in Susan Patron's *Higher Power of Lucky*. In the verse novel, *42 Miles* by Tracie Vaughn Zimmer, JoEllen needs to decide where her loyalties lie as she tries to bring together her two separate lives—one as Joey, who enjoys weekends with her father, and another as Ellen, who lives with her mother in an apartment near her school and friends.

A wide range of cultures and religions are portrayed for young readers, often providing a mirror to their own lives and a window into identities that may be different from their own. In order to help students of this age become respectful citizens, it is important to provide them with books to help them understand the backgrounds, customs, and identities found in multicultural books. For example, *Esperanza Rising* by Pam Muñoz Ryan introduces readers to a young girl who is forced to leave her family ranch in Mexico when tragedy hits. When Esperanza and her mama flee to a California camp for Mexican farm workers, the young girl isn't prepared for the hard labor and lack of acceptance she now faces. Cynthia Kadohata won the Newbery Medal for *Kira-Kira*, which chronicles Katie and her family move from a Japanese community in Iowa to the deep south of Georgia. Katie and her sister Lynn are struck by the stares of the people who pass them on the street, but it is Lynn's illness that forces them the family to come together. The Newbery Medal also went to Linda Sue Park for her novel *A Single Shard*, set in 12th-century Korea. In this book we meet an orphaned boy named Tree-ear who, through an accident, becomes mentored in the art of making pottery. *Home of the Brave*, written by Katherine Applegate, tells the story of Kek, an African refugee who arrives in Minnesota to live with his aunt and cousin. Longing to be reunited with his mother, Kek is comforted by new friendships and finds strength in his memories. He develops a sense of responsibility, taking care of a cow that he names Gol, meaning "family" in his African language. This novel is written in free-verse style, with chapters that are no longer than four pages long.

Adventure stories set in the past—such as *The Castle Corona* by Sharon Creech, *Crispin* by Avi, and *Alex and the Ironic Gentleman* by Adrienne Kress—engage readers with their plot twists and exotic settings. In a novel by Trenton Lee Stewart, an 11-year old boy reads an advertisement for "gifted children looking for special opportunities" and sets out on a series of challenging and creative tasks with a group of four who form *The Mysterious Benedict Society*. Fantasy worlds à la Harry Potter continue to be enormously popular with boys (and girls) in the middle years.

For other titles, see Chapter 6: Multicultural Literature.

As they develop their tastes and interest in reading, independent readers look forward to a number of series, including *Artimus Fowl* by Eion Colfer, *The Spiderwick Chronicles* by Tony DiTerlizzi, and *Children of the Red King* by Jenny Nimmo.

Lloyd Alexander: *The Book of Three* (series)

David Almond: *Skellig*

Avi: *Crispin: The Book Without Words*

Natalie Babbit: *Tuck Everlasting*

Judy Blume: *Blubber*

Betsy Byers: *The Pinballs*

Beverly Cleary: *Dear Mr. Henshaw*

Esme Raji Codell: *Sahara Special*

Sharon Creech: *Love that Dog*

Christopher Paul Curtis: *Bud, Not Buddy*

Alan Cumyn. *Dear Sylvia*

Karen Cushman: *The Midwife's Apprentice*

Paula Danziger: *The Cat Ate My Gymsuit*

Eion Colfer: *Artemis Fowl* (series)

Cynthia de Felice: *Weasel*

Kate DiCamillo: *The Tale of Desperaux*

Brian Doyle: *Pure Spring*

Jeanne du Prau: *The City of Ember* (trilogy)

Deborah Ellis: *The Breadwinner* (trilogy)

Sarah Ellis: *Pick-up Sticks*

Anne Fine: *Flour Babies*

Louise Fitzhugh: *Nobody's Family is Going to Change*

Jules Feiffer: *A Barrel of Laughs, A Vale of Tears*

Paul Fleischman: *The Whipping Boy*

Cornelia Funke: *The Thief Lord*

Jack Gantos: *Joey Pigza Swallowed the Key* (series)

Morris Gleitzman: *Toad Heaven* (trilogy)

Andy Griffiths: *The Day My Butt Went Psycho* (trilogy)

Kevin Henkes: *Words of Stone*

Karen Hesse: *The Music of Dolphins*

Carl Hiaasen: *Hoot*

Polly Horvath: *Everything on a Waffle*

Bernice Thurman Hunter: *That Scatterbrain Booky* (series)

Glen Huser: *Stitches*

Brian Jacques: *Redwall* (series)

Julie Johnston: *In Spite of Killer Bees*

Marthe Jocelyn: *Mable Riley: A reliable record of humdrum peril and romance*

Cynthia Kadohata: *Kira-Kira*

Gordon Korman: *No More Dead Dogs*

Madeline L'Engle: *A Wrinkle in Time* (series)

Gail Carson Levine: *Ella Enchanted*

C.S. Lewis: The Chronicles of Narnia (series)

Jean Little: *Mama's Gonna Buy You a Mockingbird*

Janet Lunn: *The Root Cellar*

Lois Lowry: *Number the Stars*

Lucy Maude Montgomery: *Anne of Green Gables* (series)

Phyllis Reynolds Naylor: *Shiloh* (trilogy)

Kenneth Oppel: *Silverwing* (trilogy)

Katherine Paterson: *Bridge to Terabithia*

Gary Paulsen: *Hatchet* (series)

Linda Sue Park: *A Single Shard*

Kit Pearson: *Awake and Dreaming*

Richard Peck: *A Year Down Yonder*

Robert Newton Peck: *A Day No Pigs Would Die*

Daniel Pinkwater: *Fat Men from Outer Space*

Pamela Porter: *Crazy Man*

J.K. Rowling: Harry Potter (series)

Cynthia Rylant: *Blue-eyed Daisy*

Louis Sachar: *Holes*

Tor Siedler: *Mean Margaret*

Richard Scrimger: *The Nose from Jupiter*

Barbara Smucker: *Underground to Canada*

Jerry Spinelli: *Maniac Magee*

William Steig: *Abel's Island*

Mildred Taylor: *Roll of Thunder, Hear My Cry*

Cynthia Voight: *Dicey's Song*

Eric Walters: *We All Fall Down*

Jacqueline Wilson: *The Worry Website*

Jacqueline Woodson: *The Lottie Project*

Fiction for Young Adolescent Readers

In these beginning years of adolescence, the lives of children are changing drastically. These developments are reflected in both the content of what they read and in their attitudes toward the act of reading. As they come to depend more on peer groups, young people become critical of parents, of adults in authority, and of siblings. Books may provide some insights into these changes, giving young people roles for identification, situations for reflection, and opportunities for examining issues.

Novels for young adults allow the reader to engage in a dialogue with the author on a wide range of topics at a deep emotional level. The personal and private reading of a novel gives young people the security to delve into situations that may reflect their lives, giving them opportunities to identify and reflect upon human traits and behavior. The themes of these novels reflect the development of young adolescents, their concern about their place in the adult world, social justice, peace, ecology, the future and the past. Young adolescent readers are coming to an understanding of life's problems, and come to accept the portrayal and examination of these issues, carefully and artfully developed in the novel, in order to strengthen their understanding and beliefs of their own world and of society. Because of their well-developed reading abilities and mature interests, some adolescents may want to move into adult novels at this stage.

Peer acceptance is at the centre of adolescence, and many authors for this age group help students reflect on the complexities of coming-of-age. It could be argued that more girls than boys are drawn to the realistic fiction written for this age group. The popularity of series books such as *The Sisterhood of the Traveling Pants* by Ann Brashares and *The Clique* collection by Lisa Harrison represent the tastes of many girls. Beyond the pulp series, many authors of the past four decades show that they are in tune with the young adolescent spirit. Paula Danziger (*The Cat Ate My Gymsuit*), M.E. Kerr (*Little, Little*), Valerie Hobbs (*Anything But Ordinary*), Caroline Cooney (*The Face on the Milk Carton*), and Paul Zindel (*The Pigman*) are some examples. Lynn Rae Perkins won the Newbery Award for *Criss Cross,* in which a group of teenagers who live in a small town experience new thoughts and feelings, question their identities and disconnect as they search for the meaning to life. *Dairy Queen* by Catherine Gilbert Murdock is about a 16-year old girl, who chooses to train the quarterback for school's football team; tired of helping out on her family farm, DJ decides to try out for the team herself, but does not anticipate the reactions of those around her. An interesting approach to the rollercoaster ride of high school is taken in Lauren Myracle's The Internet Girls Collection, told entirely in instant messages: titles in this series include *ttyl, ttfn* , and *l8r gr8r.* Canadian authors of novels for students aged 12 and up include Martha Brookes (*True Confessions of a Heartless Girl*), Julie Johnston (*Two Moons in August*), O.R. Melling (*My Blue Country*), and Marthe Jocelyn (*Would You*). Award-winning author Sheree Fitch has written a fine novel, *The Gravesavers*, set in Nova Scotia, which blends elements of ghost story, historical fiction, and family relationships.

Although many of the protagonists in this genre happen to be girls, we can learn much about 12- to 15-year-old boys by reading works by some of Canada's leading male authors. Eric Walters is one of the most prolific of these authors; *Stars, I've Got an Idea* and *We All Fall Down* exemplify contemporary realistic fiction for males. Like Deborah Ellis, Walters has written a novel told from two points of view. In *Bifocal*, Haroon (whose parents emigrated from Afghanistan) is a serious student, devoted to his family. Jay, a white boy, is the school's football star. Readers are taken inside a high school torn apart by racism when the police arrest a Muslim student on suspicion of terrorism. Christopher Paul Curtis, the author of *The Watsons Go To Burningham – 1963* and *Bud, Not Buddy*, has written *Bucking the Sarge* about a 14-year-old boy who keeps his sense of humor while running the Happy Neighbor Home Group for Men and dreaming of going to college and becoming a philosopher. A fine example of historical fiction is *Elijah of Buxton*, which introduces readers to a first-generation freedom child from the black community of Buxton, Ontario. When the town's corrupt preacher steals money intended to buy the freedom of slaves still trapped in the US, the hero of Curtis's novel sets off in pursuit of the thief. A particular strength of several of these novels is a strong sense of community and culture. Brian Doyle paints a picture of living in Ottawa in the late 1940s in *Up to Low*, *Angel Square*, *Easy Avenue*, and *Mary Ann Alice*. Kevin Major sets his books in Newfoundland, offering forthright language and strong characterization in such books as *Hold Fast*, and *Far From Shore*. Tim Wynne-Jones sets *The Maestro*—a survival story of a teenage boy who takes refuge with a famous musician—in the wilderness of Northern Ontario. Other novels by Tim Wynne-Jones—*Stephen Fair*, *The Boy in the Burning House*, and a *Thief in the House of Memory*—deal with the metamorphosis into manhood as teenage boys deal with terror, grief, and mystery.

Many books have been written to help the world understand the horrors of the Holocaust, and it is at the adolescent stage that readers can begin to grasp the complexities of events that unfolded during World War II. In *The Book Thief* by Markus Zusak, Death relates the story of Liesel, a young German girl living in Nazi Germany whose book-stealing and storytelling abilities help sustain her family and the Jewish man they are hiding, as well as their neighbors. Jerry Spinelli's *Milkweed* introduces readers to an orphan boy who lives in the streets of Warsaw and who wants to be a Nazi one day, but then witnesses the emptying of Jews from the ghettos. In *The Boy in the Striped Pajamas* by John Boyne, the horror of the Holocaust is seen through the naïve eyes of Bruno, the son of a Nazi officer who lives with his family in a place he calls "Out-With." Bruno is unaware that the boy he befriends is one of his father's enemies who lives behind a wire fence. It is at the adolescent stage that many students first find that the satiric, autobiographic graphic novels *Maus* and *Maus II* by Art Spiegelman help them understand the impact of surviving the atrocities of war.

Other novels ask adolescents to consider what one person can do to make a difference. Eric Walters offers one of the first novels for young readers about the Rwandan genocide in *Shattered*. In this book, a 15-year-old boy volunteers at a soup kitchen where he meets a man who once was a soldier in the Canadian Armed Forces, who informs the teenager about the peacekeeping mission in Rwanda. Allan Stratton's *Chanda's Secrets* gives us a character filled with enduring strength and loyalty as she is forced to confront the appalling treatment of AIDS victims in southern Africa. Meg Rosoff has written a novel set in the future, *How I Live Now*, that tells the story of one girl's perseverance in a world of chaos and terrorism.

Novels about teenagers in trouble, or with rebellious attitudes, are a strong lure for adolescent readers. Written in 1967, S.E. Hinton's *The Outsiders* is about two brothers who live on the wrong-side of the tracks and must come face to face with the privileged "socs." This novel, which the author wrote while she was still in high school, is just as popular today as it was 40 years ago. After enjoying S.E. Hinton's first book, many readers (boys, in particular) go on to read other books by the author, such as *Rumble Fish*, *Tex*, and *That Was Then, This is Now*. In *Slake's Limbo*, Felice Holman tells the story of a troubled teenager who chooses to live on his own beneath the world in the tunnels of the subway system. Walter Dean Myers brings a contemporary approach to troubled teenagers, specifically Afro-American boys: in the award-winning *Monster*, 16-year-old Steve Harmon is on trial as an accomplice to a murder; *Shooter* is the story of three troubled teenagers involved in a high-school shooting; *Autobiography of My Dead Brother*, written by Myers and his son Christopher, is about teen gang violence, and uses sketches and comic strips to have the character make sense of the lose of a close friendship.

The rebel appears in many forms. Jerry, the hero in Robert Cormier's novel *The Chocolate War*, becomes one of the first anti-heroes in young adult literature when he finds himself caught between a tyrannical priest and a secret gang leader. Phillip, a ninth-grader in *Nothing But the Truth* by Avi, challenges teacher authority and gets suspended from school by singing "The Star Spangled Banner" during homeroom. Cole Matthews, in *Touching Spirit Bear* by Ben Mikaelsen, must choose between prison and the Native American Justice Circle as his punishment for smashing the skull of another boy. In *Trouble*, novelist Gary D. Schmidt tells the story of 14-year-old Henry, who runs away from home to hike Maine's Mount Katahdin with his best friend and dog. Along the way he meets up with Cambodian refugee Chay Chouan, who had been accused of fatally injuring Henry's brother, and who reveals the trouble that predates the accident. Holling Hoodhood, from *The Wednesday Wars*, is another one of Schmidt's antiheroes. During the 1967 school year, this seventh-grader stays behind in his teachers' classroom while all his classmates go either to Catechism or Hebrew School. Reading the plays of William Shakespeare, Holling learns valuable lessons about the world he lives in.

Many adolescents are consolidating their tastes and enjoy reading novels that take them into fantastical words, and there is still a strong need at this age for readers to read more than one book in a series. Sitting alongside Harry Potter titles, books by J.R.R. Tolkien, Terry Brooks, Anne McCaffrey, Francesca Lia Block, and V.C. Andrews can be found on thousands of teenage bookshelves. *The Inheritance Trilogy* by Christopher Paolini describes the world of a 15-year-old dragon rider whose quests are guided by an ancient storyteller. The *His Dark Materials* trilogy by Philip Pullman and the *Bartimaeus Trilogy* by Jonothan Stroud take the reader into parallel worlds where demons and mythical creatures live alongside humans. Garth Nix's fantasy trilogy includes modern and medieval worlds in *Sabriel* and its sequels *Liarel* and *Abhorsen*. Nix's talents as a fantasy writer can also be found in the spirit world of *The Seventh Tower* series and *The Keys to the Kingdom* collection, in which a young boy discovers a strange key that is central to saving the world from horrible plagues and sinister characters. Always ready to be entertained and shocked, many young adults favor books of the supernatural and horror: *Septimus Heap* by Angie Sage, *Protector of the Small Quartet* by Tamora Pierce, *The Edge Chronicles* by Chris Riddell, and *Cirque du Freak* by Darren Shan are series books that frighten and delight.

A Theme that Spans the Continuum: Bullying

The stastics are irrefutable. The headlines are frightening. The stories are painful. The issue of bullying plays a strong part in the culture of today's schools as educators struggle to help young people build better relationships. If we want to help young people live with integrity, civility, and compassion, we need to introduce strategies and resources that help students come to an understanding of the complex issue of bullying. We need to help students understand why a bully behaves the way he or she does, and we need to provide students with strategies to prepare themselves if they are caught in the bully web. Reading and discussing literature are powerful tools for such preparation.

FOR YOUNGER READERS

In chapter books such as *So Long, Stinky Queen* by Frieda Wishinsky, *Jake Drake: Bully Buster* by Andrew Clements, and *Shredderman: Secret Identity* by Wendelin Van Drannen, young readers learn what its like to survive the mean people who may be in their classrooms. *Scrambled Eggs and Spider Legs* is a short novel by Gary Hogg that explains what happens when a bully is assigned to be a project partner with the boy who is intimidated by him. In the British short novel *The Angel of Nitshill Road* by Anne Fine a guardian angel helps three terribly unhappy children who are relentlessly bothered by a bully. In Katherine Paterson's *The Field of Dogs*, not only does Josh need to deal with a bully when his family moves to a new neighborhood, but his dog is also facing a bully of his own. Judy Blume, the queen of realistic fiction, wrote one of the strongest books on mean relational and verbal bullying with *Blubber*. The story centres on the teasing endured by an overweight girl named Linda, and another girl's growth as she learns that this kind of mean behavior is wrong. A comparative situation can be found in *Larger-Than-Life Lara* by Dandi Daley Mackall, who frames the story in a clever format. Using the writing techniques she has learned in school, a fourth-grader relates how an obese girl in class changes the lives of those around her, despite being bullied by her peers.

Two novels that featured the bully issue, written more than 40 years ago, are still meaningful to today's readers. With no friends and a family who seems to ignore him, Martin Hasting, *The Bully of Barkham Street,* realizes that he must do something to improve his reputation. Mary Stolz helps readers crawl inside a bully and see how a sixth grader's world looks through Martin's eyes. We get to meet a girl bully in *Veronica Ganz* by Marilyn Sachs. Bigger and meaner than everyone else, Veronica meets her match when shrimpy Peter Wedermeyer tries to gain power within the class.

The titles of several novels for students from Grades 4 to 6 capture the themes of bullying: *Starting School with an Enemy* by Elise Carbone, *Losers, Inc.* by Claudia Mills, and *The Present Takers* by Aidan Chambers each paint a picture of targets who are being tormented by scary kids. Author Jerry Spinelli knows exactly what it's like to think and feel like student in the middle years, and each of his books convey the complexities of peer pressure and challenges of being accepted: as Palmer comes of age, he must accept the violence of being a *Wringer* in his town's annual pageant, or find the courage to oppose it; *Stargirl* is the new girl in the school who dares to do things her own way, challenging those around her to consider what is normal; Donald Zinkoff in *Loser* exemplifies a kid who seems to rise above it all, as his optimism, exuberance, and the support of his loving family prevent him from feeling like the misfit his classmates view him as.

FOR OLDER READERS

For young adolescents, the issue of the bully, the bullied, and the bystander helps readers carefully consider the relationships in their own lives. *The Misfits* by James Howe is about a group of four students do not seem to fit in with their small-town middle school. When it is time for school council elections, the students join together to represent all students who have ever been called names. A strong story about a class victim named Robert is told in Nicky Singer's *Feather Boy*. When a strange senior citizen calls upon Robert to help solve the mystery of a derelict house, the target learns what courage it takes to find his own voice and never give up. Teachers play an important part in two other two young adult novels: the new teacher at the school helps Maleeka learn to be comfortable with herself in *The Skin I'm In* by Sharon G. Flake; Ali, who is the leader of a school gang, determined to make trouble, bullies a new inexperienced teacher in *Bullies Don't Hurt* by Anthony Masters.

The bullying problem, of course, continues in high-school settings. When three popular girls go on trial in government class for their ruthless bullying of a classmate, everyone has to come to terms with the fallout. The book, *Poison Ivy* by Amy Goldman Koss is interesting in its format, presented as eight first-person narrators giving different versions of the same event. When the protagonist in *Inventing Elliot* by Graham Gardner becomes a victim of school bullying, he attempts to invent a calmer, cooler persona by changing schools in the middle of the year. He soon attracts the wrong kind of attention from a group known as the Guardian who are determined to maintain order at the school. Moving to a new school and finding a place to fit in also poses a problem for Paul Fisher in *Tangerine* by Edward Bloor, Alex Fisher in *The Losers' Club* by John Lekich, and Darrell Mercer in *The Bully* by Paul Langan. The power of cliques and manipulation over others are the foundation of another two novels: *Shattering Glass* by Gail Giles and *Speak* by Laurie Halse Anderson. A horrific picture of the bullying issue is described in *Give a Boy a Gun* by Todd Strasser, which tells the story of two boys who have been mercilessly teased and harassed by the jocks at their high school. Determined to get revenge, the boys begin to gather a small arsenal of guns from a neighbor.

An Overview of Novel Types

ADVENTURE NOVELS

- Exciting, fast-paced plot more important than characters, theme
- Action moves swiftly as characters pursue clearly stated goal
- Often take the form of a journey

The End of the Beginning, Avi
The Miraculous Journey of Edward Toulane, Kate DiCamillo
Dominic, William Steig

ANIMAL STORIES

- Animals and humans mix
- Naturalistic wild animals
- Anthropomorphic

The Underneath, Kathi Appelt
Julie of the Wolves, Jean Craighead George
Silverwing (trilogy), Kenneth Oppel

BIOGRAPHICAL NOVELS

- Written as if it is about a person's life
- Can be written by someone else, or by protagoinist
- Although characters are fictitious, form shares similarities with biographies, autobiographies

Our Canadian Girl (series)
White Lily, Ting-xing Ye
Run, Eric Walters

DIARY NOVELS

- Written as private account of protagonist
- Story told as though novelist (protagonist) is unaware that anyone will read the diary

A Gathering of Days, Joan Blos
Mable Riley: A reliable record of humdrum peril and romance, Marthe Jocelyn

The Amazing Days of Abby Hayes (series), Anne Mazer

FANTASY NOVELS

- Imaginative, alternative world ruled by created laws and values
- Though set in the realm of magic, laws are consistent, credible
- Often inhabited my supernatural and/or mythical creatures

The Thief Lord, Cornelia Funke (also: *Dragon Rider; Inkheart; Inkspell*)
The Giver (trilogy), Lois Lowry

His Dark Materials (trilogy: *The Golden Compass; The Subtle Knife; The Amber Spyglass*), Philip Pullman

GRAPHIC NOVELS

- Format is easily recognizable, by storyboard or comic-book presentation
- Story is told through illustrations and dialogue balloons, with some narration
- Multi-genre approaches including adventure, fantasy, humor

The Invention of Hugo Cabret, Brian Selznick

Bone, Jeff Smith
American Born Chinese, Gene Yang

HISTORICAL NOVELS

- Teach history by telling story of people who lived in a past time
- Incorporate historical facts, though characters and events may be imaginary
- Story is accurate, authentic picture of another time

Daniel's Story, Carol Matas
The Underground Railroad, Barbara Smucker

The Bully Boys, Eric Walters

HORROR NOVELS

- Concerned with supernatural/unnatural events, creatures
- Brooding atmosphere of terror
- Combine an eerie setting, violent acts, and display of powerful forces

Coraline, Neil Gaiman
Cirque du Freak (series), Darren Shan
Goosebumps (series), R.L. Stine

HUMOROUS NOVELS

- Both funny and fun to read; intent is to make reader laugh
- Enables readers to live out fantasies by reading about adventures they wish they could have
- Humor is dependent on personal taste

A Barrel of Laughs / A Vale of Tears, Jules Feiffer

Mean Margaret, Tor Seidler
Barry, Boyhound, Andy Spearman

ISSUES/PROBLEM NOVELS

- Deal with topic issue/problem in a serious or candid manner
- Provide insights into the way people think and act

Speak, Laurie Halse Anderson
Kira-Kira, Cynthia Kadohata
Feather Boy, Nicky Singer

MYSTERY NOVELS

- Create suspense: atmosphere is an important element
- Usually involve a protagonist and an antagonist
- Plot oriented with a problem to be solved

Chasing Vermeer, Blue Balliet
Time Stops for No Mouse (sequel: *The Sands of Time*), Michael Hoye

The Tom and Liz Austen Mysteries (series), Eric Wilson

REALISTIC FICTION

- Deals with the immediate "here and now"
- Readers can identify with issues of behaviors and experiences
- Relationships, friendships, and social attitudes and values predominate

Jeremy Fink and the Meaning of Life, Wendy Mass
The Graduation of Jake Moon, Barbara Park

The Higher Power of Lucky, Susan Patron

SCIENCE FICTION

- Scientific facts, hypotheses, technology are featured to present other worlds, times
- Speculate about possibilities of real world and future world
- Similarities between fictional and real world are deliberate; they are created to lead reader to consider our world from new point of view

The City of Ember (series), Jeanne Du Prau
The Keeper of the Isis Light (trilogy), Monica Hughes

The Girl Who Owned a City, O.T. Nelson

SPORTS NOVELS

- Appeal to readers interested in sports and sports heroes

- Usually examine the effect of competition on an athlete
- May appear as part of a series by one author

Sports Classics (series), Matt Christopher

The Year of the Boar and Jackie Robinson, Bette Bao Lord

Dairy Queen, Catherine Gilbert Murdock

VERSE NOVELS

- Written in free-verse poetry
- Usually written in first-person voice
- Narrative built through a series of poems, each not more than two pages

Love that Dog, Sharon Creech
Out of the Dust, Karen Hesse

Crazy Man, Pamela Porter
Locomotion, Jacqueline Woodson

WAR NOVELS

- Setting is an important part of the story
- Teach historical facts about countries at war
- Gain readers' sympathies for a protagonist trapped by an enemy

Oranges in No Man's Land, Elizabeth Laird

Private Peaceful, Michael Morpurgo

Sunrise Over Fallujah, Walter Dean Myers

Multi-Modal Genres

Verse Novels

Karen Hesse won the 1998 Newbery Award for the novel *Out of The Dust*, a rich description of the harsh farm life during the dust storms of the 1930s. With each meticulously arranged verse entry, the author conveys a vivid picture of a young girl's desolation, longing, and hope. Karen Hesse uses the same format for the novels *Witness* and *Aleutian Sparrow*. In both *Keesha's House* and *Spinning Through the Universe*, Helen Frost weaves together stories of several characters as they struggle to hold their lives together at home and at school. *Frenchtown Summer* by Robert Cormier is a series of vignettes in which the writer reminisces about his life as a 12-year-old living in a small town in 1938. The verse form of *Where the Steps Were* by Andrea Cheng details the last year of five students in Miss D's third-grade class before their inner-city school is torn down.

Many award-winning authors have attempted the verse form. Sharon Creech's gem, *Love That Dog*, describes how one young student comes to love poetry by gaining a personal understanding of what different poems mean to him. In the sequel, *Hate That Cat*, we are reintroduced to the characters of Jack and his teacher and the world of poems. In *Heartbeat* Creech's character contemplates the many rhythms of life the year that her mother becomes pregnant and her best friend becomes distant. Cynthia Rylant's *Ludie's Life* is a collection of poems that follows the character from childhood, through marriage, motherhood, and old age. Rylant's *Boris* is a tribute to companionship and compassion as seen through the world of a big gray cat. Kevin Major has written a historical novel, *Ann and Seamus*, in poetic form. Author Pamela Porter has won a number of Canadian book awards for *The Crazy Man*, a story set in the Prairies that describes a disabled girl's friendship with a man with a mental disorder.

Several verse novels have been written for young adult readers. *Jinx* by Margaret Wild is a powerful verse novel about identity, loss, and love. The work of Australian author Steven Herrick can be recognized by the prose that comprises his novels about troubled teenagers: *The Simple Gift*, *By the River*, and *The Wolf*. *The Brimstone Journals* by Ron Koertge presents a haunting series of poems by fictional high-school students who contemplate the violence existing in their lives.

MULTI-GENRE APPROACHES

The multi-genre approach makes for an interesting twist of reading a novel. In his award-winning book *Monster*, Walter Dean Myers tells the story about the murder trial of a 16-year-old through diary entries, courtroom transcripts, and the teenager's imagined film script that helps him come to terms with the course his life has taken. In *Shooter*, Myers uses interviews, reports, and journal entries to tell the story of a tragic shooting at a high school.

Transcripts, which present the authentic conversation of characters, are important features of the novels *Days of Tears* by Julius Lester, *Seek* by Paul Fleischman, and *Nothing but the Truth: A Documentary Novel* by Avi.

In a more humorous vein, *Barry Boyhound* by Andy Spearman is the story a boy who feels and acts like a canine after a flea bite turns his human brain into that of a dog. Skimming through the book, readers can see Spearman's clever use of maps, lists, photographs, exposition, diagrams, captions, a time line, and scripts that feature conversations between two fleas. In the *The Fruit Bowl Project* by Sarah Durkee, a middle-school teacher arranges for a rock superstar to teach her Grade 8 students, who each tell a story about the same topic in the style of a rap, a poem, a monologue, a screenplay, haiku, and more. *Naked Bunyip Dancing* by Steven Herrick looks at a wacky year from the point of view of sixth-graders who are under the spell of Carey the Hairy, a teacher who introduces his class to new activities, such as writing punk poetry and belly dancing.

Many novels are written as diaries. This format gives the opportunity for a story told in first-person and invites the reader to learn about the lives of characters from their first-hand views of the world. In *The Amazing Days of Abby Hayes* series by Anne Mazer, the main character reflects on everyday events, and these thoughts are presented in a different color to accompany the Mazer's narrative. *The Diary of a Wimpy Kid* by Jeff Kinney includes cartoon drawings, and student print "written" on the lines of a journal. For mature readers, Sherman Alexie's novel *The Absolutely True Diary of a Part-time Indian* is the story of a teenager named Arnold who laments his life on a Spokane Indian Reservation. When a teacher pleads with Arnold to get a better life, the boy switches to a rich white school and becomes as much of an outcast as he was in his own community. Another humorous novel, *Spud* by John van de Ruit, is written in journal format. This book invites young adult readers into the mind of John "Spud" Milton as he goes through the stages of puberty at a South African private school.

Novels written as diaries or notebook entries include the titles *The Amazing Life of Birds: The Nineteen Day Puberty Journal of Duane Homer Leech* by Gary Paulsen, *A Gathering of Days: A New England Girls' Journal 1830–32* by Joan W. Blos, *Catherine, Called Birdy* by Karen Cushman, *The Secret Diary of Adrian Mole, Aged 13 3/4* by Sue Townsend, and the *Anastasia Krupnik* series by Lois Lowry.

The world of electronic communication is represented in a number of new novels, most notably *ttyl* and its sequels *ttfn* and *l8r g8r* by Lauren Myracle, which chronicle in Instant Message format the day-to-day experiences and plans of three tenth-grade friends known as the Internet Girls. Michael J. Rosen has written *Chaser* in e-mails to tell the story of a young man who shares his outlook on life when his parents choose to move to a new home in the country. E-mail messages are also spread throughout the novel *The Gospel According to Larry* by Janet Tashijan, which is about 17-year-old who creates a secret identity as the author of a web site that ends up receiving national attention. Battling cancer, a

Many novels are available to young readers as audiobooks. Hearing the voices of narrators is a way of experiencing a novel that can appeal to many readers who may feel burdened with a book's length or challenged by some of the book's language. Listening to a story being read aloud can offer a rich experience for many students of this age. *The Miraculous Journey of Edward Toulane* by Kate di Camillo, *The Invention of Hugo Cabret* by Brian Selznick, *Monster* by Walter Dean Myers, and *The Book Thief* are some good examples.

The term "graphic novel" is commonly used to disassociate works from the juvenile or humorous connotation of comics or comic books. Although many graphic novels are written for developing readers, their content, language, and theme can be considered better accessible to mature readers.

In recent years, a number of books have been transformed into graphic novels to appeal to a new generation of readers who are engaged with striking visual images on the page, just as onscreen. The Hardy Boys and Nancy Drew, The Babysitters Club, and The Time Warp Trio are all series that have undergone the metamorphosis into graphic novel format. Single titles such as *Artimus Fowl* by Eion Colfer and *Coraline* by Neil Gaiman also appear as graphic texts, as do such literary classics as *The Hobbit*, *Frankenstein*, and *Macbeth*.

teenage girl tires to complete her classes online in the novel *Sun Signs* by Shelley Hrdlitschka, a novel told through e-email communications.

The Graphic Novel

A graphic novel is a type of comic book, usually with a lengthy and complex storyline. Though the format can encompass short story collections, a graphic novel may be described as a stand-alone and complete narrative presented through visual and textual elements. Like a text-only novel, the graphic novel may deal with a complex plot, varied characters and settings, and various subject matters.

Graphic novels deliver a range of genres, from superhero to romance, historical fiction, fantasy, science fiction and *manga* (the Japanese word for "comic book"). Graphic novels are closely related to comics—stories are told with the fusion of sequential picture-frames and written text—but the two genres, though similar, are distinct. Graphic novels suggest a story that has a beginning, middle, and end, as opposed to an ongoing series with continuing characters. Although the length of graphic novels varies, they are usually longer than comics.

For young readers moving into novels, the graphic novel has a strong appeal because of the use of pictures and more limited text. *The Geronimo Stilton* series features a variety of fonts and sizes, illustrations, and comic formats to tell the adventures of the rodent journalist. One of the reasons for the popularity of the *Captain Underpants* series is the comic-strip format, which appeals to many young readers. Even the popular *Time Warp Trio* series by Jon Scieszka has been transformed into the comic format. In *Babymouse: Our Hero* by Jennifer L. Holm and Matthew Holm, black, white, and pink images feature an imaginative young mouse who deals with her fears of facing an her enemy in a game of dodgeball.

The graphic format is particularly suited to fantasy or adventure genres. Avi, along with illustrator Brian Floca, has written *City of Light, City of Dark* entirely in comic format. *Travels of Thelonious* by Susan Schade and Jon Buller is an adventure story that is told in traditional narrative interwoven with graphic-novel storytelling. The *Bone* series by Jeff Smith, the *Akiko* series by Mark Crilley, and the *Leave it to Chance* series by James Robinson are popular with, and suitable for, all ages.

The popularity of Japanese *manga* has exploded the world of novel reading, usually featuring the adventures of superheroes and villains. Series titles include *Hikaru No Go* by Yumi Hotta, *Knights of the Zodiak* by Masami Kurumada, *Shaman King* by Hiroyuki Takei, and *Prince of Tennis* by Takeshi Konomi.

Historical events (*Time Line* series), classic novels (*The Hobbit* by Dixon Chick, *Frankenstein* by Gary Reed), and powerful stories based on autobiographical events have been retold in graphic-novel format, more suited to older readers. *Maus: A Survivor's Tale: My Father Bleeds History* by Art Speigelman was the first graphic novel to win a Pulitzer Prize. The story of a Jewish survivor of Hitler's Europe and his son, a cartoonist who tries to come to terms with his father's story, provides readers with gripping details of the Holocaust. *Maus II* continues the story of the mice (Jewish people) and cats (Germans). *Persepolis*, along with its sequels, offer Marjane Satrapi's poignant story of a young girl growing up in Iran and her family's suffering following the 1979 Islamic revolution, drawn in small black-and-white panels that evoke Persian miniatures. *American Born Chinese* by Gene Luen Yang was the first graphic novel recognized by the National Book Foundation. It starts out with three seemingly different tales, then merges them together to present readers with the legendary folk tale *The Monkey King*, a story of second-generation immigration from China, and a perspective on extreme Chinese stereotypes in terms of accent, appearance, and hobbies.

Novels that are heavily illustrated can be considered graphic novels. Artist Christopher Myers has supplied black-and-white sketches and comic strips throughout *Autobiography of My Dead Brother*, a book about gang violence written by his father, Walter Dean Myers. With *The Invention of Hugo Cabret*, Brian Selznick expands the novel form to create a new reading experience: the book features 284 pages of original pencil drawings. It combines elements of picture book, graphic novel, and film to tell a story about an orphan, a clock keeper, and a thief in a Paris filled with secrets and mystery. This novel was awarded the Caldecott Medal in 2008 for best illustrated book.

Teaching with Novels

A novel program, like any other area of the curriculum, requires long-term planning to determine practices that will need to occur regularly in order to achieve its goals. Decisions need to be made about what kinds of class groupings will best facilitate learning, and how to maximize the use of novels you share with the students and have them read for themselves. Programs need to evolve to suit the needs and interests of students and our developing knowledge. The following five components are essential to the development of students as critical and competent readers of literature.

You do not always need to ask for external responses from the students. The reading of a novel can be a complete experience in itself. Students may call upon their reactions at some distant time, but have no need to respond immediately or often.

1. Time for Reading Aloud
   Daily read-aloud time is an opportunity to broaden the students' world of literature as they are introduced to new authors, the first book in a series, or novels on a particular theme. Novels that are slightly above most students' reading abilities should be considered appropriate material to be read aloud.
2. Time for Independent Private Reading
   Regardless of when it occurs, daily independent reading is an essential part of a literature-based program. To begin, at least 15 minutes per day should be devoted to this activity. Our students can witness the fact that we are readers when we discuss our own reading interests and habits, how we choose novels, and our reactions to the books we read.
3. Time for Direct and Indirect Instruction
   Once the resources and basic structure for experiencing novels have been established, we need to let the students take some control over their learning. Our main role at this time is one of guide and facilitator. That said, direct instruction can play a significant role in building a community of readers. Mini-lessons need to be woven into the program.
4. Time to Respond
   Through response activities, our students come to make sense of what they have read, and make links from the world of books to their own life experiences. The forms students take to let their voices be heard

Mini-lessons can be presented to the whole class, but much of our significant teaching can be done with individuals or small groups during reading conferences.

allow for individual differences in learning styles at the same time that they develop critical-thinking skills. Over time, our students should vary the ways that they tell others about their novels and should share responses through response journals and literature circles, through talk, writing, art, and drama activities.

5. Time for Celebrating

   When students share their viewpoints with their classmates in small- or large-group settings, they have the chance to reveal some of their reactions to story elements as well as to appreciate the viewpoints of others. The process of students recommending books to peers needs to be part of the classroom reading community.

Personal Response

- The impact of a novel is stronger when the reader makes strong connections. Students use the That Reminds Me form on page 124 to keep a record of situations from the novel that reminded them of something that happened to them, someone they know, others in the world, or other texts they have heard, seen or read.
- The reading response journal (also called a dialogue journal or literature log) is a convenient and flexible tool that students can use to reflect on their independent reading. A reading-response journal makes the connection between reading and writing.
- See Your Response to a Novel on page 125 for a list of prompts that invite students to share their personal responses.

Reading and Writing Skills

- Summarizing: Students consider the plot of a novel they have read by preparing a 100 word summary of the book. To make the activity more challenging, instruct the student to write a synopsis that is *exactly* 100 words long. When the summary is completed, students can work with a partner who has written a synopsis for the same novel. The students can compare ideas and then, as a further activity, combine ideas to make a new summary that is 100 words in length.
- Persuading: Students write a review of a book that they liked (or not) to help others consider whether they might want to read the book or not. If available, provide students with samples of book reviews from local publications as models. The might want to use the Becoming a Book Reviewer form on page 126 to organize their thoughts.

As children become independent readers, they learn to choose a book by more than just the cover. They become very aware of the authors they like. A study of the work of a particular author can take the children beyond a bunch of good stories and pleasant reading experiences, it can yield an understanding of theme, style, plot, and characterization.

Literary Elements

- Plot: Invite students to imagine that they have just begun a new job as a reporter for a local newspaper. For the first assignment, students choose an exciting event from a novel they have just read to write a newspaper article about the event. Remind the stuudents of the five W's of journalism (*Who? What? Where? When? Why?*) Students write a headline and draw a "photograph" to capture readers attention. Completed articles can be published for others to read.

- Character: Ask students to choose a character from a novel they are reading. In the role of the character, the students write their thoughts and feelings about an event or an experience. As a follow up, students exchange fictitious journal entries with a partner and interview each other in role.
- Setting: Tell the students to imagine that the novel that they have read is going to be made into a movie. The students, as directors of the movie, need to determine the different locations needed to shoot the film. To help identify the most important locations, the students can work with others who have read the same novel to list different locations needed to shoot the film.
- Style and Language: Students select a half-page passage from a novel. If the novel is written in first-person voice, students rewrite the passage in third-person. If the novel is written in third-person voice, the passage can be rewritten in first-person. As students rewrite, they may change certain words to match the voice. Encourage the students to keep the tone of the passage as close to the original as possible. Students can share their opinions about why the author chose a certain voice to tell the story.

Critical Reading and Writing

- Students consider the gender role of the novel's protagonists. They can meet in groups to share their opinions about whether they think this novel is more suited to male readers or female readers. Encourage them to identify specific incidents and characters as they discuss the novel. How might aspects of this novel change if it were told from the point of view of someone of the opposite gender?
- To consider the author's intent, the students can complete each of the statements below. Students can share responses with others who read the same book.
  - I think the central theme of this novel is…
  - I think the author wrote this novel because…
  - I think this novel would be interesting to someone who…
  - Here is a question(s) I would like to ask the author…

That Reminds Me

This activity invites you to make notes on how a novel remind you of one or more of the following. Once completed you can share your personal connections with a partner who is familiar with your novel and discuss how your responses were similar or different

People you know:

Relationships in your life:

Adventures/ events from your past:

Places you've visited:

News events:

Stories you've heard from others:

Feelings you've experienced:

Problems with which you are familiar:

Other books you've read:

Films or television shows you've seen:

Your Response to a Novel

What did you like about the novel?

What puzzles or questions came to mind as you read the novel?

As you read the novel, did you "see" the story in your mind?

What problem(s) emerged in the novel? How were these problems resolved (or not)?

What words, phrases or sentences had an impact on you?

What interests you about the character(s) in the novel?

What advice might you give to a novel character?

What comments might you offer to the author about the way he or she told the story?

Have you, or someone you know, experienced similar events to the one's in the novel?

What did the novel make you think about?

What will you tell your friends about the novel?

Becoming a Book Reviewer

Record your thoughts—positive and negative—about a novel you have read by writing responses to the following items. Your review may help others decide if they want to read the novel.

Novel Title: _____   Author: _____

Reviewers:

1. Main character's personality and behavior

2. Action of the novel

3. Theme of the novel

4. Believablility

5. Vocabulary

6. Dialogue

7. Setting

8. Narration (how the story was told)

9. Interest level

10. Why you recommend this novel.

Novel Lists

Chapter Book Series

Adler, D.A.: Cam Jansen.
Clements, Andrew: Jake Drake.
Dadey, D and Jones, M. T.: The Adventures of the Bailey School Kids.
Delton, J.: The Pee Wee Scouts.
Giff, P. R.: The Kids on Polk Street School.
Jones, M. T & Dadey, D.: Barkley's school for dogs.
MacGregor, Roy: Screech Owls.
Osbourne, Mary Pope: The Magic Tree House.
Park, Barbara: Junie B. Jones.

Paulsen, Gary: The Culpepper adventures.
Pilkey, Dav: The adventures of Captain Underpants.
— Ricky Ricotta's Mighty Robots.
Roy, R.: A to Z Mysteries.
Sachar, L.: Marvin Redpost.
Scieszka, Jon: The Time Warp Trio.
Sharmat, M.W.: Nate the Great.
Sobol, Donald: Encyclopedia Brown.
Stilton, Geronimo: Geronimo books.
Wishinsky, Frieda: Canadian Flyer Adventures.

Fiction for Developing Readers

Blume, Judy (1972) *Tales of a fourth grade nothing (sequels: Superfudge; Fudge-a-mania; Double Fudge)*
Byars, Betsy (1974) *Summer of the swans.*
— (1981) *The midnight fox.*
Clements, Andrew (2001) *The janitor's boy.*
— (2002) *The school story.*
— (2004) *The Landry News.*
— (2005) *The report card.*
— (2007) *No talking.*
Dahl, Roald (1961) *James and the giant peach* (also: *Charlie and the chocolate factory; The Twits*)
Gardiner, John Reynolds (1980) *Stone Fox.*
Henkes, Kevin (1998) *Sun & Spoon.*
Howe, Deborah & James (1979) *Bunnicula* (sequels: *The celery stalks at midnight; Howliday Inn; Nighty nightmare*)
Little, Jean (1988) *Lost and found.*
— (1989) *Different dragons.*
MacLachlan, Patricia (1985) *Sarah, Plain and Tall* (sequels: *Skylark; Caleb's story; More perfect than the moon*)

Park, Barbara (1996) *Mick Harte was here.*
Richler, Mordechai (1975) *Jacob Two Two meets The Hooded Fang* (sequels*: Jacob Two Two and the dinosaur; Jacob Two-Two's first spy case*)
Rockwell, Thomas (1973) *How to eat fried worms.*
Rylant, Cynthia (1992) *Missing May.*
Scrimger, Richard (1998) *The nose from Jupiter* (sequels: *A nose for adventure; Noses are red; The boy from earth*)
Schein, Miriam (1990) *In the year of the panda.*
Smith, Robert Kimmel (1972) *Chocolate fever.*
Smith, Doris Buchanan (1973) *A taste of blackberries.*
Smucker, Barbara (1989) *Jacob's little giant.*

SERIES FOR DEVELOPING READERS

Cleary, Beverly: Ramona.
Clements, Andrew: Jake Drake.
Danziger, Paula: Amber Brown.
Hurwitz, Johanna: Aldo Applesauce
Korman, Gordon: Bruno & Boots
Korman, Gordon: Danger series
(trilogies: Dive; Everest; Island;
Kidnapped)

Martin, Ann M.: The Babysitters
Club.
Snicket, Lemony: The Series of
Unfortunate Events

Fiction for Independent Readers

Applegate, Katherine (2007) *Home of the Brave.*
Avi (2004) *Crispin* (trilogy)
Baker, Deirdre (2007) *Becca at sea.*
Birdsall, Jeanne (2005) *The Penderwicks.*
Black, Holly (2003) *The Spiderwick Chronicles* (series)
Choldenko, Gennifer (2007) *If a tree falls at lunch period.*
Colfer, Eion (2001) *Artimus Fowl* (series)
Creech, Sharon (2007) *The Castle Corona.*
Ellis, Deborah (2007) *Jakeman.*
Gantos, Jack (1998) *Joey Pigza swallowed the key* (sequels: *Joey Pigza loses control; What would Joey do?; I'm not Joey Pigza*)
Graff, Lisa (2006) *The thing about Georgie.*
Henkes, Kevin (1992) *Words of stone.*
Kadohata, Cynthia (2004) *Kira-Kira.*
Kress, Adrienne (2007) *Alex and the ironic gentleman.*
Lord, Cynthia (2006) *Rules.*
Morpurgo, Michael (1977) *Friend or foe.*

— (1982) *War horse.*
— (2003) *Private Peaceful.*
— (2005) *The amazing story of Adolphus Tips.*
— (2007) *Born to run.*
Nimmo, Jenny (2002) *Charlie Bone: Children of the red king* (series)
O'Connor, Barbara (2008) *Greetings from nowhere.*
— (2007) *How to steal a dog.*
Park, Linda Sue (2002) *A single shard.*
Paterson, Katherine (1977) *Bridge to Terabithia.*
Patron, Susan (2006) *The higher power of Lucky.*
Ryan, Pam Muñoz (2000) *Esperanza rising.*
Spinelli, Jerry (2000) *Stargirl* (sequel: *Love, Stargirl*)
— (2007) *Eggs.*
— (2008) *Smiles to go.*
Stewart, Trenton Lee (2007) *The Mysterious Benedict Society* (sequel: *The Mysterious Benedict Society and the perilous journey*)
Zimmer, Tracie Vaughn (2008) *42 Miles.*

Fiction for Young Adolescent Readers

Avi (1991) *Nothing but the truth.*
Brookes, Martha (2002) *True confessions of a heartless girl.*
Cooney, Caroline (1990) *The face on the milk carton.*
Cormier, Robert (1974) *The chocolate war.*

Curtis, Christopher Paul (1998) *The Watsons go to Burningham—1963.*
— (1999) *Bud, Not Buddy.*
Danziger, Paula (1974) *The cat ate my jumpsuit.*

Doyle, Brian (1983) *Up to Low.*
— (1984) *Angel Square.*
— (1988) *Easy Avenue.*
— (2001) *Mary Ann Alice.*
Fitch, Sheree (2005) *The gravesavers.*
Hinton, S.E. (1967) *The outsiders.*
Hobbs, Valerie (2007) *Anything but ordinary*
Holman, Felice (1977) *Slake's limbo.*
Johnston, Julie (1991) *Two moons in August*
Kerr, M.E. (1981) *Little, little.*
Koertge, Ron (2004) *The brimstone journals.*
Major, Kevin (1978) *Hold fast.*
— (1980) *Far from shore.*
Melling, O.R. (1996) *My blue country.*
Mikaelsen, Ben (2001) *Touching spirit bear.*
Murdock, Catherine Gilbert (2006) *Dairy queen.*
Myers, Walter Dean (1999) *Monster.*
— (2004) *Shooter.*
Myers, Walter Dean & Christopher (2005) *Autobiography of my dead brother.*

Myracle, Lauren (2004) *ttyl* (also *ttfn; l8r g8r*)
Perkins, Lynn Rae (2005) *Criss cross.*
Rosoff, Meg (2004) *How I live now.*
Speigelman, Art (1973) *Maus* (sequel: *Maus 2*)
Spinelli, Jerry (2003) *Milkweed.*
Stratton, Allan (2005) *Chandra's secrets.*
Walters, Eric (1996) *Stars.*
— (2004) *I've got an idea.*
— (2006) *Shattered.*
— (2006) *We all fall down.*
Wynne-Jones, Tim (1995) *The maestro.*
— (1998) *Stephen Fair.*
— (2000) *The boy in the burning house.*
— (2005) *A thief in the house of memory.*
Zindel, Paul (1968). *The Pigman.*
Zusak, Markus (2006) *The book thief.*

SERIES FOR YOUNG ADOLESCENTS

Brashares, Ann: The Sisterhood of the Traveling Pants
Cooper, Susan: The Dark Is Rising
Harrison, Lisi: The Clique
MacHale, DJ: Pendragon
Nix, Garth: Sabriel (trilogy)
— The Seventh Tower
Paolini, Christopher: The Inheritance (trilogy)
Pierce, Tamora: Protector of the Small (quartet)

Pullman, Philip: His Dark Mateials
Sage, Angie: Septimus Heap
Shan, Darren: Cirque du Freak
Stewart, Paul & Riddell, Chris: The Edge Chronicles
Stroud, Jonathan: The Bartimaeus Trilogy
Tolkien, J.R.R.: The Lord of the Rings
Dean, Zoey: The A-List

Bullying Novels

Anderson, Laurie Halse (1999) *Speak.*
Bloor, Edward (1997) *Tangerine.*
Blume, Judy (1974) *Blubber.*
Carbone, Elise (1998) *Starting school with an enemy.*
Chambers, Aidan (1983) *The present takers.*
Clements, Andrew (2001) *Jake Drake: Bully buster.*

Fine, Anne (1992) *The angel of Nitshill Road.*
Flake, Sharon G. (1998) *The skin I'm in.*
Gardner, Graham (2003) *Inventing Elliot.*
Giles, Gail (2002) *Shattering glass.*
Hogg, Gary (1998) *Scrambled eggs and spider legs.*

Howe, James (2001) *The misfits.*
Koss, Amy Goldman (2006) *Poison Ivy.*
Langan, Paul (2002) *The bully.*
Lekich, John (2002) *The loser's club.*
Masters, Anthony (1995) *Bullies don't hurt*
Mills, C. (1997) *Losers, Inc.*
Paterson, Katherine (2001) *The field of dogs.*
Sachs, Marilyn (1968) *Veronica Ganz.*
Singer, Nicky (2001) *Feather boy.*
Spinelli, Jerry (1997) *Wringer.*

— (2000) *Stargirl* (sequel: *Love, Stargirl*)
— (2002) *Loser.*
Stolz, Mary (1963) *The bully of Barkham Street.*
Strasser, Todd (1999) *Give a boy a gun.*
Tolan, Stephanie S. (2002) *Surviving the Applewhites.*
VanDraanen, Wendelin (2004) *Shredderman: Secret identity.*
Wishinsky, Frieda (2000) *So long, stinky queen.*

Verse Novels

Cormier, Robert (1999) *Frenchtown summer.*
Creech, Sharon (2001) *Love that dog.*
— (2004) *Heartbeat.*
— (2008) *Hate that cat.*
Frost, Helen (2003) *Keesha's house.*
— (2004) *Spinning through the universe.*
— (2006) *The braid.*
Hesse, Karen (1997) *Out of the dust.*

— (2001) *Witness.*
— (2003) *Aleutian Sparrow.*
Koertge, Ron (2004) *The Brimstone journals.*
Major, Kevin (2004) *Ann and Seamus.*
Porter, Pamela (2005) *The crazy man.*
Rylant, Cynthia (2005) *Boris.*
— (2006) *Ludie's life.*
Wild, Margaret (2002) *Jinx.*

Multi-Genre Approaches

Avi (1991) *Nothing but the truth: A documentary novel.*
Blos, Joan W. (1979) *A gathering of days: A New England Girl's Journal, 1830–32.*
Cushman, Karen (1994) *Catherine, called Birdy.*
Durkee, Sarah (2006) *The fruit bowl project.*
Flieschman, Paul (2001) *Seek.*
Hrdlitschka, Shelley (2005) *Sun Signs.*
Kinney, Jeff (2007) *Diary of a wimpy kid: A novel in cartoons.*
Lowry, Lois (1979) *Anastasia Krupnik* (series)

Mazer, Anne *The Amazing days of Abby Hayes* (series)
Myers, Walter Dean (1999) *Monster.*
— (2004) *Shooter.*
Myracle, Lauren (2004) *ttyl* (sequels: *ttfn; l8r g8r*)
Rosen, Michael J. (2002) *Chaser: A novel in e-mails.*
Spearman, Andy (2005) *Barry boyhound.*
Tashjian, Janet (2001) *The gospel according to Larry* (sequel: *Vote for Larry*)
Townsend, Sue (1982) *The secret diary of Adrian Mole, aged 13 3/4.*

Graphic Novels

Avi & Floca, Brian (1993) *City of Light City of Dark.*

Chick, Dixon (1989) *The Hobbit.*

Myers, Walter Dean & Christopher (2005) *Autobiography of my dead brother.*

Reed, Gary (2005) *Frankenstein.*

Selznick, Brian (2007) *The invention of Hugo Cabret.*

Satrapi, Marjane (2003) *Persepolis: The story of a childhood.* (trilogy)

Schade, Susan & Buller, Jon (2006) *Travels of Thelonious: The Fog Mound* (sequel: *The Fog Mound #2: Faradawn*)

Spiegelman, Art (1986) *Maus: A survivor's tale* (sequel *Maus II*)

Yang, Gene Luen (2005) *American born Chinese.*

GRAPHIC NOVELS SERIES

Crilley, Mark: Akiko

Holm, Jennifer L. & Matthew: Babymouse

Hotta, Yumi: Hikaru No Go

Kurumada, Masami: Knights of the Zodiac

Pilkey, Dav: The Adventures of Captain Underpants

Scieszka, Jon: Time Warp Trio

Smith, Jeff: Bone

Stilton, Geronimo: Geronimo Stilton

Takeshi, Hiroyuki: Prince of Tennis

Time Line series

CHAPTER 6 Multicultural Literature

> Multicultural literature heightens respect for individuals and other cultures and helps children to see the humanity and similarities in all of us, while acknowledging contributions of minority and majority groups. (Barta & Grindler, 1996: 269)

While we could argue that any children's literature worth its salt broadens children's views of the world and introduces them to ways of looking at the world that they might not otherwise have encountered, there are some books that do more than this. They give voice to individuals and groups whose perspectives are not often heard or respected. As Landt (2006: 294) points out, "Not seeing one's self, or representations of one's culture, in literature can activate feelings of marginalization and cause students to question their place within society." They show the effects of unequal power relations and celebrate those who make a difference in the lives of marginalized groups and individuals. They provide vicarious experience of a diversity of ways of being, and honor cultural diversity and the shared national culture (Banks, 1994). Today several publishers, such as Coteau Books, Pemmican Publications, and Second Story Press in Canada, and the Children's Book Press, Just Us Books, and Lee and Low Press in the United States, primarily publish books featuring populations that have felt victimized, oppressed, or discriminated against in some way. Across the community of children's book publishers, more and more books are being published that are recognized as multicultural literature.

Multicultural children's literature as a category of children's literature emerged in the 1960s in response to African American demand for the infusion of Black history into the curriculum. Later, other groups who had experienced institutionalized discrimination on the basis of race also placed pressure on schools for representation in the curriculum (Banks, 1993). Although there are contemporary educators and librarians who continue to define multicultural literature as works that focus on "people of color" (Yokota, 2001), by the mid-1990s others had expanded the definition of multicultural literature to include "gender, class, sexual orientation, ableism, age, religion, and geographical location" (Botelho, 2004: 52).

We also share Cai's (1998) concern about authors of multicultural literature who take a tourist approach, presenting cultural differences as exotic curiosities. Readers might take away a superficial understanding of the culture because the book ignores the social and political issues that marginalize various groups. Chieri Uegaki seems to take such an approach at the beginning of her book, *Suki's Kimono* (2003), about a spirited first-grade Japanese-Canadian girl who, on the first day of school, proudly wears the kimono that her grandmother gave her. Stéphane Jorisch's cartoon-like watercolors help introduce readers to

In this book, we use the more inclusive definition of multicultural literature, agreeing with Cai (1998) that narrowing the definition of multicultural children's literature to that which represents perspectives and lives of visible minorities unjustifiably excludes other marginalized groups.

Japanese dances, food, music, and visual arts as Suki takes part in a Japanese street festival with her visiting obachan, or grandmother. If the book had ended here, it would be relegated to Cai's "tourist approach" category. However, difficult issues of being different from others, along with pride in one's culture, are examined. Suki's mother and sisters advise against wearing the kimono to school because Suki will not fit in. Their fears are borne out as Suki's peers ask questions about Suki's "funny" clothing, and embarrass her by calling her a bat. At the bidding of her teacher, Suki demonstrates the dancing she learned at the festival to show what she did over the summer. She receives rousing applause and acceptance. In this case, Suki is a strong protagonist who determinedly asserts her cultural identity and takes action to open her peers' minds to differences.

Selecting Multicultural Literature

In selecting multicultural literature for classrooms, it is important to assess particular books' potential for achieving social justice goals, such as combating intolerance, fostering a sense of inclusion, and acting for change in education and society (Cai & Bishop, 1994). But multicultural books cannot achieve social justice goals on their own. It takes readers who attend to the issues and themes, asking questions and rethinking assumptions, to take action and effect those changes. Hade (1997: 243) asserts that teachers "need to examine how we read and how we teach children to read" in order to realize the social justice goals of multicultural literature.

Drawing from the work of Finazzo (1997) and Landt (2006), we recommend considering the following issues:

1. STEREOTYPING OF CHARACTERS

Are the actions, the speech and language, the physical appearances, and the interactions and relationships among the people in the book true to life and not stereotypical? Is there diversity within cultures? Do characters have unique personalities?

When selecting books to read with students, teachers must be critical of the ways in which *all* characters are portrayed. For example, in Luis J. Rodriguez's *América is Her Name*, América, a Mixteca Indian girl from Oaxaca, Mexico, has immigrated to Chicago with her family. It is a hopeful story and sympathetic to Mexican immigrants living in the United States. Yet, stereotypes of heavy-drinking immigrants and bigoted non-immigrants abound. In contrast, in *The Christmas Gift* Franciso Jiménez honors the lives of migrant families living in labor camps. Panchito, a young boy, rises above his disappointment when his parents give him a bag of candy, instead of a heartily longed-for red ball, and shares his candy with his parents. Class differences are evident, but Claire B. Cotts' acrylic illustrations, like the text, show the characters to be strong-featured and expressive. Readers come to know and respect the family's love and the strength they gain from that bond.

2. INSIGHT INTO SOCIO-POLITICAL ISSUES

Do the books delve into issues, rather than just dealing with them superficially and trivializing the issues? Do characters show agency in solving their problems, rather than being dependent on more powerful others?

Of course, a criterion that also must be considered is the literary and aesthetic quality of the book. The chapters on novels and picture books provide more specific selection criteria for these qualities.

"If multicultural education and debates over authenticity in multicultural children's literature have always addressed power, we must ask why selection criteria for multicultural children's literature commonly subordinate power and focus more on interethnic understanding." Ching (2005: 134)

When addressing this selection criterion, teachers assess whether the author oversimplifies social issues or seems to skirt them. Two books about one woman—Alia Muhammad Baker, the chief librarian of the Central Library in Basra, Iraq, who was responsible for saving 7 percent of the library's books before the library was burned to the ground—illustrate how you might use this criterion to select multicultural literature. Cartoonist Mark Alan Stamaty uses black-and-white cartoon form to tell this true story in *Alia's Mission: Saving the Books of Iraq*. An anthropomorphized book narrates the story, starting the story with an explanation of the context for the war against dictator Saddam Hussein and a brief history of Iraq. The format allows for a moment-by-moment chronicling of the enormous community effort that was needed to move the 30,000 books to safety after Alia's appeal for government help was refused. The book shows Iraqis to be sophisticated, educated people who treasure their culture and their history. Another book written by Jeannette Winter, *The Librarian of Basra: A True Story from Iraq*, simplifies the story to such an extent that the war appears to be something inflicted on the Iraqi people during a time of peace and happiness, and implies that, once the war ends, Iraq will return to its original blissful state. The events are not as meaningful and the heroism of Alia Muhammad Baker not as powerful when readers are not aware of the iron-fisted rule of dictator Saddam Hussein over the Iraqi people and the grave dangers that Alia Muhammad Baker must have faced to move the books. There is not the same sense of the larger community supporting her efforts and she appears to be a one-woman crusader for Iraqi culture.

3. AUTHORITY OF THE AUTHOR

What gives the author and illustrator the authority to write a book about this group or this place in the world?

From *The Storymakers: Writing Children's Books—83 Authors Talk about Their Work* (2000) we know that the author of *Baseball Bats for Christmas*, Michael Arvaarluk Kusugak, was born in Cape Fullerton, Northwest Territories. He went to school in two communities in Nunavut and one in the Northwest Territories. His connection with and love for northern Canada are evident in the way he tells the story of an unusual event in the life of an Inuit boy living in Repulse Bay, Northwest Territories, in 1955. In an easygoing, humorous style, he provides information about the rocky environs of Repulse Bay to give readers a sense of the extraordinariness of having trees. Naïve folk art by Vladyana Krykorka complements Kusugak's story.

From the Canadian Children's Book Centre website we know that author Deborah Ellis spent time in Afghan refugee camps in Pakistan and Russia in 1999. While talking with women and girls about their experiences under Taliban rule, she met the family of a girl in Kabul who had cut her hair, worn boys' clothes, and sold goods in the marketplace to support her family. The young girl inspired Ellis to write two books: *The Breadwinner* and *Parvana's Journey*. Ellis brings readers into the despotic lives that women and girls lived under Taliban rule; however, it seems as if the story is told from a North American perspective, in terms of the views on women's roles and the absence of references to religion in a story set in a country ruled by a religious-based regime. Uma Krishnaswami, in *Children's Literature* writes:

> Where is Islamic practice in the lives of these people? No mosques, no calls to prayer, no religious observances? The shariah, Muslim law so severely

For biographical information on authors and illustrators, check websites such as **http://www.bethanyroberts.com/ childrensbookauthors.htm and http://www.cbcbooks.org/contacts**

Issues for Discussion

Authors and professors have weighed in on the debate regarding authenticity in multicultural children's literature (see Fox & Short, 2003). What are your thoughts on these quotes?

- "A writer can have all the right credentials in terms of ethnic background and culture but can still fail if he or she does not have the aesthetic heat." (Kathryn Lasky, author: 91)
- "Some say there is a move by people of color to keep whites from writing about us, but this isn't true…. We want the chance to tell our stories, to tell them honestly and openly." (Jacqueline Woodson, author: 45)

interpreted and applied by the Taliban, isn't mentioned once, not even in the glossary.

4. CURRENT PERSPECTIVES

Where and when was the book published? Does the book reflect a dated perspective?

Literature is written by people whose perspectives are flavored by the social, cultural, and political understandings of their times and places. Books that were published at times when readers were not acutely aware of uneven power relationships across social and cultural groups may seem intolerant and chauvinistic today. For example, the 1960 book *Cricket in Times Square* portrays a Chinese-American storeowner in very stereotypical ways. Sai Fong's speech is written to mock his language: "Oh velly good. . . You got clicket!" (p. 45). The book was a Newbery Honor book in 1961 and it was published in a second edition in 1977; clearly the socio-political content was not seen as problematic at that time. Today, however, teachers would encourage student readers to question the characterization of Sai Fong, recognizing how his language and actions position him as childlike and undignified, not someone to be taken seriously or respected.

In contrast, a book that was first published in 1986 and later republished in 2005, *Naomi's Road*, portrays Japanese-Canadians as acting honorably and intelligently while being forcibly removed from their homes in Vancouver to the interior of British Columbia. Joy Kogawa's partly autobiographical book shows the devastation wrought on Japanese-Canadian families following the Japanese invasion of Pearl Harbor in 1941 through the eyes of a six-year old girl. Readers of the newly published edition will find that the book's themes and perspectives resonate harmoniously with today's thinking about Japanese- Canadians' contributions to Canada, portraying young Naomi's sense of loss and struggle to understand why her life has changed so greatly, but also conveying a sense that she is starting a new life. Ruth Ohi's pencil drawings, while highlighting significant events in the story, are child-like, gentle, and in keeping with the tone that Kogawa has set in the text.

5. ACCESSIBILITY OF CONTENT

In this chapter we introduce a range of genres, from poetry to fiction to nonfiction. Unlike many works on multicultural literature, we have not organized our discussion by particular racial groups or by country of origin. We have listed multicultural literature books in terms of their purposes:
• to celebrate diversity in terms of race, social class, gender, ableness, and sexual orientation
• to highlight injustices that arise because of unequal power relations among social and cultural groups

In the case of books that are set in places that are unfamiliar to student readers, does the author provide sufficient information and a glossary to ensure that readers who are not from the culture or society will understand the theme?

This criterion is straightforward, as teachers assess how accessible the ideas and issues are to its intended readers through the use of unobtrusive tools such as appended glossaries, maps, pronunciation guides, or explanations woven into the text in non-didactic ways. Through her clear, descriptive writing, Suzanne Fisher Staples makes an unfamiliar setting and lifestyle, that of a nomadic Muslim family raising camels in the Cholistan Desert of Pakistan, accessible in her Newbery Honor Book, *Shabanu*. The author draws on her experience as a journalist living in Pakistan, threading in indigenous words, names, and phrases, providing a helpful glossary, a map, and a list of characters' names with pronunciations to make Shabanu's story more accessible.

Celebrating Diversity and Highlighting Injustices

Racial Diversity and Social Class

Botelho (2004: 55) explains that "race and ethnicity are social constructions and should be at the centre of any discussion about all literature, but it is a limited perspective all by itself, because racial oppression interfaces with classism and sexism." Far too often, assumptions are made about working class people and their relationships that overlook the sense of dignity and honor that goes with working with one's hands and exerting physical effort to accomplish tasks. Books that respect working-class lives position people whose work is as physical as it is cerebral, together with those whose incomes support a subsistence standard of living, as having a sense of pride in their identities and in having a sense of power in overcoming injustices and prejudices against working class ways of being and living. These books also represent working-class people as individuals with unique personalities and perspectives on the world, rather than as a homogeneous group.

BOOKS FOR YOUNGER READERS

Vivi, daughter of a truck driver, admires the lives of the "Pinks," the rich children who attend her school in *Pink*. "Dizzy with wanting pink," her longing for an expensive bride doll in glistening pink leads her to take up odd jobs to earn money to buy it, and results in crushing disappointment when one of the Pink children receives it as a gift from her aunt. Vivi finds happiness dancing to her father's harmonica music, as the melodies play the love he has for her and his understanding about what it means to want and be disappointed. There is pink around the edges and in the grain of Vivi's life, and the world of the Pinks is drenched in pink in Luc Melanson's illustrations, making them a faithful complement to the narrative.

Canadian and former Nicaraguan Luis Garay dedicated his book, *The Kite*, to children living in poverty in Latin America. Respect for working-class people, earning an honest day's living to care for their needs, is evident as readers follow Francisco through his day selling newspapers, encountering others selling their wares in the marketplace, and earning a few extra cents by gathering up plantain leaves for one of the vendors. Luis Garay shows Francisco to be resolute and grateful for what he has, in spite of his sadness over the death of his father. Garay says his textured acrylic-and-ink on canvas paintings use a "social realistic" style. Their brilliant colors, with shades of pink in every one, are an unmistakable signature of his artistry.

Eleven African American poets celebrate the inner and physical strength, as well as the gentle humanity, of their fathers and grandfathers in the poetry collection by Lee and Low Books, *In Daddy's Arms I am Tall*. The vigor and power of the poets' relationships with their fathers throb in Javaka Steptoe's striking illustrations created with torn paper, cut paper with pastel, appliqué, and found objects. The illustrations are poems, themselves, honoring fathers who work with their hands to make bricks, create artwork, bring in the harvest, play basketball, catch fish, and bring happiness to their children.

A Song for Ba is Paul Yee's tale of a boy, his father, and his grandfather, all singers who struggled to keep Chinese culture alive while adapting to life in North America. Wei Lim, living in a family of men after his mother died, helped his Ba (father) to train his voice to sing the female parts in the Chinese opera. The book ends with an uncertainty about the future of Chinese opera in North

Never able to find books about the world of immigrants in Canada while growing up, **Paul Yee** has tried to fill the void by writing about Chinese immigrants to Canada. Two of Paul Yee's picture books have won multiple awards: *Ghost Train,* and *Tales from Gold Mountain. Bamboo,* his first book set in China, marks a change in Paul Yee's writing. He says that he had previously resisted writing about China because it felt like a surrender to pressures to create a Chinese identity that did not encompass his Canadian identity and his Canadian experiences.

America. Wei Lim's aspirations to follow in his father's footsteps may never be realized, but Wei Lim accepts this possibility without feelings of despair. In Jan Pen Wang's realistic illustrations, as in Harvey Chan's, brown, orange, and red are dominant colors, while Shaoli Wang's folk-art style sets the story in a more primitive time in Yee's *Bamboo,* which presents a light-hearted view of the hard-working, ambitious Chinese farmer, Bamboo, his wife Ming, and his brother and sister-in-law. The bamboo, grown from seeds given to Bamboo by his wife on their wedding day, rewards the industrious, loyal Ming by helping her with field work when her husband leaves the farm to augment their earnings. Very discriminating, the same bamboo punishes the treacherous and lazy sister-in-law, and rescues Bamboo when his ship sinks at sea. Farmers are portrayed in a positive light, as Ming counters Jin's whining about being laughed at by townspeople with, "the work is hard and the townspeople scorn us. But they feast on the food we grow and can't live without us."

The natural landscape of northern parts of Canadian provinces is as important as the characters in two books written by Canadian Aboriginal authors. In Jan Bourdeau Waboose's *SkySisters,* two Ojibway sisters walk through the snowy night, seeking SkySpirits. Brian Deines's impressionistic oil paintings are very much part of the narrative, as an apparition of the two girls dances amidst the colors and motion of the lights. Sisterly love and a reverence for spirituality and silence are threaded throughout the text and the illustrations. Leo Yerxa's *Last Leaf First Snowflake to Fall* tells of a canoe trip through a natural paradise that existed "before rain fell and became mud puddles and seas and rose again to become clouds…" The textures, earthy colors, and layering in Yerxa's tissue-paper collage illustrations recreate the peacefulness and magnificence of that pristine landscape. Yerxa uses a technique to make paper look like leather in *Ancient Thunder,* a poetically written book that celebrates the wild horses of the North American prairies.

American Yangsook Choi's *The Name Jar* is about Unhei, who has just arrived in the United States from Korea. Unhei's classmates try to help her out by writing possible names for her, but she comes to the conclusion that her Korean name, which means "grace" and was carefully selected for her by her parents, is the best name for her. Gentle, earth-tone oil illustrations, reflect the Korean culture; however, Unhei and her classmates are represented as individuals within their cultures, not as stereotypical representations of their cultures. They act together for change in taking up questions about assimilating and maintaining cultural identity in everyday ways.

Bullying and racial issues are taken up in *Mr. Lincoln's Way* by highly-regarded author and illustrator Patricia Polacco. The coolest principal in the world, according to his students, African-American Mr. Lincoln sees European-American Gene beat up his peers and use racial slurs. Giving a bird field guide to Gene, spending time with Gene building bird feeders, consulting him on plants, seeds, and grain to buy to attract birds to the school atrium, Mr. Lincoln builds a trusting relationship with Gene. He helps Gene to question the racist views his father promotes and to treat all his peers with the same respect that Gene shows Mr. Lincoln. Both Mr. Lincoln and Gene show agency in changing Gene's racist views, with the birds being intermediaries who transcend human hatreds and fears that lead to racism.

Coteau Publishers in Regina, Saskatchewan, have published a number of book series celebrating diverse cultures in Canada. Ruby Slipperjack's *Little Voice*, part of the In the Same Boat series, features Ray, a girl of mixed heritage named after her grandfather and the ray of sunlight that shone through the window when she was born. Slipperjack honors the life of Ray's mother, who works hard to provide for her children on welfare and later marries an Aboriginal man. The author also honors traditional Native life in northern Ontario when describing Ray's visits with her grandmother and her later decision to live with her grandmother over the winter. The book ends with Ray's grandmother showing great respect for her granddaughter, a young woman "who can handle both worlds— the Native and the non-Native, the old and the new."

Aboriginal ways of life that value independence in providing for basic needs and surviving on the land rub up against urban ways of life in Jordan Wheeler and Dennis Jackson's *Christmas at Wapos Bay*. Three cousins—Talon, T-Bear, and Raven—and their families travel from their urban homes to visit their grandparents on a northern Saskatchewan lake for Christmas. Stranded in a tent with their grandfather, who is ill from lack of food, the three boys have to test their survival skills to get everyone back to the cabin. T-Bear's love for living off the land is finally nurtured as his father, who had been apprehensive about T-Bear sacrificing educational opportunities in the city, agrees to send him often to visit his grandparents.

The Year of the Dog, by Grace Lin, is the story of a Taiwanese-Chinese-American girl, Pacy, along with her friends and her family, during the Year of the Dog; a year of self-discovery. Genuinely told from a young girl's perspective, with entertaining drawings that look like the doodles of a young girl, this book provides insight into the joys and struggles of growing up in new immigrant families. The family's celebration of Chinese traditions and Pacy's mother's stories of her childhood in Taiwan and later life as a new immigrant to North America are woven into Pacy's contemporary American life.

The protagonist in Ellen Schwartz's *Stealing Home* is Joey Sexton, a boy whose Jewish mother had rebelliously left her home in Brooklyn to be with Joey's father, an African-American musician, to live in the Bronx. Schwartz portrays Joey's parents quite stereotypically: they die violently, his father in a fight and his mother from a drug overdose. However, her story of Joey's coming to terms with his mixed-race identity is more sensitively portrayed. Joey goes to live with his stern grandfather, his widowed aunt, and her baseball-loving, tomboy daughter. With the support of his family, and by taking Jackie Robinson (the first African-American to play Major League baseball) as a role model, Joey develops a sense of pride in having a Jewish and an African heritage. Ellen Schwartz artfully weaves together Joey's struggles with his grandfather, the discrimination Joey experiences in his new neighborhood, and his growing admiration for Jackie Robinson. The baseball metaphor, stealing home, works beautifully to highlight the ways in which Joey has finally found a home in both the physical and emotional sense.

In a note from author Barbara Joose at the end of *Stars in the Darkness*, we find out that she had met a young man who had been a gang banger, and many of the events in the book are based on his life. The disruption of ordinary life brought about when a family member joins a gang are symbolized by the Blockhead and Officina font used for text, and in Gregory Christie's surrealistic acrylic paintings. The story highlights the independent spirit of Richard's mother and brother, as they see the complex issues around Richards' gang membership and bring their community together to reclaim their neighborhood from the gangs.

Poverty and unemployment bring great pain to families, as portrayed movingly in Hope Anita Smith's *The Way a Door Closes*. Through more than 30 free-verse poems told in the first-person by 13-year old C.J., we see C.J. as more than "the poster child for families with problems." C.J., his parents, siblings, and grandmother are shown to be strong, proud, loving individuals who draw on all their resources to work through C.J.'s father's job loss and the sorrow and hurt when he walks out on his family. Shane W. Evans's realistic alkyd paintings, and references C.J.'s brother's "smooth brown cheeks" in a poem called "Legacy" show the family to be African-American. Otherwise, this story could be one of any racial group—there is no sense of stereotyping African- American families as ones that have problems.

Jacqueline Woodson's *Locomotion* is a highly acclaimed work of art. Introducing fifth-grader **Lo**nnie **C**ollins **Motion** (aka Locomotion) to poetry writing, his teacher Ms. Marcus gives him tools to work through the difficulties in his life. In one- and two-page poems, mostly free verse, Locomotion writes about the people in his life and the changes he has endured since his parents were killed in a house fire.

Gender, Sexual Orientation, and Ableness

Over many decades, researchers have analyzed children's literature for gender patterns (Albers, 1996; Nilsen, 1971). These studies decried the well-traveled and separate paths that female and male characters took in children's stories. Male characters, possessing characteristics such as courage, aggressiveness, and independence, carried out a wide range of activities outside the home. The characteristics and activities of female characters were confined to more family and home-like activities, and as passive, powerless, and dependent on others, particularly males. Social, political, and economic injustices have arisen from these dualistic gender roles because the male characteristics and the world beyond the home have been valued more highly.

BOOKS FOR YOUNGER READERS

Shirin Yim Bridges' *Ruby's Wish* is about a strong female character living in a very wealthy Chinese family. She has all that any girl could want—fine living quarters and a loving family, and a tutor that comes to her home to teach her and her cousins. She also has the best future a Chinese girl can hope for—marriage to any man she wishes because of her family's stature. But she wants to go to university. There is no sense of the protagonist having to give up anything to get what she wants, but it is clear that it takes courage to go against the cultural traditions and expectations of her family. Sophie Blackall's gouache illustrations have a subtle historical air; stylized borders frame some of the pages and every page sings with the red that characterizes Ruby's vitality and spirit.

Scully, a hearing-impaired girl who is typical in every other way, is the protagonist in Rachna Gilmore's *A Screaming Kind of Day*. Gordon Sauvé's realistic acrylic paintings are remarkable for capturing the wide range of emotions on Scully's face—from despair over what seems like endless waiting, to naughtiness in removing her hearing aid so she can't hear her mother's scolding, to wild

Jacqueline Woodson grew up in Greenville, South Carolina, and Brooklyn, New York. Her works include *The Dear One, From the Notebooks of Melanin Sun*, three "Maizon" novels, *I Hadn't Meant to Tell You This, Show Way, House You Pass on the Way*, and *Hush*. Her website explains that, as a child, Woodson was to be found writing every moment she could using whatever surface was available to her at the time: paper bags, her shoes, her denim binders, sidewalks, and notebook margins.

Researchers conclude that bringing children together with strong female characters in children's literature will provide a starting point for questioning gender inequities and taking action to provide greater opportunities for social, political, and economic power to women and girls.

See Appendix A: Censorship and Selecting Books for a closer look at concerns about books depicting same-sex marriage.

delight in being out in the rain on her own, to outrage at being reprimanded and being grounded.

Ken Setterington's *Mom and Mum are Getting Married* chronicles the days leading up to Rosie's mothers' wedding. Rosie changes her mothers' plans somewhat so that she and her brother are part of the wedding party, as bearers of the rings and scatterers of flower petals. There is no sense of the social struggle in which society has engaged over same-sex marriage, simply a celebration of two people uniting in marriage. Alice Priestley's merry illustrations add to the celebratory tone. Issues related to same-sex families are brought into classrooms in Nancy Garden's *Molly's Family*. Molly, a Kindergarten student, draws a picture of her birth mother and her adoptive mother as her family. Her peers are unkindly incredulous and leave Molly feeling hurt and questioning whether she wants her drawing included in the display for Open School Night. Conversations with her teacher and her parents assure her and her classmates that families take many configurations. Sharon Wooding's cheery colored pencil drawings work well to depict the bustle of a Kindergarten classroom, though not as well to express the characters' emotions.

BOOKS FOR OLDER READERS

Like the Chinese female character in *Ruby's Wish*, the female protagonist in *White Lily* is from a wealthy family. Ting-xing Ye creates a headstrong female character who is a disappointment to her father because she was not a boy. In spite of her confident demeanor, White Lily cannot escape the footbinding custom of her culture. In secret, her brother Fu-gui teaches White Lily to read and write, and wraps the paper containing her calligraphy around her feet, allowing them room to grow. When White Lily's aspirations to become a scholar are revealed, her father relents, remembering that he, too, had gone against his father's wishes to prepare for the Imperial Civil Service Examinations. The book ends with all family members showing great pride in White Lily's courage, and with an Afterword explaining the origins of footbinding and the harsh realities of women's lives.

Michelle Porter's *Rebel Women of the East Coast* is a collection of stories about extraordinary women who either lived on Canada's east coast or had some connection to it. Part of a series of books that tell "True Canadian Amazing Stories," this book is fairly well-researched, with original and secondary sources consulted. A swashbuckling story from 1645 tells of Francoise Marie Jacquelin La Tour, who picked up arms alongside her soldiers to defend (sadly, unsuccessfully) a fort from an ambitious French gentleman who wanted to take the title of governor of Acadia away from her husband. Mina Benson Hubbard, who explored and mapped Labrador (an exploit that killed her husband), and the last Beothuk, Shanawdithit, are among the nine women who are honored in this collection.

Jane Kurtz's *Bicycle Madness* weaves together the stories of feminist activist Frances Willard learning to ride a bicycle as an adult, and of her neighbor, Lillie, a girl coping with the death of her mother and preparing for a school spelling bee. The language, perspectives, and actions of the characters and Beth Peck's pencil illustrations have an authentic feel of the late-19th century. Through the restrictions placed on Lillie in having any contact with Frances Willard, readers learn of the opposition to her views on female suffrage, child labor, and workers' rights.

Penny Colman created a different kind of book honoring strong women in her nonfiction work, *Rosie the Riveter: Women Working on the Home Front in World War II*. This book celebrates the enormous contributions of the more than 18 million women who worked in shipyards, airplane factories, farms, transportation, assembly lines, and everywhere that workers were needed during World War II in the United States. These heroic stories are complemented with more than 60 archival black-and-white photographs and an abundance of primary source material, including transcripts and quotations from period magazines, a chronology, and a bibliography. Set in the early 1900s, Canadian Barbara Greenwood's *Factory Girl* tells the story of 12-year-old garment worker Emily, who endures long hours and harsh conditions to help support her family in the early 1900s, alternating chapters with a more straightforward history of child labor. Archival photographs by Lewis Hine and others, as well as a glossary and index, provide additional information about child laborers, the Triangle Shirtwaist Factory, hazards of factory work, the beginnings of labor unions, and living conditions for the poor in the early 1900s.

Glen Huser's *Stitches*, a Governor General's Award winner, brings together two strong characters: a boy, Travis, who is viewed by peers as effeminate because of his interests in sewing, puppetry, and theater, and his female friend, Chantelle, who walks with a limp and has a harelip. Travis survives horrific bullying, as well as an assault that could have ended up in his death were it not for adult intervention. The characters of the protagonists, their teachers, and their families are sensitively developed. This thought-provoking novel never overtly addresses Travis's sexuality because Travis himself is barely beginning to consider that aspect of his identity. Yet the portrayal of the blue-collar rural community, itself, is stereotyped, with an implication that bullies who torment an effeminate peer are part of small-town life.

In Jean Little's *Willow and Twig*, a Mr. Christie's Book Award winner, memorable ten-year old Willow takes on responsibilities and shows wisdom far beyond her years. She is the only one who understands her four-year old brother, Twig, who has attention deficit disorder and impaired hearing. The children's lives in Vancouver under the care of an elderly woman are filled with uncertainty and deprivation. That changes when the woman dies and Willow remembers that they have extended family living on a farm in Ontario. The bumps and joys of reuniting with their grandmother, an eccentric uncle, and a disapproving aunt are told sensitively.

Picture Books in Two Languages

In Canada, a number of books have been written in English and Aboriginal languages. In the United States, dual-language books tend to be written in Spanish and English.

Classrooms in Canada and the United States, particularly in large urban communities, are becoming more and more diverse, as newcomers from every continent make these North American communities their homes. The majority of these students come to their classrooms speaking a language other than English. In addition, a number of Aboriginal children living in rural areas speak Aboriginal languages at home. They and immigrant students are more likely to develop a stronger sense of self and to succeed academically when teachers show them that their language and culture are welcomed in school. Cummins (2001: p. 121) sums up the key findings of research by saying, "When promoted together, the two languages enrich each other rather than subtracting from each other." Books that are written in students' mother tongue and in English are important resources for developing minority language students' literacy.

Canadian Brian Deines uses warm yellows and oranges to show the summer home of two brothers near a lake in northern Manitoba, the setting of Tomson Highway's *Dragonfly Kites*. English text followed by a Cree translation on the same page tell how the brothers tie threads around the middle of dragonflies to create kites. In real life, the boys let the dragonflies go by letting go of the strings, but in their dreams, the boys soar over the lake and through the forest, carried by the dragonflies. This is a companion book to *Caribou Song*, also set in northern Manitoba, which tells of the two brothers and their parents following the caribou in winter. The illustrations and descriptions of the boys perched on a rock as a caribou herd thunders around them are breathtaking. In the final book in the series, *Fox on the Ice*, one of the boys is ice fishing with his father when their sled dogs take off after a fox. One of the boys and his mother are dragged along in a sled behind the dogs in a wild chase that ends with a rescue by the family dog, Ootsie. This trilogy celebrates and preserves a language and memories of family and a culture that Thomson Highway wants to see endure.

Pemmican Publications in Winnipeg has begun publishing bilingual books in the Métis language, Michif. This language, which began as a trade language about 300 years ago, combines Cree and Canadian French with some borrowing from English and other First Nations languages like Ojibway. The Michif Children's Series includes Bonnie Murray's *Thomas and the Métis Sash*. The goal of the book, keeping the Métis language and culture alive, is clear. The dialogue and events are used to highlight the cultural and historical significance of the weaving of the sash and its colors. The two languages are formatted in a way that is easy to follow. Like the text, Sheldon Dawon's brilliantly colored illustrations are prosaic and suited for the educational purpose of the book.

A Spanish/English book, Benjamin Alire Sáenz's *A Gift from Papá Diego*, was published by Cinco Puntos Press, a non-profit organization that publishes books by authors living in Mexico and along the Mexican-American border. The endearing story features a reality of many children whose families have immigrated to the United States from Mexico—their extended family is living in another country. Little Diego thinks often about his Papá Diego and wishes desperately that the senior Diego would come for a visit. He practices his Spanish so he will be able to converse with his Papà and requests a Superman costume for his birthday to enable him to fly and bring home his Papà from Chihuahua. Though the Superman costume is a big disappointment (flying capabilities are not inherent), Little Diego's wish comes true and his Papà appears at his doorstep, saying, "A border is nothing for people who love." Illustrator Geronimo Garcia's illustrations are clay figures and scenes painted with acrylic, with borders of painted clay. The illustrations, with characters' moon- shaped faces and beautiful brown eyes, are like a third language that tells the story as clearly as the words do.

Racial and Cultural Injustices

Sonia Nieto (2000): 305 writes that "schools cannot be separated from social justice." She goes on to explain that classrooms should be forums for discussing what it means to live in democratic societies. Students need to be aware of their democratic rights and responsibilities, including the challenge of ensuring and maintaining the privileges of democracy. Such awareness arises from many sources, including becoming familiar with the stories of people whose democratic rights have been systematically denied and who have not had socio-political power to access justice systems that would support them in reclaiming those rights.

BOOKS FOR YOUNGER READERS

As Long as the Rivers Flow is a fond recollection of Larry Loyie's summer of 1944 near Slave Lake, Alberta, before he was loaded into the back of a truck with his three siblings and taken south to a residential school for four years. In this respect, the book is a celebration of aboriginal life and of the beauty of the natural world. Although the weight of the devastating changes to come at the end of the summer is not fully borne until the end of the book, there is a sense of inevitability throughout. The epilogue contains an explanation of what children did at the residential schools and how the schools contributed to the loss of aboriginal traditions and lifestyles, and to native children's illiteracy. Heather D. Holmlund's watercolors are realistic in depicting the Loyie family summer activities, and impressionist in depicting the thick green forest and cloud-filled blue skies that provide a comforting background for those activities. Nicola I. Campbell's *Shi-shi-etko* is another recollection by an Aboriginal child. A fictional young girl spends the week before she is taken to residential school gathering memories to see her through the months and years away from her family. Shi-shi-etko's Yayah gives her a memory bag for the tangible parts of her life, such as a sprig from a fir tree. There is a gentle quietness and a strong reverence for the natural world in this book. Illustrator Kim LeFave has applied a fiery reddish-orange to the impressionist landscapes, which adds to the reader's tension. The author, herself of Interior Salish and Métis ancestry, includes a preamble with an explanation of the impact of residential schools on native people in Canada, the United States, Australia, and New Zealand.

Paul Yee's *Ghost Train*, with Harvey Chan's ethereal oil illustrations, identifies historical injustices to Chinese workers in Canada. This much-celebrated book has won the Ruth Schwartz Children's Book Award, the Elizabeth Mrazik-Cleaver Canadian Picture Book Award, the Governor General's Literary Award for children's literature, and the Amelia Frances Howard-Gibbon Illustrator's Award. Arriving in North America from South China, Choon-yi finds that her father had been killed while working on the railway. His ghost appears in a dream, urging Choon-yi to paint the fire train. Her painting of the train becomes real enough for her to board it. Her father's specter explains that the ghost train transports home the souls of the men whose lives had been lost to lay the tracks that would carry countless millions of people across North America for centuries to follow.

Two books written by American writers tell stories of strong African-American women who were born into slavery in the southern United States. *Show Way* is Jacqueline Woodson's tribute to the mothers in her family through the generations, starting with Soonie's great-grandma (her name has been lost to the author), who was sold from the Virginia plantation, where her parents lived, to a plantation owner in South Carolina. Big Mama, who took care of her, told stories about children getting themselves freed when they became adults. The children sewed "Show ways," quilts with stars, moons, and roads that showed the way to freedom. The narrative follows women in Soonie's family through the generations to Jacqueline Woodson and her daughter in the present day. The book ends with the promise that the generations to come will continue to tell the stories of women's Show Ways. Illustrator Hudson Talbott builds the road traveled by the generations of women with watercolors, chalk, and fabrics, as well as gray interpretations of contemporary documents. In a visually dramatic picture book by Carole Boston Weatherford, *Moses: When Harriet Tubman Led her People to Freedom*, Harriet Tubman, breathtakingly courageous and unswervingly committed to living free, bursts onto the page. Kadir Nelson's larger-than-life paintings provide dazzling perspectives of Harriet and her environment as she escapes slavery on a Maryland plantation and brings her family and 300 others to northern states and Canada. God's voice arches through each page in uppercase, reassuring Tubman that, like Moses from the Judao-Christian Bible, she has all that she needs to lead herself and her people to freedom.

Ruxhana Khan's *The Roses in my Carpets* tells of one boy's life in a refugee camp, where daily life includes taking cover from jet fighters flying overhead, hauling water from a communal well, eating scraps of bread, going to sex-segregated schools, and answering the call of the muezzin for daily prayers. The story's authenticity is evident—the boy is Ruxhana Khan's sponsored child, whom she has met. The boy's unique personality is portrayed in his desire to become a master weaver to free his family of their dependency on his sponsor's money. He chooses a red rose pattern to bring beauty into his life of browns. His dream of running in a field of roses where bombs cannot touch his family and himself are his source of hope in an environment over which he has little control. Ronald Himler's watercolor illustrations soften, yet portray realistically, the severity and bleakness of refugee life.

BOOKS FOR OLDER READERS

In Chilean Antonio Skármeta's *The Composition*, the distrust and fear fomented by military dictatorships are viewed through the eyes of Pedro, a small but fast nine-year old who holds his own on the soccer field. It is clear that he understands the dangers of his world when his composition about what his family does at night, written at the "invitation" of General Perdomo, contains innocuous information about playing chess. Skármeta is a master at creating suspense, as readers and Pedro's parents are uncertain whether Pedro's writing will innocently condemn his parents. Alfonso Ruano's illustrations are powerful political messages themselves. At the end of the book, the author explains what dictatorships are, how they rule, and what people do to overthrow them and restore democracy to their countries.

Peter Sís's Caldecott Honor book, *The Wall: Growing Up Behind the Iron Curtain*, is rich with symbols representing the tyranny of life in Czechoslovakia during the time of the Soviet Union's occupation. Many of the illustrations are textured black-and-white drawings with jarring red flags, Soviet stars, and the hammer and sickle. Graphic forms are accompanied by italicized text identifying compulsory activities for all Czech citizens. Sís's personal story, overwhelmed by increasing Soviet control over everyday life up to and following the Prague Spring in 1968, is told in sparse text.

Cambodia in early 1980, five years after the Communist Khmer Rouge took control of the country, is the setting of Minfong Ho's *Clay Marble*. The author was working with an international relief agency in refugee camps set up along the Thai-Cambodian border during that time. Meeting a young Cambodian refugee girl holding a clay marble inspired the writing of this book about 12-year old Dara, who flees with her mother and older brother because of the war between Vietnamese soldiers and Pol Pot's Khmer Rouge soldiers. Minfong Ho weaves information about the political strife in Cambodia with a light touch, so readers have a sense of the context but are not bogged down in historical detail.

Three books by Canadian authors tell the lives of Jewish children living in Nazi-occupied countries during World War II. Kathy Kacer's *Hiding Edith* tells the true story of a young Jewish girl, Edith Schwalb, who escapes to Belgium with her family when the Nazis invade Vienna, Austria, in 1938. After her Mutti (mother) gains the release of her imprisoned father in 1940, the family is again on the run. After Edith's father is imprisoned and sent to the Auschwitz concentration camp (where he died in 1944), her mother brings Edith to an orphanage in a town where all inhabitants are aware of and work together to hide the Jewish children seeking refuge from the Nazis. Photographs taken by one of the orphans who later became a member of the French Resistance, together with Kathy Kacer's sensitive writing, make the horrors of Edith's childhood very real to readers.

Hana's Suitcase tells the story of a Jewish girl from Czechoslovakia who died in a Nazi concentration camp. This book has been well recognized, garnering both the Information Book Award and the Silver Birch Award for Non-fiction. It was a finalist for the Norma Fleck Award and for the Governor General's Award. In 2000 Hana Brady's suitcase, confiscated by Nazis at the Auschwitz concentration camp, comes to the attention of director Fumiko Ishioka and the children in her Small Wings group. The suitcase is in a Tokyo museum that is dedicated to teaching global tolerance and understanding through educating Japanese children about the Holocaust. This book chronicles the detective work of Fumiko and her Small Wings group side-by-side with the short life of Hana Brady, the girl who was killed in the Auschwitz gas chambers the day she arrived. The book ends with the Small Wings' poem about Hana and the hope that

> We children can make a difference in building peace
> In the world—so that the Holocaust will never
> Happen again.

In *Brave Deeds: How One Family Saved Many from the Nazis*, Ann Alma tells of the fearless and selfless efforts of the Braal family in the Netherlands during the Nazi occupation. This compelling true story, told to the author by members of the Braal family who had moved to British Columbia following the war, is accompanied by photographs, historical notes, and a glossary of terms related to the occupation and World War II, as well as commonly-used Dutch words and phrases.

Nadja Halibegovich's *My Childhood Under Fire: A Sarajevo Diary* chronicles 12-year old Nadja's life under siege in Sarajevo in 1992, when the bombing started. The horrors of thousands of children being killed and of families' lives being torn apart are documented in brief daily entries, as Nadja writes to remain human in a place and time of incomprehensible inhumanity, hatred, and destruction. Many black-and-white photos show the girl and her family, before and during the war, including a dramatic view of the tunnel through which she finally escaped. Brief notes provide limited background about the Balkans war, but the author does not discuss the issues in depth, even in reflections written after her escape from Bosnia.

An avoidance of issues is not the case in *Our Stories, Our Songs: African Children Talk about AIDS*, a collection of short narratives taken from conversations that author Deborah Ellis had with Malawian and Zambian children and

Deborah Ellis was a runner-up in Groundwood Books' contest for writers who had never written for children, with her novel, *Looking for X* (1999), which went on to win the Governor General's Award. She has been a political activist, advocating nonviolence, women's rights, and economic justice since she was 17-years-old. Her books are noteworthy for their detail about the environment, as she conducts research by traveling for extended periods to the location of her books.

Schmidt (1999) explains that the first step in developing cultural sensitivity is to discover one's own cultural identity and identify the similarities and differences between oneself and others.

their caregivers whose lives have been torn apart by AIDS. Helpful appendices include a list of "AIDS terms," a map of the communities that Deborah Ellis visited in Africa, lists of books and AIDS organizations, and an index.

Teaching with Multicultural Literature

Personal Response

- Students write about memorable life events in their histories and those of their family. Ask them to make connections between the events in their lives and those of the multicultural books they read.
- Students write a series of diary or blog entries for a character in a multicultural book, showing what they feel it would be like to be in that character's situation.

Reading and Writing Skills

- Students generate questions about a multicultural book that they want to discuss in literature discussion groups. During or after the discussion, students mark a star beside questions that generated a lot of discussion in their literature discussion books and put a line next to those that did not. What is the difference between the questions? What makes good discussion questions? (Adapted from Lee Heffernan, whose teaching is featured in Vasquez (2003).)
- Students think about the ways they feel about particular characters in a multicultural book. These feelings are often drawn from information in the written and visual elements of the text and from students' own knowledge, experiences, values, perspectives, beliefs, etc., and are thus inferences about the characters. Show students that making inferences involves bringing together information from the text and the reader's background knowledge and experiences.

Literary Elements

- Students compare and contrast the text and illustrations of a number of multicultural books set in a particular country, a urban area, or a rural area, in terms of how the book portrays people living in that location and how the book portrays the characters' relationship to their physical environment. How do readers feel about the geographic location in each case: Is it a place where they would like to live? What makes it appealing or unappealing? How are lives of the characters in the book influenced by their physical setting?
- Ask students to consider the author's purpose for writing a multicultural book of their choice. What has the author done to achieve that purpose? How has the author achieved the purpose without making the book boring or overly preachy?

Critical Reading and Writing

- Using the four dimensions of critical literacy below, create questions based within each dimension for a multicultural book. Students read the book and respond to the questions as a class or in small groups.
  1. Disrupting the commonplace
     - Ask how the text is trying to position the reader
  2. Interrogating multiple viewpoints
     - Ask questions about whose voices are heard and whose are missing
  3. Focing on sociopolitical issues
     - Ask questions about the power relationships among characters
  4. Taking action and promoting social justice
     - Challenge and redefine stereotypes that marginalize certain groups of people

  (Adapted from Lewison, Flint & Sluys, 2002)
- Students work with a partner to create interview questions for one of the characters, for particular readers of the book, or for the author of a multicultural book of their choice. Ask students to consider what responses the interviewee might give. Students might practice and later perform their interviews for small groups of peers.

Multicultural Literature List

Alma, Ann (2008) *Brave deeds: How one family saved many from the Nazis.*

Bridges, Shirin Yim (2002) *Ruby's wish.*

Campbell, Nicola I. (2005) *Shi-shi-etko.*

Choi, Yangsook (2001) *The name jar.*

Colman, Penny (1995) *Rosie the riveter: Women working on the home front in World War II.*

Curtis, Christopher Paul (1999) *Bud, not Buddy.*

Ellis, Deborah (2000) *The breadwinner.*

— (2002) *Parvana's journey.*

— (2004) *The heaven shop.*

Garay, Luis (2002) *The kite.*

Garden, Nancy (2004) *Molly's family.*

Gilmore, Rachna (1999) *A screaming kind of day.*

Gregory, Nan (2007) *Pink.*

Halibegovich, Nadja (2006) *My childhood under fire: A Sarajevo diary.*

Highway, Tomson (2001) *Caribou song.*

— (2002) *Dragonfly kites.*

— (2003) *Fox on the ice.*

Ho, Minfong (1993) *The clay marble.*

Hundal, Nancy (2001) *Number 21.*

Huser, Glen (2003) *Stitches.*

Jiménez, Francisco (2000) *The Christmas gift.*

Joose, Barbara (2002) *Stars in the darkness.*

Kacer, Kathy (2006) *Hiding Edith.*

Khan, Ruxhana (2004) *The roses in my carpets.*

Kogawa, Joy (2005: 2nd ed) *Naomi's road*

Kurtz, Jane (2003) *Bicycle madness.*

Kusugak, Michael Arvaarluk (1990) *Baseball bats for Christmas.*

Lee & Low Books (1997) *In daddy's arms I am tall: African Americans celebrating fathers.*

Levine, Karen (2002) *Hana's suitcase.*

Lin, Grace (2006) *The year of the dog.*

Little, Jean (2000) *Willow and Twig.*

Loyie, Larry (2002) *As long as the rivers flow.*

Murray, Bonnie (2004) *Thomas and the Metis sash.*

Polacco, Patricia (2001) *Mr. Lincoln's way.*

Porter, Michelle (2005) *Rebel women of the east coast.*

Rodriguez, Luis J. (1998) *América is her name.*

Sáenz, Benjamin Alire (1998) *A gift from Papá Diego.*

Schwartz, Ellen (2006) *Stealing home.*

Selden, G. (1960) *The cricket in Times Square.*

Setterington, Ken (2004) *Mom and Mum are getting married.*

Sis, Peter (2007) *The wall: Growing up behind the Iron Curtain.*

Skrypuch, Marsha Forchuk (2006) *Aram's choice.*

Slipperjack, Ruby (2001) *Little voice.*

Smith, Hope Anita (2003) *The way a door closes.*

Skármeta, Antonio (1998) *The composition.*

Stamaty, Mark Alan (2004) *Alia's mission: Saving the books of Iraq.*

Staples, Suzanne Fisher (1989/2003) *Shabanu, daughter of the wind.*

Stephenson, Wendy (2006) *Idaa Trail: In the steps of our ancestors.*

Uegaki, Chieri (2003) *Suki's kimono.*

Waboose, Jan Bourdeau (2000) *Skysisters.*

Weatherford, Carole Boston (2006) *Moses: When Harriet Tubman led her people to freedom.*

Wheeler, Jordan (2005) *Christmas at Wapos Bay.*

Winter, Jeannette (2004) *The librarian of Basra: A true story from Iraq.*

Woodson, Jacqueline (2003) *Locomotion.*

— (2005) *Show way.*

Ye, Ting-xing (2000) *White lily.*

Yee, Paul (1996) *Ghost train.*

— (2004) *A song for Ba.*

Yerxa, Leo (1993) *Last leaf first snowflake to fall.*

— (2006) *Ancient thunder.*

CHAPTER 7 Nonfiction

Nonfiction is not just about information. The truth is that for many young adult readers nonfiction serves the same purposes as fiction does for other readers: it entertains, provides escape, sparks the imagination, and indulges curiosity There's a lot more to a good nonfiction book than mere information. (Sullivan, 2001: 44)

Through reading informational literature, children learn more about the familiar and are introduced to people, places, and things they might never encounter in everyday life. In addition, as Russell Freedman (1992: 3), award-winning writer of nonfiction for children, explains, "[a]n effective non-fiction book must animate its subject, infuse it with life. It must create a vivid and believable world that the reader will enter willingly and leave only with reluctance." A well-crafted nonfiction book captures and holds children's attention as readily as any well-written fictional narrative would do.

According to Bamford and Kristo (2003), nonfiction literature takes a wide range of forms:

- Concept books, which explore a class of objects (e.g., John Paul Zronik's *Oil and Gas*) or an abstract idea (e.g., Shari Graydon's *Made You Look: How Advertising Works and Why You Should Know*)
- Biographies (e.g, Elizabeth MacLeod's *Albert Einstein: A Life of Genius*)
- Photographic essays (e.g., Kathy Conlon's *Under the Ice: A Marine Biologist at Work*)
- Survey books (e.g., Silvey's *The Kids' Book of Aboriginal Peoples in Canada*)
- How-to books (e.g., Judy Ann Sadler, Gwen Blakley Kinsler, Jackie Young, and Biz Storms' *The Jumbo Book of Needlecrafts*)
- Reference books (e.g., Stanford's *The Canadian Oxford Junior Atlas*)

As an editor, **Shelley Tanaka** has worked with many of the best children's authors in Canada and has edited twelve Governor General's Award-winning books. As a writer, she has won several awards, including the Silver Birch Award, the Mr. Christie's Book Award, the Information Book Award, and the Science in Society Award. Her books are about historical events and times, environmental topics, and the arts.

Increasingly, information books defy classification, however, because they take on hybrid forms, sometimes even interweaving fiction and nonfiction. In Linda Bailey's *Adventures in the Middle Ages*, for example, the Binkerton children travel through time and find out about the Middle Ages through a guide book provided by the Good Times Travel Agency. Similarly, Shelley Tanaka's *On Board the Titanic: What It Was Like When the Great Liner Sank*, an Information Book Award winner, is a hybrid book. The events of the days leading to the sinking of the Titanic are told through the eyes of two young survivors. Detailed photograph-like paintings by Ken Marschall are accompanied by explanatory text providing information about the size of the ship, Morse code, and how the

Titanic sank. In addition, there is a picture graph showing the lives saved and lost among the three classes of passengers and the crew.

Historically, much of children's nonfiction did not match the quality of fiction. Nonfiction literature was "often characterized by inaccuracy, pedestrian writing and minimal visual appeal" (Moss, 1995: 122). As a result, works of nonfiction received little recognition from the larger literary community for many decades.

Today, the proliferation of awards for nonfiction is in step with the increased attention paid to children's nonfiction by publishers. In 2003, the Library of Congress reported (Bamford & Kristo, 2003) that nearly 60 percent of the children's books it catalogued were nonfiction.

Selecting Nonfiction Literature

Although age appropriateness is always a consideration when selecting books for children, "adult ideas about what is appropriate for a given age level are often less important than a child's desire to know about a particular topic" when it comes to informational books (Huck, Hepler, Hickman, & Kiefer, 1997: 578). This point was underscored by a study of adults who had been diagnosed as dyslexic in their elementary grades and had become successful readers and writers in their professional careers. The one thing all subjects had in common was that a passionate interest in a topic had compelled them to read widely and voraciously. Their desire to learn by reading nonfiction books on a topic of interest helped them to overcome the obstacles that their dyslexia posed (Fink, 1995/96). Similarly, Carter and Abrahamson (1990) found that adolescents read nonfiction texts outside of school that were far more challenging than their teachers believed they were capable of reading.

Of course, when selecting books suitable for curriculum units, the curriculum objectives must be considered. Together with curriculum appropriateness, however, teachers should take into account the following criteria, also used to determine nonfiction book awards.

Accuracy

The book should offer accurate and current information about the topic. Russell Freedman (1998: 225) explains that

> writers can only interpret the truth as they hear it. They are answerable in that interpretation to their readers, with whom they have an unwritten but clearly understood pact to be as factually accurate as human frailty will allow.

Criteria for determining a book's accuracy include

- the qualifications of the author and/or evidence of extensive research conducted by the author
- appropriate breadth and depth of the information on the book's topic
- presentation of varying viewpoints
- avoidance of stereotypes and anthropomorphism

There should be evidence that the author is appropriately qualified to write on the topic. For example, Kathy Conlon, the author of the photodocumentary *Under the Ice: A Marine Biologist at Work*, is unquestionably qualified to write the book. She is a marine biologist who has documented her experience with color photographs on every page, showing ocean life under the ice of the Antarctic Ocean, as well as human and animal life in and around the United States, and at McMurdo Station, the largest of 37 research stations operating year-round in Antarctica.

If the author is not an expert in the field explored in a nonfiction book, there should be evidence that the author has consulted a range of sources. In Linda Granfield's Information Book Award-winning concept book, *Where Poppies Grow,* for example, Granfield acknowledges people who work in museums, the National Archives of Canada, and the Toronto Reference Library, among many others that she consulted to gather information and verify its accuracy. She also identifies where the original source materials (e.g., post cards sent home by WWI soldiers, photographs of soldiers and their loved ones, pages from books written for children in the early 20th century) have come from in the Picture Credits.

Another concept book, Jane Springer's *Listen to Us: The Worlds' Working Children* defines child labor, describes the history of working children, identifies the ways in which children are working for pay throughout the world, and examines the social/economic/cultural conditions that lead to their having to work. Having worked with CUSO and UNICEF in the developing world, Springer has first-hand experience with the topic. Her book has a clear bias, however, as it focuses on the most exploitive and hazardous work that children do and features children who have been injured by their work or whose rights have been denied.

Anthropomorphism (attributing human thought and speech to animals) usually works against the authenticity of the book. Rice (2002) analyzed 28 science trade books for accuracy of content. She found titles that reinforced stereotypes (e.g., *The Yucky Reptile Alphabet Book*), inaccuracies (e.g., *The Reason for a Flower* classifies mushrooms as flowers), and misinformation (e.g., in *The Mixed Up Chameleon*, a chameleon changes to bright red, yellow, and white; chameleons generally change from shades of green to shades of brown). Laurence Pringle's Orbis Pictus Award-winning *An Extraordinary Life: The Story of a Monarch Butterfly* walks close to the anthropomorphic line as it follows the life cycle of one butterfly named Danaus. The narrative of Danaus's life is interwoven with paragraphs of information about monarch butterflies in general. However, at times readers get a sense of Danaus as having human emotions, such as feeling fear when a hummingbird flies near, having an "extraordinary day" of riding a thermal, and "becom[ing] accustomed to seeing fellow migrators." In spite of the anthropomorphic leanings, there is evidence that the book is well researched with a lengthy list of acknowledgements and further readings.

Design

A nonfiction book's layout should be attractive and readable, with illustrations, maps, diagrams, charts, and other explanatory visuals that complement the text. For example, full-page photographs and Greg Ruhl's realistic depictions of life in Pompeii in AD 79 draw readers' attention in Shelley Tanaka's *The Buried City of Pompeii.* On pages opposite the visuals, the text, in two columns with

Dresang (1999) explains that the changing nature of today's reader-viewer, due to the proliferation of digital technology and multimedia, has prompted children's book designers to create books that have non-linear structures, so that our eyes can "point and click" as we would if we were using digital texts.

drawings, maps, photographs, and reproductions of art works, is easy to follow. The visuals both complement the text and provide information that goes beyond the text.

Mark Kurlansky's *The Cod's Tale*, an Orbis Pictus Honor book, contains descriptive pages explaining what a cod looks like, how it lives, and what its life cycle is like. There are also maps showing where cod live, recipes for dishes such as accra (codfish balls from the French Caribbean), timelines of the Basques' and Vikings' travels across the Atlantic Ocean, and lyrics for sea shanties. The eyes can follow the blocks of text introduced with a heading, or they can skip to the sidebars and illustrations with verses, captions, and explanations. The text is above, below, or embedded within S.D. Schindler's watercolor cartoon illustrations.

Organization

There should be a logical development and clear sequence of ideas in a nonfiction book. Reference aids (e.g., headings, table of contents, index, glossary) should facilitate readers' search for information. Elizabeth MacLeod's *Albert Einstein: A Life of Genius*, for example, is organized chronologically. Each two-page spread contains information about a particular aspect of Einstein's life and work. Headings such as "Meet Albert Einstein" are in the top left corner, followed by paragraphs about the topic. The text is framed by captioned photographs, quotes, and artifacts. On the right page are more photographs, artifacts, and a cartoon drawing of Einstein with speech balloons. Readers quickly catch on that the information in the text is supported by short explanations of the visuals on the right page; this is the pattern in all of MacLeod's biographies. A table of contents and an index make it easy to find specific information.

Concept books, such as *Search of the Spirit: The Living National Treasures of Japan* by Sheila Hamanaka and Ayano Ohmi, are often organized by subcategories within the overall concept. In this case, the traditional Japanese crafts and performing arts are introduced individually through a master who practices them. Following an introduction identifying who the living national treasures are, the works of each master are illustrated, the art form is described, and illustrated instructions show how the master creates his national treasure. A table of contents and a short index help readers to locate specific national treasures.

Style

Issues for Discussion

How can trade books be used in the content areas? What role should they play in content area teaching?

The writing should be interesting and stimulating. Appropriate terminology and rich language should be used. Linda Granfield's story of the poem *In Flanders Fields* uses the formal and informal language of war, such as "artillery" and "funk holes" (shelves scraped into the sides of trenches). She also uses rich language to create vivid images of the horrors of the battlefield: "After dark, a stretcher squad of four men would lift the wounded to their shoulders and stumble across the bomb-scarred field, all the while dodging snipers' bullets and mud holes that could claim them."

Even in the title *Out of Sight: Pictures of Hidden Worlds*, Seymour Simon crafts his language artfully. The title is a play on words, as the images in the book are taken by electron microscopes, endoscopes inserted into the body, x-rays, electronic strobes, Landsat satellites, and the Hubble Space Telescope. As such, they are both out of sight to the human eye and out of sight in the colloquial sense—awe-inspiring. Throughout the book, Simon uses the terminology of science with readily-understood explanations, examples, and analogies. A gentle sense of humor mitigates the revulsion readers might have when they see a magnification of the surface of a tooth showing plaque and tartar build-up. Simon writes, "See what happens when you don't brush your teeth?"

Nonfiction Literature and the Curriculum

Trade books are more up to date than textbooks, and provide greater depth of information about a topic than the shallow look at a broad range of topics offered by a textbook. Butzow and Butzow (2000) contend that trade books provide more textualized information to support concept learning, and are often more interesting and relevant to children's lives. As a result, teachers are making nonfiction literature an ever-larger part of the curriculum in all content areas.

Visual Arts and Music

Kiefer (2003: 172) writes that "books cannot replace firsthand experiences with creating art but they can encourage children to experiment with art, music making, drama, and dance." Some nonfiction books have done an honorable job of overcoming the limitations of the two-dimensional page to complement children's first-hand experience with visual arts and music.

VISUAL ARTS AND CRAFTS: FOR YOUNGER READERS

Lucy Micklethwait carries the "I Spy in a highly-regarded art work" theme into a number of other books, including *Animals: A First Art Book, Colors: A First Book, I Spy: Shapes in Art*, and *I Spy Two Eyes: Numbers in Art.*

Many of the nonfiction books appropriate for visual arts classes introduce and analyze works of art. Lucy Micklethwait's *I Spy: An Alphabet in Art*, for example, introduces 26 paintings from the world's greatest museums containing objects from A to Z. Its layout is consistent—the paintings are featured on the right page and the text, starting with "I spy with my little eye something beginning with (*a letter of the alphabet*)" is on the left page. Text and illustration complement each other, as readers are invited to find the everyday object in the painting.

An instructional book for making artwork such as clay sculptures, chalk creatures, dot-painted T-shirts, and styroblock prints is well named: *I Can Make Art.* Author Mary Wallace, an award-winning artist, craftsperson, and former elementary school teacher gives easy-to-follow directions with three to six steps, each step described in concise text with accompanying photographs. The *Jumbo Book of Art*, intended for children aged eight and up, is also put together by artists, this time from Toronto's Avenue Road Arts School. The 200 pages of art ideas are presented according to four themes—"Drawing out your ideas," "Creating with color," "Transforming ideas into sculptures," and "Mixing up your media"—with a graphic table of contents for each one. Irene Luxbacher, author and illustrator of the book, draws or paints examples of the art works, and the procedures are numbered so they are easy to follow. Because its intended audience is slightly older than that of Mary Wallace's book, many steps of the process do not have accompanying illustrations.

VISUAL ARTS AND CRAFTS: FOR OLDER READERS

Jon Scieszka has brought his zany sense of humor to the art world in *Seen Art? Misunderstood by a lady on the avenue in New York, the first-person narrator is* directed to the Museum of Modern Art as he tries to find his way to the corner of Fifth and Fifty-third to meet his pal, Art. The narrator walks past artwork by Vincent Van Gogh, Andy Warhol, Henri Matisse, Salvador Dalí, Edward Hopper, Claude Monet, and Paul Klee, among many others, having a terrible time convincing those he meets that he really is looking for Art, not art. Lane Smith's cartoon-like characters are made of a combination of collage elements and line drawings. The long white pages, less than 15 cm (6 inches) high by almost 30 cm (12 inches) wide, allow for arrangements of the many small reproductions of the museum's collection in varying ways, strung along a wall in typical museum fashion, totally filling a page, or as parts of a double-page mural.

In *Seurat and La Grande Jatte*, Robert Burleigh invites readers to begin an analysis of Seurat's painting by identifying particular people and animals. He then helps readers to see how the painter's pointillist style brings a vibrancy to the scene, and how his composition balances curved and vertical forms. Photographs of details in the painting, of Seurat's studies for *La Grande Jatte*, and of his other paintings help to create a sense of Seurat's intentions as a painter and who he was as an artist. Readers can find further information about Seurat in the short bibliography.

A number of art-related nonfiction books are biographies. The life of Canadian artist Emily Carr is chronicled in two recent books: one by Jo Ellen Bogart (*Emily Carr: At the Edge of the World*), and the other by Nicolas Debon (*Four Pictures by Emily Carr*). Nicolas Debon retells Emily Carr's life in comic strips, anchoring the events on the circumstances surrounding her work on four paintings. The cartoons, with their speech and thought balloons, make Emily Carr seem very much a real person. However, the comic strip format limits the amount of information that can be conveyed. Evidence of the author's research into Carr's life is found only in a list of paintings that inspired Debon's cartoon illustrations. Jo Ellen Bogart, on the other hand, has consulted a number of sources, as evidenced in the extensive bibliography and a list of painting sources. In her book are many more of Carr's paintings. Her lively and easy-to-follow narrative of Emily Carr's life is illustrated by Maxwell Newhouse's pencil drawings. Canadian artist William Kurelek has been featured in a book by May Ebbitt Cutler, *Breaking Free: The Story of William Kurelek*. May Ebbitt Cutler, founder of Tundra Books, knew the artist well because she published his award-winning books for children. She calls him "Bill" in the book and quotes him frequently as she narrates the story of his life and work. All of the artwork is Kurelek's.

The realistic oil paintings of artists Laura Fernandez and Rick Jacobson carry the life story of Spanish artist, Pablo Picasso, harmoniously with the text in *Picasso: Soul on Fire*. Although the authors acknowledge museums that gave permission to have Picasso's artwork included in the book, there is no mention of sources of information about Picasso for the text of this biography. The text fleshes out the timeline of Picasso's life that is included at the end of the book. American Diane Stanley's *Leonardo da Vinci* and *Michelangelo* are Orbis Pictus Award-winning and Honor books respectively. Stanley illustrates the books in the style of the old masters, with reproductions from da Vinci's notebooks and archival photographs of Michelangelo's work from the Vatican Museum. Her narrative follows their lives and their art.

MUSIC: FOR YOUNGER READERS

A concept book, *The Story of the Incredible Orchestra* by violin and jazz guitar player Bruce Koscielniak, begins by introducing readers to instruments originating prior to 1597. This was when Venetian organist Giovanni Gabrieli wrote the *Sacrae Symphoniae*, with separate parts for specific groups of instruments, thus initiating the first orchestra. The text, explaining historical music periods and instrumental families, is extended with watercolor cartoon illustrations that are well labeled, identifying the instruments and providing explanations of how the instruments are played.

In her well-known cartoon style, artist and writer Aliki has created a survey book, *Ah Music!*, that defines elements of music (e.g., rhythm, melody, pitch and tone, volume and feeling), and covers a vast range of music-related topics. She devotes a page to showing music scores and identifying a staff, treble clef, time signature, etc., then moves to identifying orchestral instruments within their families, types of dances from around the world, and early instruments. No topic is given an in-depth treatment, but Aliki's book does provide an introduction to terminology and concepts related to music.

MUSIC: FOR OLDER READERS

A number of books on music topics are biographies of renowned musicians. Vladimir Konieczny, amateur musician and former English and music teacher, has been a fan of virtuoso Canadian pianist Glenn Gould since he first heard him play on CBC radio in the early 1960s. Konieczny's admiration for Gould's artistry and his sensitivity towards Gould's eccentricities are evident in the book, *Struggling for Perfection: The Story of Glenn Gould*. Photographs from the Estate of Glenn Gould and the National Archives of Canada, together with Chrissie Wysotski's black-and-white drawings, work with the text to tell the story of Gould's life. Although chronologically organized with subheadings at the top of most pages, the book lacks a table of contents or index to help readers find sought-after information.

Black-and-white photographs, programs, and newspaper clippings add to the authenticity of Russell Freedman's *The Voice that Challenged a Nation: Marian Anderson and the Struggle for Equal Rights*. The book, scrupulously researched in Freedman's award-winning style, chronicles Marian Anderson's life and work in a social and political climate that presented barriers to her success as an African-American contralto. The back pages include notes linking quotes to their original sources, a selected bibliography of sources on Marian Anderson's life, a selected discography of recent compact discs of Marian Anderson's music, and an index.

Some concept books on music, such as Meredith Hamilton's *Story of the Orchestra* and Neil Ardley's *A Young Person's Guide to Music*, include compact discs. The CD in Ardley's book contains a work by Paul Ruders that was commissioned by the British Broadcasting Corporation to commemorate the 300th anniversary of Henry Purcell's death and the 50th anniversary of Benjamin Britten's *A Young Person's Guide to the Orchestra*, based on a theme by Purcell. Directions about which track of the CD to play while reading particular sections are on each page. The book is divided into two parts, the first explaining how music is made, illustrated with well-captioned photographs of musicians and their instruments, and the second dealing with the history of classical music, illustrated with both photographs and reproductions of paintings. At the end of the book is an "A–Z of Composers" with brief paragraphs on composers from John Adams to Kurt Weill, another reference of musical forms, and a final glossary of musical terms.

Russell Freedman, author of more than 40 books, worked as a reporter and editor for the Associated Press and as a publicity writer. When choosing topics for his books, Freedman selects those that he, himself, wants to learn more about. His books are about people in history who have character traits that stand out and make them memorable. Rigorous in his research, Freedman may identify as many as 1000 possible photographs, finally selecting 140 or so for his book. Freedman's work earned him a Newbery Medal and two Newbery Honor medals.

Health and Physical Education

Books for health classes tend to take the form of survey and concept books about self-esteem, healthy living, and interacting with others safely. The activity of physical education classes can be complemented with how-to books, concept books, and biographies of athletes.

HEALTH: FOR YOUNGER READERS

Gail Gibbons is the author and illustrator of more than 130 nonfiction books for young children. She has always loved drawing and painting, and came up with the idea for her first book while doing artwork for children's television shows. Gail Gibbons artfully makes complex subjects understandable and entertaining for young readers.

Gail Gibbons is well loved by younger readers for her lively cartoon illustrations that fill a page, accompanied by minimal text to highlight certain features and to extend the information in the pictures. In *Emergency!*, Gibbons introduces people who help others in an emergency: police, ambulance personnel, fire fighters, pilots, and the Coast Guard. The book ends with a historical look at emergency equipment. Young children are also enamored of Joanna Cole's Magic School Bus books on health and science topics. In *The Magic School Bus Explores the Senses*, Principal Wilde ends up behind the wheel of the Magic School Bus, taking Ms. Frizzle's students on a ride into the eye of a passing policeman, the ear of a child, and the nose of a dog. Bruce Degen's lively cartoon illustrations bring readers along for the ride.

HEALTH: FOR OLDER READERS

Two books for older readers, with their focus on body image and self-esteem, target female readers. Ann Douglas and Julie Douglas teamed to write *Body Talk: The Straight Facts on Fitness, Nutrition and Feeling Great about Yourself.* The authors acknowledge 30 girls who contributed to the "Girl Talk" quotes sprinkled liberally throughout the book, and a nurse, a fitness instructor, and authors of books about girls. They identify a dozen websites on topics related to body image, as well. There is a mix of primary and secondary sources of information for the seven well laid-out chapters that deal with diets, eating disorders, physical activity, skin care, and media influences on self-image. Claudia Dávila's lively cartoon illustrations include girls of many races and graphics for features such as "Chew on This!," which provides bites of related information and tips for enhancing one's body image. This book provides a survey of topics related to body image, whereas Shari Graydon's *In Your Face: The Culture of Beauty and You* is a concept book that focuses on beauty—humanity's fascination with beauty, historical perceptions of beauty and what men and women have done to match those perceptions, as well as the forces that shape views on beauty. Extensive notes for each chapter indicate that the book is thoroughly researched. Photographs come from a wide number of sources, including the portfolios of one male and one female model, a painting of Peter Paul Rubens' wife, and photographs of the 1953 contestants for the Miss America beauty-pageant crown. The information is conveyed in a conversational style with an appealing and instructional mix of colloquial and formal language. Graydon encourages readers to evaluate messages about body image critically, ending each chapter with questions and considerations in a section entitled "Image Reflections."

Trudee Romanek, the author of *Squirt: The Most Interesting Book You'll Ever Read about Blood,* thanks cardiologists and staff from the UK International Blood Group Reference Laboratory, showing that the book is well-researched. A table of contents and an index make it easy to find information. Cartoon illustrations add a lighthearted touch. There is a sufficient breadth of information about topics such as blood pressure, blood types, blood flow through the heart,

Since the publication of his first book in 1968, **Seymour Simon** has written more than 200 highly acclaimed science books. He has introduced readers to a staggering array of subjects. Having spent 23 years as a science teacher, Seymour Simon has a keen sense for topics that appeal to children and a direct way of explaining scientific concepts without talking down to his young readers.

and organs such as the liver, kidneys, and pancreas. Seymour Simon, nonfiction writer extraordinaire, has written a number of books on organ systems: *Guts: Our Digestive System*, *Brain: Our Nervous System*, and *Lungs: Your Respiratory System*. He uses detailed colored X rays, computer- generated pictures, and microscopic photos to show the fascinating workings of the human body. Simon is a thorough researcher who goes the extra mile to ensure the accuracy of the information in his books. He uses scientific terminology in ways that are accessible to readers.

PHYSICAL EDUCATION: FOR YOUNGER READERS

Camilla Gryski's *Let's Play: Traditional Games of Childhood* is a survey book of active games—such as various versions of tag, hopscotch, skipping games, and ball games—and more sedentary hand games, clapping games, and hand-shadow games. Written instructions for playing the games are accompanied by lively cartoon illustrations by noted illustrator Dusan Petricic.

PHYSICAL EDUCATION: FOR OLDER READERS

Former *OWL* magazine editor Keltie Thomas has written *How Baseball Works*, *How Hockey Works*, and *How Soccer Works* as both how-to guides and concept books about the sports. Each provides information for longtime fans and newcomers about the historical origins of the sport, legends, gear and equipment, ways to improve one's game, the rules, and a glossary of terms. Divided into chapters with a table of contents and an index, the books are easy-to-use references. Less comprehensive and acknowledging fewer people consulted are *Field Events in Action* and *Soccer in Action* by Bobbie Kalman and Niki Walker, respectively. Part of a series on sports, these books introduce the sport and its components (e.g., the long jump, shot put, and pole vault are all field events), and illustrate each event with photographs of athletes. A two-page spread is devoted to each topic. Subheadings, a table of contents, and an index guide readers to specific information.

Many books on physical education topics are biographies of noteworthy athletes. Jack Batten, a sports and crime writer, drew on information from a number of archives and libraries, and consulted with writers from the *Toronto Star* to write the Information Book Award winner *The Man Who Ran Faster Than Everyone: The Story of Tom Longboat*. The book begins by celebrating Tom Longboat's fame as the greatest long-distance runner in the early 20th century, when races were as popular in North America as hockey, football, basketball, and baseball are today. The subsequent nine chapters chronicle Longboat's beginnings as a champion lacrosse player on the Onondaga team in a Six Nations league in Ontario. Information is easily accessed using the table of contents and an extensive index.

Russell Freedman's *Babe Didrikson Zaharias: The Making of a Champion*, together with Canadian Anne Dublin's *Bobbie Rosenfeld, The Olympian who Could Do Everything*, are biographies of exceptional female athletes. Dublin's book, shortlisted for the Norma Fleck Award in 2005, chronicles Canadian Bobbie Rosenfeld's life from her birth in the Ukraine and her youth in Ontario, to her Olympic triumphs and work as a sports columnist at the *Globe and Mail*. Photographs from the City of Toronto Archives and Canadian Sports Hall of Fame are included throughout the book, and there is evidence of extensive consultation in the acknowledgments. Russell Freedman's book follows a similar pattern. He traces Mildred Ella Didrikson's life from her childhood in Texas, where she was nicknamed "Babe" because she played baseball like Babe Ruth, through her remarkable sports career as an All-American basketball player, Olympic gold medalist in track and field, and champion golfer. The book ends with a tribute to her courage as she suffered from and finally succumbed to spinal cancer in 1956 at the age of 45.

Mathematics

Standards set out by the National Council of Teachers of Mathematics (1989) support the use of children's literature in teaching mathematics. More and more, teachers are using literature to extend students' mathematical understanding and show how mathematics is a part of everyday life.

NUMERACY AND OPERATIONS: FOR YOUNGER READERS

It was difficult to find nonfiction books for young children on numeracy and operations topics. One book, *The Numbers Dance: A Counting Comedy* by Josephine Nobisso, is a rhyming poem that features numbers boogying, western line dancing, and classical dancing with each other. The poetry describes what the numbers look like, and Dasha Ziborova's digital illustrations present stylized numbers in various combinations and contortions, along with a constant border of the numerals from on to ten on every two-page spread. *One is a Snail, Ten is a Crab* has the subtitle "A Counting By Feet Book." Authors April Pulley Sayre and Jeff Sayre take readers on a walk-along to the beach. Addition is practiced as readers look and count the number of feet found on a number of creatures: "6 is an insect. 7 is an insect and a snail." Originally written in 1986, Celia Barker Lottridge's *One Watermelon Seed* has recently been reissued with brightly-colored digital art. Readers follow along and count the number of seeds planted by Max and Josephine in their garden, one-by-one up to ten, then in groups of ten up to one hundred.

The other books we found could easily be classified as fictional narrative. *Anno's Counting House*, by widely-known author and illustrator Mitsumasa Anno, is a wordless picture book of ten little people who move from their fully furnished home to an empty house next door. Anno's watercolor and ink illustrations include an overlay with cut-out windows that can be moved in front of either house. Children use the overlay to determine who is in each of the houses on each two-page spread, adding and subtracting from each house as the people move back and forth between them. The concept of 1000 is approached from many angles in Canadian Helen Nolan's *How Much, How Many, How Far, How Heavy, How Long, How Tall is 1000?* Tracy Walker's cartoon characters take readers through situations where 1000 seems like a small number (e.g., 1000 hairs on one's head) and those where 1000 seems like a lot (e.g., 1000 freckles on one's face, when one is not fond of freckles). The humorous rhymes in Trudy Harris's *100 Days of School* show different ways to count to 100 that involve adding combinations of numbers and multiplying various numbers. The colorful, child-like paintings illustrating the book are by Beth Griffs Johnson.

NUMERACY AND OPERATIONS: FOR OLDER READERS

In David M. Schwartz's *On Beyond a Million*, Professor X and his dog Y explore powers of 10 to a googol (a 1 followed by 100 zeros) and beyond. Real-life examples provide plenty of fun facts, such as how much popcorn Americans eat in one year, or how many hairs are on a square inch of a person's head. One book

Whitin (2002), who reviews children's books for the journal *Teaching Children Mathematics*, cautions that the new interest in using literature in mathematics has motivated publishers to produce a number of low-quality books that are marketed as teaching tools for specific concepts taught at particular grades. He recommends that teachers choose nonfiction for teaching mathematics with quality, as well as curricular criteria, in mind.

that is clearly nonfiction is written by archaeologist Denise Schmandt-Besserat: *The History of Counting.* The realistic, textured paintings of Michael Hays are prominent on every page, providing visual representations of the text information. The evolution of counting to meet the demands of changing societies is detailed chronologically, from the body counting of the Paiela of Papua New Guinea, to the Sumerians' abstract numbers used for trade, taxes, and calculations used in everyday life. The book then describes the Roman system of place value and the Arabic system that invented a symbol for zero and made limitless counting and simple computation possible.

Written for children who are developing a more sophisticated understanding of operations, Greg Tang's *Math Appeal: Mind-stretching Math Riddles* requires readers to use Harry Brigg's colorful illustrations to solve problems requiring addition, multiplication, and subtraction. The answers and how to figure them out are at the back of the book.

Polar Bear Math: Learning about Fractions from Klondike and Snow teaches fractions with practical problems arising from the story of two polar bear cubs abandoned by their mother in the Denver Zoo; *Panda Math* teaches subtraction; *Chimp Math* teaches about time; and *Tiger Math* teaches graphing.

In collaboration with various zoos, Ann Whitehead Nagda has written a number of books that explain basic mathematical operations and present problems for students to solve. *Cheetah Math: Learning about Division from Baby Cheetahs*, for example, is the story of two baby cheetahs born at the San Diego Zoo. Photographs accompany the narration of their story. On opposite pages are division problems related to the amount of milk they drink at each of their feedings, the number of ounces of meat each cheetah eats out of the total consumed in a day, how many times faster the cheetahs run compared to their companion dogs at the zoo, etc. The story provides an authentic context for the math problems, and the easy-to-follow solutions to the problems are explained with diagrams.

MEASUREMENT AND GEOMETRY: FOR YOUNGER READERS

Useful for a mathematics/visual art integrated lesson, the Metropolitan Museum of Art's *Museum Shapes* is beautifully illustrated with paintings and artifacts from the museum. The book has a predictable pattern: readers are asked to identify the shape in the artwork on one page, and then the shape and its name are identified along with four additional examples from museum art on the following page. The works of art and their creators are indexed in the back of the book. Identification of geometric shapes is a feature of Catherine Sheldrick Ross's *Circles*, as well. Cartoon watercolors illustrate the circles in the natural and technological world, and in mathematics, and guide readers in following directions to create circle prints, moebius strips, pinwheel disks, and other circle-related objects.

In David M. Schwartz's *Millions to Measure*, Marvelosissimo the Mathematical Magician explores the invention of length, weight, and volume measurements, introducing the basic pattern of meters, liters, and grams. Steven Kellogg's unmistakable watercolor illustrations add a lighthearted touch to the information about metric measurement.

MEASUREMENT AND GEOMETRY: FOR OLDER READERS

Kathryn Laskey's *The Librarian who Measured the Earth* is a biography and an explanation of how Eratosthenes figured out how to measure the circumference of the earth. The author's passion for the topic shows in the "Author's Note" at the beginning of the book, where she explains her fascination with Eratosthenes' accuracy (within 200 miles of the measurements made using modern technology) in measuring the circumference of the earth using camels, plumb lines, and the angles of shadows. Both Kathryn Laskey and the illustrator, Kevin Hawkes, provide an extensive bibliography of sources they consulted to create this book.

Social Studies

Myra Zarnowski (2003: 121) proposes that social studies "is a rigorous exercise program for the mind" because it involves students in "activities such as selecting and synthesizing, interpreting and speculating, discussing and debating." Through the author's notes and acknowledgments, good nonfiction literature reveals the traces of the author's research and thinking. Nonfiction authors who raise questions about conflicting sources of information model the inquiry processes of social studies.

FOR YOUNGER READERS

Peter Kuitenbrouwer's *Our Song: The Story of "Oh Canada"* is illustrated by Ashley Spires with eye-catching cartoon characters on a textured background. The words appear in both of Canada's official languages, as a whole song with the musical score at the front of the book and then on every other spread. Timelines starting at 1875 provide a historical context for the evolution of the national anthem. Information is provided about Calixa Lavallée (the anthem's composer), Adolphe-Basile Routhier (the French lyricist), and the many writers of the English lyrics, including Robert Stanley Weir, whose version is the one we sing today, save for a few phrases changed by Canada's Secretary of State, Francis Fox, in 1980. There are no acknowledgments to any sources consulted during the research process, alas. Although quotes are used in Maxine Trottier's *Our Canadian Flag*, their sources are not referenced. The illustrations are the truly notable aspect of this book. Brian Dienes's readily-identifiable Impressionist-style illustrations place the Canadian flag at an international hockey tournament, on Parliament Hill in Ottawa with fireworks below, and in a schoolyard with running children. Text in large print explains where and on what occasions the flag is flown. Underneath are boxes with smaller print providing the historical background of the flag.

Life in modern India and issues of protecting the vulnerable are possible social studies topics arising from Veronika Martenova Charles's *The Birdman*. This is a true story of a Calcutta tailor, Noor Nobi, who buys the leftover illegally-captured birds that are sold in the market. Annouchka Gravel Galouchko and Stéphan Daigle's gouache scenes radiate the exotic heat and bustle of Calcutta, filling one page per spread and spilling over onto the pages with text. The patterns and jewel-like colors add to the mythical ambiance of this true story. The book ends with the author's story of discovering Noor Nobi in a Canadian newspaper feature, and seeking him out on a Monday in Calcutta. Photographs of Noor Nobi show that he is, indeed, a real-life person.

FOR OLDER READERS

A good number of the shortlisted and award-winning nonfiction books are on social studies topics and written for older readers. Many books are biographies or autobiographies. In *Red Land, Yellow River*, a book shortlisted for the Norma Fleck Award, Ange Zhang recounts his youth in China during Mao's Cultural Revolution. Readers come to understand how the horrors of that time influenced the lives and identities of individuals. Zhang sees his father, a writer, humiliated and arrested. Ange himself is bullied and compelled to watch others

The nonfiction literature discussed here provides students with social studies content while promoting the inquiry and deliberation that characterize active citizenship. All of the social studies literature was written and illustrated by Canadians.

Other picture books that help readers travel across the ten provinces and learn facts drawn from Canadian culture are *M is for Maple: A Canadian alphabet* by Mike Ulmer, *Eh? To Zed: A Canadian ABCedarium* by Kevin Major, and Ted Harrison's colorful illustrations accompanying the words of the Canadian anthem, *O Canada*.

being bullied by the Red Guard. He is later forced to work as a rural laborer. Ange Zhang illustrates his personal story with dramatic paintings and reproductions of newspaper cartoons, photographs, and artifacts from that period in China's history.

The Norma Fleck Award-winning biography, *Heart And Soul: The Story Of Florence Nightingale*, chronicles the life of a woman who made immeasurable contributions to the training of nurses, to views on the importance of nurses to health care, to hospital conditions, and to the quality of life for soldiers. The book is well-researched: author Gena K. Gorrell provides source notes for each chapter and a selected bibliography. The many photographs and other artifacts come from British, Canadian, and American museums, libraries, and archives. A detailed caption, marked with a lantern icon, accompanies each photograph. Gorrell provides a context for Florence Nightingale's work, seamlessly weaving in information about major historical events, such as the Crimean War, and about technological advances, such as iron steamships, that greatly influenced the lives of Europeans during Florence Nightingale's lifetime of 1820–1910.

If the World Were a Village is a book that helps readers learn about our global village. Author David J. Smith challenges students to think about the whole world as a village of just 100 people, where only 76 people would have electricity, and 24 would not. If the world were a village… 61 people would be from Asia, only 5 from Canada and the United States, and 1 from Oceania. A DVD is available to support the information in this resource.

The stories behind maps we take for granted, such as the Mercator projection of the world and the London A–Z map books of London, UK, are chronicled in Val Ross's *The Road To There: Mapmakers and Their Stories*. Less familiar maps are highlighted, as well, as readers learn about al-Idrisi's planisphere of the known world in the early 12th century and John Murray's 19th-century Bathymetrical Chart of the World's Oceans. Libraries and museums around the world, as indicated in the photo credits, gave Val Ross permission to use the reproductions of some of the most important maps in history. She acknowledges cartographers and provides several books for further reading on the maps and the mapmakers of each chapter. Winner of the Norma Fleck Award, this book is written in a straightforward style and organized chronologically, with each chapter featuring particular mapmakers and the historical events of their time. Information is readily located using the table of contents and an index.

Some of the Information Book Award-winning books chronicle particular historical periods or groups of people. Barbara Greenwood's *The Last Safe House: A Story of the Underground Railroad* is a hybrid book that tells a story of a fictional family. Each chapter is followed by nonfiction text accompanied by Heather Collins's black-and-white illustrations. This text includes biographical information about Harriet Tubman and Frederick Douglas, instructions for making cornhusk dolls and gingerbread cookies and for storytelling, as well as background information about the cotton gin and slave catchers. There are maps showing Underground Railroad routes and the layout of a typical cotton plantation. Greenwood acknowledges books and museums she consulted to inform her writing. She provides a bibliography of novels, biographies, picture books, and histories that extend readers' knowledge of the Underground Railroad. Another Information Book Award winner, Deborah Hodge's concept book *The Kids Book of Canada's Railway and How the CPR was Built,* is based on consultation with many people, as evident in the acknowledgments at the beginning of the book. This book uses color paintings by John Mantha to illustrate the

Barbara Greenwood has also won a number of Canadian awards for *A Pioneer Story*, which is a useful and accessible resource about the daily life of a Canadian family in 1840.

people, machines, and geography involved in building the Canadian Pacific Railway between 1881 and 1885. Two-page spreads are devoted to specific topics, such as surveying the land, laying track, the navvies, and the last spike, as well as types of trains, maintaining the track, and a train disaster. The book ends with an index and glossary of "words from the past."

Kathleen Kenna's *A People Apart*, a photodocumentary, was a Canadian Children's Book Centre Our Choice award selection in 1996. It tells of the Old Order Mennonites in Canada, and shows how the traditional ways of life have been maintained over the last 100 years. The photographs, taken by award-winning Andrew Sawicki, are one-of-a-kind, because Mennonites believe that photographs are evidence of pride, which they consider a sin.

Wendy Stephenson's *Idaa Trail: In the Steps of Our Ancestors* has a nonfiction feel to it, although the story of children who take a month-long canoe trip from Rae to Hottah, Northwest Territories, retracing a major trading route of their Dogrib ancestors, is fictional. The author, Curator of Education at the Prince of Wales Northern Heritage Centre in Yellowknife, Northwest Territories, drew on extensive archaeological research and the oral tradition of the Dogrib people. She acknowledges a number of resource people and provides extensive information about the Dogrib and the sites along the trail that were described in the story. In addition, the authenticity of information is confirmed with a glossary and pronunciation guide for common words and expressions, as well as a pronunciation guide for proper names. The plot is uneventful and the characters are not well-developed, as the story is simply a vehicle for providing information about a part of Canada that deserves attention in children's literature. Autumn Downey's impressionist watercolor illustrations convey a love of the natural world and bring readers alongside the paddlers on the Idaa Trail, giving no doubt that this Yellowknife inhabitant has firsthand experience with this route.

Two award-winning authors have written thoughtful, informative tributes to soldiers in World War I. Linda Granfield's *The Unknown Soldier* provides a starting point for classroom discussion about the fallen soldiers whose bodies lie in unmarked graves, helping to ensure that they and their sacrifices are never forgotten. Granfield takes readers to the Tombs of the Unknown Soldier erected in many countries around the world, sharing more than 100 photos, a summary of tomb and gravestone symbols, a glossary, and a timeline of significant events. Hugh Brewster's *At Vimy Ridge: Canada's Greatest World War I Victory* tells the story of the capture by Canadian soldiers of a heavily fortified German position during the First World War. It is clear that Brewster has done extensive research to present an accurate account, as he acknowledges staff at the Vimy Memorial and at the Passchendaele Memorial Museum, and provides a selected bibliography. Quotes from soldiers' letters and interviews, newspaper clippings, and many captioned photographs provide information that no narrative could convey about the courage and steadfastness of Canadian soldiers during a horrific battle.

Science

Anthony Fredericks (2003: p. 141) explains that science "should allow children to examine new ideas, play around with concepts and precepts, and discover that there is no such thing as a body of finite knowledge." These goals are important to keep in mind when selecting nonfiction literature as science curriculum materials. The literature should provide breadth and depth to the science curriculum and a starting point for students' self-initiated discoveries.

Lutz (1996) advises against using literature in science solely to enhance motivation and "energize" science curriculum. Instead, the nonfiction books should have an authentic connection to science and scientists, and should show why the topic is important to the scientists and to others. The books should not simply report facts—there should be a theme or identifiable purpose/passion to those selected for use in science classes.

BIOLOGY: FOR YOUNGER READERS

An Orbis Pictus Honor Book, Cheryl Bardoe's *Gregor Mendel: The Friar Who Grew Peas* is masterfully put together, with Jos. A. Smith's watercolors highlighting the yellows and greens of the two types of peas that Mendel cross-fertilized to draw his conclusions about dominant and recessive genes. The diagrams and clear explanations make Mendel's theory accessible to young readers. This is a sensitively-told autobiography about a farm boy whose family made sacrifices so he could get a high school education in the early-19th century. An author's note and a select bibliography provide additional sources of information for readers who wish to pursue their learning about Mendel, the Father of Genetics. Cheryl Bardoe is Senior Project Manager of Exhibitions at The Field Museum in Chicago and well-positioned to write authoritatively about Mendel's work.

The life cycles of animals and plants are documented with lively, colorful illustrations in two books. The watercolors in Gail Gibbons's *Chicks and Chickens* are meticulously labeled, providing as much information as the straightforward, concise text. This concept book answers many *what* and *who* questions about chickens—about common breeds, and their digestive tract and other body parts. It also answers a number of *how* questions about the beloved fowl—how eggs are created, how fertilized eggs become chicks, and how eggs are gathered on small and large farms. Gail Gibbons acknowledges a professor of animal veterinary sciences as a source of information for the book. In a similar style, Gibbons' book *Corn* offers information about the history of humans' use of corn, together with details about planting, cultivating, and harvesting corn, and the many ways in which corn is used. Plant life cycles are the topic of Lola M. Schaefer's book *Pick, Pull, Snap! Where Once a Flower Bloomed*. Readily-accessible language works well with Lindsay Barrett George's life-size realistic images, cross-section diagrams, and tri-fold pages to show the pollination, seed formation, and fruit production of six plants. Readers are invited to observe first-hand the life of a plant by following the planting instructions at the end of the book.

Fire!: The Renewal of a Forest, a book written and illustrated by professional biologist and scientific illustrator Celia Godkin, provides another perspective on life cycles—this time about the regeneration of a boreal forest following a forest fire. A Norma Fleck Award winning book, *Fire!* tells the story of the fire and its aftermath with insets of specific mammals, birds, and trees affected by the fire. The final pages include a spread of definitions overlaid on a diagram of a forested area, and a similar spread showing "How Life Returns to a Forest After a Fire." An author's note at the end suggests websites that readers can consult to find out more about forest fires.

BIOLOGY: FOR OLDER READERS

Jan Thornhill's book, *I Found a Dead Bird: The Kids' Guide to the Cycle of Life and Death*, has won multiple award in Canada and the US. This encyclopedia of information about life and death addresses a breadth of topics about lifespans and what it means to be alive, the many ways living things can die, what can happen to things after they die, grieving, and funeral customs—not delving into great depth about any one topic. Thornhill approaches the topic of death in a straightforward non-sentimental way. Information is easy to find in boxed text accompanied by clear headings and carefully chosen, well-placed photographic illustrations.

Diane Swanson is a knowledgeable guide who has consulted museum staff before taking readers on an underwater interpretive excursion in *Safari Beneath the Sea: The Wonder World of the North Pacific Coast*. Well laid-out in five chapters, with plenty of subheadings, bulleted lists, sidebars, and an index, it is an easy-to-use reference on sea life in the Pacific Ocean. The book is especially appealing to the eye, with crisp, colorful photographs taken by the Royal British Columbia Museum.

It is not surprising that the illustrations in the field guide *Backyard Birds: An Introduction* are equally impressive. They are the paintings of world renowned artist Robert Bateman. Accompanying the breathtaking artwork are quick specs on each bird (e.g., length, wingspan, voice, food, range, habitat) and a brief description of the bird. The text is written informally and provides information about everyday features that one would observe about the birds. There are no acknowledgments or other evidence of sources consulted, but because of Robert Bateman's work as a nature photographer, readers can feel assured that the author is an authority.

Also notable for its breathtaking photographs is the Orbis Pictus Award-winning *Quest for the Tree Kangaroo: An Expedition to the Cloud Forest of New Guinea*. Written by naturalist/documentary scriptwriter/radio commentato, Sy Montgomery, this book follows scientist Lisa Dabek's expedition to locate the endangered Matschie's tree kangaroo in a remote mountainous cloud forest in New Guinea. The book centres on the expedition, with descriptions of Dabek, her team, and the people from the village of Yawain, New Guinea who work with her. There are nuggets of information about the cloud forest and its inhabitants, and Nic Bishop's photographs give stunning close-up views of these unique living things and their cloud forest home. This book provides starting points for discussions of the developed world's influence on traditional lives of people who live in remote parts of the world (e.g., Lisa Dabek and missionaries before her have convinced the people of Yawain to give up their hunting in the name of conservation of rare species of animals.) The book is divided into sections, with an index to access information easily.

Large and small animals from around the world are featured in Steve Jenkins' Orbis Pictus Honor Book, *Actual Size*. The collage illustrations of parts of the larger animals, such as the foot of the largest land animal, the African elephant, are the actual size of the body part. The book begins with a close-up of the eye of a giant squid. Fold-out pages are used to show the snout of the largest reptile, the saltwater crocodile. They are accompanied with information about the animal's height and weight. At the end of the book are short paragraphs about each animal. *Prehistoric Actual Size* is a worthy companion to Jenkins's original book.

TECHNOLOGY, SPACE, AND THE PHYSICAL WORLD: FOR YOUNGER READERS

Don Kilby's *In the Country* and *On a Construction Site* are part of the Wheels at Work series on machines. Kilby's crisp, realistic paintings showing the vehicles at work are the most noticeable feature of each page. The text provides some information about how each vehicle works, though there is often more of a "these are the people in your community" bent than a technological one. There is no evidence of resources consulted in either book, so it is not clear where Kilby got the idea that modern-day farmers are using square bales. Look around you when you travel the countryside—most of the straw and hay bales these days are round.

Steve Jenkins writes and illustrates books to share his personal fascination with the natural world, and to show how science helps us understand why the world is the way it is. Watercolor cut-paper collage illustrate such books about the animal world as *Animals in Flight*, *Sisters & Brothers*, and *Birdsongs*. Factual information at the end of each picture book is a bonus feature of a Steve Jenkins masterpiece.

Joanna Cole ventures into the physical world in *The Magic School Bus and the Science Fair Expedition.* Mrs. Frizzle's students think they've avoided the whacky side trips that the magic school bus takes when Mrs. Frizzle decides to take them to the science museum within walking distance. But, while in search of ideas for science fair projects, the class gets aboard a mockup bus that takes them back in time to the world of great scientists. Scientists such as Newton, Marie Curie, and Albert Einstein demonstrate elements of the scientific methods, as well as scientific principles that they developed. A gallery of scientists, who point out inaccuracies in some of the assumptions we tend to hold about their discoveries and principles, concludes the book.

In her engaging style, with watercolor paintings that appeal to young readers, Gail Gibbons opens up the universe in *Galaxies, Galaxies.* She starts with the Milky Way Galaxy, explaining how astronomers have learned more about it through the centuries. Following a description of refracting and reflecting telescopes, Gibbons identifies characteristics of various types of galaxies and features astronomers and telescopes that have advanced our knowledge of galaxies. The book ends with eight illustrated tidbits of knowledge about galaxies.

TECHNOLOGY, SPACE, AND THE PHYSICAL WORLD: FOR OLDER READERS

Bill Slavin's Norma Fleck Award-winning *Transformed: How Everyday Things are Made* is a jaunty encyclopedia of the machines and processes used to create more than 60 of the manufactured goods that are part of everyday life. Slavin's cartoon illustrations contribute to the sprightly tone of the text. A table of contents shows that the objects are grouped according to their function (e.g., "Fun and Games" and "Cover-Ups"). A helpful index also provides a map to the objects—such as cat litter, denim, stick-on bandages, and whistles—whose manufacture is explained in the book. A glossary and list of books, encyclopedias, and videos provide further information for readers who seek more information. Although the author/illustrator acknowledges that "many other individuals and companies helped me with the technical aspects of the writing," he identifies only two people and does not provide their qualifications.

Catherine Thimmesh's highly regarded *Team Moon: How 400,000 People Landed Apollo 11 on the Moon* was a Robert F. Sibert Information Book winner and gained an Orbis Pictus Honorable Mention. This book provides a rare perspective on the first moon landing, exploring the work of the engineers and technicians who worked for years behind the scenes. Accompanying Thimmesh's easy-going narrative are quotes revealing the concerns and joys of those involved—"We didn't worry too much until the guys on the moon started jumping up and down" says one of the spacesuit seamstresses—as well as period and NASA photographs.

Brimming over with photographs from NASA, *The Amazing International Space Station* has the feel of a scrapbook of Expedition One, the first crew of the International Space Station. Information is conveyed using scientific terminology, insider terms (such as 'nauts for astronauts and cosmonauts), and colloquial phrases; e.g., "While Mission Control Centre radios you about how great the launch was, you're pinned against an uncomfortable metal seat, feeling like a gorilla is parked on your chest. Hey, what can you expect when you're in the nose of a rocket blasting into space." Sidebars take the form of colored shapes with scientific information, excerpts from the ship's log, and explanations of experiments conducted in space. Detailed captions and the speech balloons quoting the 'nauts show the human side of space technology.

Walter Wick's *A Drop of Water: A Book of Science and Wonder* is a photo essay of water's states and of experiments taken from science books for children, some of them more than 100 years old. Close-ups of drops of water on a pin and time-lapse photos of a water drop hitting a pool of water to show surface tension are some of the many illustrations that extend the clearly-written text to explain phenomena such as surface tension, how clouds and snowflakes form, capillary attraction, and evaporation. Walter Wick acknowledges individuals who helped with the photography and in verifying the accuracy of the information. The experiments for each topic are further explained in an appendix-like list at the end of the book.

Also on the topic of water, Rochelle Strauss's *One Well: The Story of Water on Earth* addresses the distribution of water on earth and access to clean water, recycling water, and living things' dependence on water, among other subjects. Each large, double-page spread includes insets that provide snippets of information about specific topics. Not surprisingly, the dominant color is blue in Rosemary Woods's pastel and colored-pencil illustrations. An afterword addressed to parents, teachers, and guardians provides further information about "A Crisis in the Well" and what can be done to ensure the sustainability of water for all people and other living things in the world.

Biographies of scientists complement the technology curriculum, as well (see earlier description of Elizabeth Macleod's *Albert Einstein*). Another noteworthy biography is that of Wilbur and Orville Wright by Peter Busby: *First to Fly: How Wilbur and Orville Wright Invented the Airplane.* Fred C. Culick, a leading expert in aeronautics, is the acknowledged consultant for this book. In addition, a selected bibliography of books (for younger and older readers) and of websites follows a glossary and timeline of important dates. The well-written text is supported and extended with photographs of the Wright brothers with family and colleagues (and of course, their aircraft), as well as postcards and telegrams from the Library of Congress, and various museums and archives. Jack McMaster's drawings provide information about the Wright brothers' airplane and the principles that make flight possible. Striking full-page realistic paintings by David Craig add contextual information about the inventors and their world.

Another notable biography, Carla Killough McClafferty's *Something out of Nothing: Marie Curie and Radium*, was an Orbis Pictus Honor Book. McClafferty's interest and authority in the topic of radiation is evident in the publishing of a previous book: *The Head Bone's Connected to the Neck Bone: The Weird, Wacky, and Wonderful X-Ray* and in the back matter, which includes detailed chapter source notes, an extensive bibliography and list of recommended websites, and an index. Alongside the story of Curie's life as a scientist who won two Nobel Prizes, and as a wife and mother, is the story of radium's status as a cure-all for more than cancer. This story is told in photographs of products—such as the Standard Chemical Company's Solution for Drinking, which contains two micrograms of radium and is still radioactive more than 80 years after it was made—as well as the text.

Teaching with Nonfiction Literature

In some cases nonfiction literature will relate directly to the objectives of the content subjects you teach. In others, the literature will extend the objectives in new directions. Depending on how closely the nonfiction literature connects to curriculum topics, it can be used for a number of pedagogical purposes (Pappas, Kiefer, & Levstik, 1990).

Nonfiction books that are closely related or that extend curriculum objectives may also be available in the classroom for students' independent reading. The books should be inviting and of interest to students. Students may read these books during silent reading times, when they complete assigned tasks, or they may consult them when carrying out independent writing, drama, and visual arts activities.

Personal Response

- Students create poems from two to four sentences from a nonfiction book. The poem's rhythm is created from the accents and syllables of the words, and from the lines and where they are broken on the page. Students might add or cut words from the sentences as they create their poems. The goal is for students to create their own meaning from the ideas in the nonfiction book.
- Students create tableaux of scenes that are significant to them from the life of someone featured in a biography, or of something interesting that they have read about in other types of nonfiction.

Reading and Writing Skills

- Help students develop skills for selecting relevant information by modeling guiding questions or having the questions visible for students to consider while they read and take notes from nonfiction text. The following questions have proven to be helpful:
  1. What kinds of information do you hope to find?
  2. What kinds of information do the headings indicate that you will find?
  3. Which information directly answers your questions?
  4. Which information is interesting, but doesn't really answer your questions?
- Students identify the questions or types of information they want to know more about. Ask them to scan the table of contents and index to search for the needed information. When they have found the appropriate pages, ask students to scan the page for picture captions and headings, converting each into a question to predict what each section will be about.

Literary Elements

- Students examine the information provided in the text and in the graphics/visuals, and determine how the graphics or other visuals contribute to the book's success in conveying information on the topic.
- Invite students to examine three books on a particular topic to see how the information is organized (e.g., headings highlight main ideas and supporting details are in paragraphs; procedures are explained sequentially with numbered steps). How does the organization of the information in the text and visuals make it easier for you to find the information you're seeking? What gets in the way?

Because of the visuals in nonfiction books, it is possible that students will learn from the books even if the sophistication of the text is beyond what the students usually read independently.

Students might change the pace of a poem or create tension by using a technique called *enjambment*, where the natural rhythm or meaning of a line is interrupted by being carried onto the next line.

- Students determine the accuracy of the information and credibility of the authors of nonfiction books by investigating the following:
  - date of publication (to see how current the information is)
  - authors' credentials
  - who/what the author acknowledges as sources of information
  - lists of references consulted and additional readings
- Ask students to compare and contrast three books on one topic to determine the scope and depth of the books' treatment of the topic. Does the author seem to have a particular perspective on the topic that narrows what the book communicates about the topic?

Nonfiction Literature Lists

Fine Arts

Aliki (2003) *Ah, music!*

Ardley, Neil (2004) *A young person's guide to music.*

Bogart, Jo Ellen (2003) *Emily Carr at the edge of the world.*

Burleigh, Robert (2004) *Seurat and La Grande Jatte.*

Cutler, May Ebbitt (2002) *Breaking free: The story of William Kurelek.*

Debon, Nicolas (2003) *Four pictures by Emily Carr.*

Freedman, Russell (2004) *The voice that challenged a nation: Marian Anderson and the struggle for equal rights.*

Jacobson, Rick & Fernandez, Laura (2004) *Picasso: Soul on fire.*

Hamanaka, Sheila & Ohmi, Ayano (1999) *In search of the spirit: The living national treasures of Japan.*

Hamilton, Meredith (2001) *Story of the orchestra.*

Konieczny, Vladimir (2004) *Struggling for perfection: The story of Glenn Gould.*

Koscielniak, Bruce (2000) *The story of the incredible orchestra.*

Luxbacher, Irene (2003) *The jumbo book of art.*

Micklethwait, Lucy (1992) *I spy: An alphabet in art.*

— (2001) *I spy two eyes: Numbers in art.*

— (2004) *I spy shapes in art.*

— (2005) *Colors: A first art book.*

— (2006) *Animals: A first art book.*

Sadler, Judy Ann, et al. (2005) *The jumbo book of needlecrafts.*

Scieszka, Jon (2005) *Seen Art?*

Stanley, Diane (1996) *Leonardo da Vinci.*

— (2003) *Michelangelo.*

Wallace, Mary (1997). *I can make art.*

Health and Physical Education

Batten, Jack (2002) *The man who ran faster than everyone: The story of Tom Longboat.*

Cole, Joanna (2001) *The magic school bus explores the senses.*

Douglas, Ann & Julie (2002) *Body talk: The straight facts on fitness, nutrition and feeling great about yourself!*

Dublin, Anne (2004) *Bobbie Rosenfeld, the Olympian who could do everything.*

Freedman, Russell (1999) *Babe Didrikson Zaharias: The making of a champion.*

Gibbons, Gail (1994) *Emergency!*

Graydon, Shari (2003) *Made you look: How advertising works and why you should know.*

— (2004) *In your face: The culture of beauty and you.*

Gryski, Camilla (1995) *Let's play: Traditional games of childhood.*

Kalman, Bobbie (2005) *Field events in action.*

Romanek, Trudee (2006) *Squirt: the most interesting book you'll ever read about blood.*

Romanek, T. (2006) *Squirt: The most interesting book you'll ever read about blood.*

Simon, Seymour (2005) *Guts: Our digestive system.*

— (2006) *The brain: Our nervous system.*

— (2007) *Lungs: Your respiratory system.*

Thomas, Keltie (2004) *How baseball works.*

— (2006) *How hockey works.*

— (2007) *How soccer works.*

Walker, Niki (1999) *Soccer in action.*

Mathematics

Anno, Mitsumasa (1982) *Anno's counting house.*

Harris, Trudy (2003) *100 days of school.*

Laskey, Katherine (1994) *The librarian who measured the earth.*

Lottridge, Celia (1986/2008) *One watermelon seed.*

Metropolitan Museum of Art (2006) *Museum shapes.*

Nagda, Ann Whitehead (2002) *Tiger math: Learning to graph from a baby tiger.*

— (2005) *Panda math.*

— (2007) *Cheetah math: Learning about division from baby cheetahs.*

— (2007) *Polar bear math: Learning about fractions from Klondike and Snow.*

— (2007) *Chimp math: Learning about time from a baby chimpanzee.*

Nobisso, Josephine (2005) *The numbers dance: A counting comedy.*

Nolan, Helen (1995) *How much, how many, how far, how heavy, how long, how tall is 1000?*

Ross, Catherine Sheldrick (1992) *Circles.*

Sayre, April Pulley & Jeff (2003) *One is a snail; Ten is a crab.*

Schmandt-Besserat, Denise (1999) *The history of counting.*

Schwartz, David M. (1999) *On beyond a million.*

— (2006) *Millions to measure.*

Tang, Greg (2003) *Math appeal: Mind-stretching math riddles.*

Social Studies

Brewster, Hugh (2006) *At Vimy Ridge: Canada's greatest World War II victory.*

Charles, Veronika Martenova (2006) *The birdman.*

Gorell, Gena K. (2000) *Heart and soul: The story of Florence Nightingale.*

Granfield, Linda (1993) *Cowboy: A kids' album.*

— (2005) *In Flanders Fields: The story of the poem by John McCrae.*

— (2008) *The unknown soldier.*

Greenwood, Barbara (1994) *A Pioneer story.*

— (1998) *The last safe house: A story of the underground railroad.*

— (2006) *Factory girl.*

Hodge, Deborah (2000) *The kids book of Canada's railway and how the CPR was built.*

Kenna, Kathleen (1995) *A people apart.*

Kruitenbrouwer, Peter (2004) *Our song: The story of "Oh Canada."*

Kurlansky, Mark (2001) *The cod's tale.*

Ross, Val (2003) *The road to there: Mapmakers and their stories.*

Silvey, Diane (2005) *The kids book of Aboriginal peoples in Canada.*

Smith, David J. (2002) *If the world were a village: A book about the world's people.*

Springer, Jane (1997) *Listen to us: The worlds' working children.*

Stanford, Quentin H. (1998) *The Canadian Oxford junior atlas.*

Stephenson, Wendy (2005) *Idaa Trail: In the steps of our ancestors.*

Tanaka, Shelley (1996) *On board the Titanic: What it was like when the great liner sank.*

— (1998) *The buried city of Pompeii: What it was like when Vesuvius exploded.*

Trottier, Maxine (2004) *Our Canadian flag.*

Zhang, Ange (2004) *Red land yellow river: A story from the Cultural Revolution.*

Science

Bardoe, Cheryl (2006) *Gregor Mendel: The friar who grew peas.*

Bateman, Robert (2005) *Backyard birds: An introduction.*

Busby, Peter (2002) *First to fly: How Wilbur and Orville Wright invented the airplane.*

Cole, Joanna (2006) *The magic school bus and the science fair expedition.*

Conlon, Kathy (2002) *Under the ice: A marine biologist at work.*

Editors of *YES* magazine (2003) *The amazing international space station.*

Drake, Jane & Love, Ann (2008) *Alien invaders: Species that threaten our world.*

Gibbons, Gail (2003) *Chicks and chickens.*

— (2007) *Galaxies, galaxies!*

— (2008) *Corn.*

Godkin, C. (2006) *Fire!: The renewal of a forest.*

Jenkins, Steve (2002) *What do you do with a tail like this?*

— (2004) *Actual size* (sequel: *Prehistoric actual size*)

— (2005) *Animals in flight.*

— (2007) *Birdsongs.*

— (2008) *Brothers & Sisters.*

Kilby, Don (2004) *In the country.*

—(2006) *At a construction site.*

MacLeod, Elizabeth (2003) *Albert Einstein: A life of genius.*

McClafferty, Carla Killough (2006) *Something out of nothing: Marie Curie and radium.*

Montgomery, Sy (2006) *Quest for the tree kangaroo: An expedition to the cloud forest of New Guinea.*

Patkau, K (2008) *Creatures yesterday and today.*

Pringle, Laurence (1997) *An extraordinary life: The story of a monarch butterfly.*

Schaefer, Lola M. (2003) *Pick, pull, snap! Where once a flower bloomed.*

Simon, Seymour (2000) *Out of sight: Pictures of hidden worlds.*

Slavin, Bill (2005) *Transformed: How everyday things are made.*

Strauss, Rochelle (2007) *One well: The story of water on earth.*

Swanson, Diane (1994) *Safari beneath the sea: The wonder world of the north Pacific coast.*

Thimmesh, Catherine (2006) *Team moon: How 400,000 people landed Apollo 11 on the moon.*

Thornhill, Jan (2006) *I found a dead bird: The kids' guide to the cycle of death.*

Wick, Walter (1997) *A drop of water: A book of science and wonder.*

Censorship and Selecting Books

Whenever teachers select certain books for children, they are choosing not to bring other books into children's lives. Selection involves introducing and making available particular books because they help children become readers, deepen their experiences, and meet other pedagogical objectives. When the choices about which texts to bring into classrooms involves taking books away from children because adults feel that the children will be negatively influenced or harmed in some way, the choices move into the realm of censorship (Booth, 1992).

Censorship comes from a wish to shield children from what is considered to be adult experiences: such as nudity in American Maurice Sendak's *In the Night Kitchen*; international relationships involving bombings and violent reprisals as in Canadian Deborah Ellis's *Three Wishes: Palestinian and Israeli Children Speak*; and sexual content and obscenity, as in American Judy Blume's *Forever*. Censorship also arises when adults attempt to create a buffer around children so that they do not take up societal biases: for example, making books such as American Mark Twain's *Huckleberry Finn* inaccessible because of the portrayal of racism against African-Americans. In some cases, adults restrict children's access to books in order to promote particular religious beliefs: for instance, L. Frank Baum's *The Wizard of Oz* was put on a list of banned books by some religious groups that believed stories of witches and fantasy promoted witchcraft and the occult.

Censorship can take blatant forms, such as a school district's decision to remove a book from its reading list. Many schools, parents, and school boards resist taking such action, however, because they believe that children benefit from knowledge about sensitive topics, particularly knowledge gained through talking about the issues with a caring adult. This knowledge helps children to work through issues they will encounter as adults so they can make healthy, informed decisions.

Censorship can also take indirect forms. In the National Council of Teachers of English *Guidelines for*

Dealing with Censorship of Nonprint and Multimedia Materials (1998), indirect censorship is defined as occurring "when teachers, in an attempt to avoid controversy, self-censor their classrooms, limiting their students' education." Even teachers who believe strongly in freedom of expression may think twice when facing decisions over whether to bring in Australian Pamela Allen's *Mr. McGee and the Biting Flea* or American Nancy Wilcox Richards's *Farmer Joe's Hot Day*. There are strong pedagogical reasons for introducing the books—they are cumulative tales with predictable patterns that support beginning readers' reading. They are both humorous stories with endearing characters. The former promises a potentially much bumpier ride because of Mr. McGee removing all his clothes to get rid of the flea that has jumped on him from his dog during a walk in the park. Farmer Joe adds and removes clothes, as well, as his wife shows him that the toiling he does in the fields is not so bad after all. He never even gets down to his underwear, however. Teachers who choose to read *Mr. McGee and the Biting Flea* may feel the need to check with administrators before using the book, in spite of having solid rationale for bringing this delightful book into their classroom.

Selecting Literature with a Safety Net

Teachers and librarians who wish to be prepared for censorship issues that arise and who wish, especially, to develop policies and protocols and their own philosophies regarding the selection of books that are potentially controversial, have many resources at hand.

- The American Library Association (ALA) website for Banned Books Week (usually in September) has a wealth of information about books that have been censored over the past year and advice on what teachers and librarians can do to avoid challenges and to deal with chal-

lenges to books they select for children http://www.ala.org/ala/oif/bannedbooksweek/bannedbooksweek.htm
- The National Council of Teachers of English website is also a useful resource for finding out about censorship challenges that have been mounted against children's books, and about what to do if challenged over the selection of a particular book http://www.ncte.org/about/issues/censorship/five/116515.htm

To create a safety net that allows for greater freedom in selecting texts for your classroom, we recommend the following:

1. Communicating with Parents: Criteria for selecting books should be shared early in the school year so parents can have their questions answered before the books come into the classroom. Teachers need to be sensitive to and respectful of the communities in which they teach. It is necessary to balance the responsibility to provide new perspectives that help children see the world in new ways and the responsibility to respect the perspectives of the families and neighbors who nurture children outside the school walls. Complaints about the use of particular books must be listened to with an open mind and always with the goal of working together with parents and the community to serve the children's interests. Open and ongoing communication with parents is important to ensure that they understand why certain books are used in classrooms. Seeking out reviews of books provides additional support as teachers develop solid rationales for selecting texts.
2. Policy Development: Teachers need to be aware of school and school-district policies on the selection of print and nonprint materials. These policies should include complaint procedures that start with the teacher and/or principal meeting with the individual lodging the censorship challenge. There should also be protocols for seeking support from administrators and perhaps parent organizations, if the relationships between the school and parent organization make this possible.

Issue for Discussion

What are your thoughts on the following quotes?

> "I'm afraid to use Nancy Garden's *Molly's Family* because some parents will object to the portrayal of a lesbian couple having a child."
> "I changed some of the words when I read this book aloud to my students."
> "I decided not to include Mark Twain's *The Adventures of Huckleberry Finn* in my classroom library because of the racism in it."

Children's Book References

Allen, Pamela (1998) *Mr. McGee and the biting flea*.
Baum, L. Frank (2000, original 1900) *The Wonderful Wizard of Oz*.
Blume, Judy (2007, original 1975) *Forever*.
Ellis, Deborah (2005) *Three wishes: Palestinian and Israeli children speak*.
Richards, Nancy Wilcox (1987) *Farmer Joe's hot day*.
Sendak, Maurice (1970) *In the night kitchen*.
Twain, Mark (2002, original 1885) *The adventures of Huckleberry Finn*.

APPENDIX B Children's Literature Awards

The following list, while not exhaustive, provides a solid starting point for those seeking out award-winning children's literature. Awards are organized according to the country in which they are awarded. Instead of listing award-winning titles, we provide websites for you to consult for up-to-date lists.

Australia

The Children's Book Council of Australia sponsors five awards for excellence in children's books:

- CBCA Book of the Year: Older Readers
- CBCA Book of the Year: Younger Readers
- CBCA Book of the Year: Early Childhood
- CBCA Picture Book of the Year
- Eve Pownall Award for Information Books

It also administers the Crichton Award for New Illustrators. For a complete list of these awards, go to **http://cbca.org.au/awards.htm**

Canada

The Governor-General's Awards for Children's Literature are presented annually to the best books by Canadian citizens, whether published in Canada or elsewhere. Recipients are selected by two separate juries, one for the English-language books, one for French-language books. See **http://www.canadacouncil. ca/prizes/ggla/**

In 2004, the Canadian Children's Book Centre and the TD (Toronto Dominion) Financial Group established an annual children's book award, the TD Canadian Children's Literature Most Distinguished Book of the Year. "Distinguished" is defined as individually distinct and noted for significant achievement with excellence in quality. All books, in any genre, written by a Canadian for children ages one through 12 are eligible. See **http://www.bookcentre.ca/awards/cclit/index.shtml**

Children's Choice

In Ontario, The Ontario Library Association (OLA) sponsors the Blue Spruce (Kindergarten to Grade 2), Silver Birch (K–Grade 6), and Red Maple (Grades 7–8) awards. Students need to read five books out of a list of 10 to qualify to vote. The British Columbia Library Association sponsors the Red Cedar Book Awards program (Grades 4–7). In Saskatchewan, the Willow Awards include Shining Willow (K–Grade 3), Diamond Willow (Grades 4–6), and Snow Willow (Grades 7–12). See **http://www.bookcentre.ca/awards/Canadian_awards_index**

Genre Awards

PICTURE BOOKS

The Marilyn Baillie Picture Book Award, inaugurated in 2006, is organized and administered by the Canadian Children's Book Centre. To be eligible, a book must be an original book aimed at children ages three to six, written and illustrated by Canadians and first published in Canada. Genres include fiction, nonfiction, and poetry.

NOVELS

The Geoffrey Bilson Award for Historical Fiction for Young People is awarded annually to an outstanding work of historical fiction written by a Canadian author, published in the previoius calendar year. The winner is decided by a jury selected by the Canadian Children's Book Centre.

NONFICTION

In 1987 the Children's Literature Round Tables established the Information Book Award for nonfiction books for readers aged five to fifteen. See **http://www.bookcentre.ca/awards/information_book_award**

In 1999, the Norma Fleck Award for Canadian Children's Non-fiction was established by the Fleck family and the Canadian Children's Book Centre.

New Zealand

Storylines, the Children's Literature Charitable Trust, sponsors five major awards and a notable books list. These include

- Storylines Tom Fitzgibbon Award for fiction for ages 7–13 years written by a previously unpublished author
- Storylines Joy Cowley Award for picture books
- Elsie Locke Award for nonfiction
- Russell Clark Award for picture books
- Esther Glen Award for the book that has made the most distinguished contribution to literature for children.

The complete lists of award winners can be found at **http://www.storylines.org.nz/awards.asp?pid=55**

United Kingdom

The Carnegie Medal was established in 1937 and is presented annually to an outstanding book published in the United Kingdom. Any book written in English and published first, or concurrently, in the United Kingdom has been eligible. The Kate Greenaway Medal, established in honor of the nineteenth-century children's book illustrator and writer, is awarded annually to an illustrator of children's books. See **http://www.carnegiegreenaway.org.uk/home/index.php**

The Nestle Children's Book Prize is an annual award given to children's books written in the previous year by a UK citizen or resident. Booktrust, an independent charity that promotes books and reading, sponsored the prize up until 2008. The shortlist for the award is chosen by a panel of adult judges, and children across the UK vote on the first, second, and third place winners. See **http://www.booktrusted.co.uk/nestle/**

Formerly the Whitbread Awards, the Costa Book Awards acknowledge outstanding books of literature, not only for the qualities praised by the critics, but for the popular qualities that make them readable on a wide scale. The Costa Children's Book Award is open to books for children aged seven and up, written by a British author. See **http://www.costabookawards.com/**

United States

The American Library Association Children's Literature Awards are announced each year on the Monday of the American Library Association mid-winter meeting. Awards include Newbery Medal and Honor Books (novels), The Caldecott Medal and Honor Books (picture books), the Coretta Scott King Award presented to a black author and black illustrator. The Laura Ingalls Wilder Medal is presented every three years to an author or illustrator for a body of work.

Children's Choice Awards

Children's Choices began as an annual joint project of the International Reading Association (**http://www.reading.org**) and the Children's Book Council in 1974. Each year, 100 favorite books donated by children's book publishers are chosen by thousands of American children. An annotated list of these books is published in the October issue of *The Reading Teacher*.

Genre Awards

POETRY

Awards given for the best poetry book published for children in the US include

- the Lee Bennett Hopkins Poetry Award, established in 1993 by the Children's Literature Council of Pennsylvania and awarded by the Pennsylvania State University since 1999. See **http://www.pabook.libraries.psu.edu/activities/hopkins/**
- the Myra Cohn Livingston Award, created by the Children's Literature Council of Southern California in 1999 to honor the memory of the distinguished poet Myra Cohn Livingston. See **http://www. childrensliteraturecouncil.org/myra_cohn_livingston_award.htm**

PICTURE BOOKS

The Caldecott Medal, established in 1938 and sponsored by the Association for Library Service to Children division of the American Library Association, is given to the illustrator of the most distinguished picture book for children published in the previous year in the United States.

NOVELS

The Newbery Medal was named for eighteenth-century British bookseller John Newbery. The Association for Library Service to Children offers this annual award to the author of the most distinguished contribution to American literature for children.

MULTICULTURAL LITERATURE

Since 1969, the Coretta Scott King Award, commemorating Dr. Martin Luther King Jr. and his wife, Coretta Scott King, has been given to African-American authors; since 1974, to African-American illustrators. Award-winning books are those which have made outstanding contributions to literature and to promoting an understanding and appreciation of Dr. King's dream of freedom and social justice for African Americans. This award is sponsored by the Social Responsibilities Round Table of the American Library Association. See **http://www.ala.org/ala/emiert/corettascottkingbookaward/corettascott.cfm**

Every year, the Children's Literature and Reading Special Interest Group of the International Reading Association puts together a list of Notable Books for a Global Society for K—12 students that are not tied to specific cultural groups. This list, found at **http://www.TCNJ.Edu~childlit**, identifies folklore, poetry, picture books, realistic and historical fiction, and nonfiction for enhancing student understanding of people and cultures throughout the world.

NONFICTION

Although awards for children's fiction have been in existence in the United States since 1922, it was not until 1967 that the *Boston Globe* and *Horn Book* teamed up to establish the Boston Globe-Horn Book Award for outstanding nonfiction published in the United States. See **http://www.hbook.com/bghb/**

In 1990, the National Council of Teachers of English initiated the Orbis Pictus Award for Outstanding Nonfiction for Children. *Orbis Pictus,* thought to be the first nonfiction book published for children by Johann Comenius in 1657, is translated as *the World in Pictures.* See **http://www.ncte.org/elem/awards/ orbispictus**

International Awards

IBBY, a non-governmental organization with an official status in UNESCO and UNICEF, was founded in Zurich, Switzerland, in 1953. Its membership includes authors and illustrators, publishers and editors, translators, journalists and critics, teachers, university professors and students, librarians and booksellers, social workers and parents from every continent. IBBY's goals include promoting international understanding through children's books and giving children around the world access to high quality books. See **http://www.ibby.org/index. php?id=about**

Winners of the Hans Christian Andersen Award, the highest international recognition given to an author and an illustrator of children's books, have been from every continent. Her Majesty Queen Margrethe II of Denmark is the Patron of the H.C. Andersen Awards. The nominations are made by the National Sections of the International Best Books for Youth (IBBY) organization. The Author's Award has been given since 1956 and the Illustrator's Award since 1966. See **http:// www.ibby.org/index.php?id=273**

Professional Resources

References

Albers, P. (1996) "Issues of representation: Caldecott gold medal winners 1984–1995." *The New Advocate, 9,* 267–285.

Bamford, R. A. & Kristo, J. V. (2003) "Choosing quality nonfiction literature: Examining aspects of accuracy and organization." In R. A. Bamford & J. V. Kristo (Eds.), *Making facts come alive: Choosing quality nonfiction literature K-8* (pp. 19–38). Norwood, MA: Christopher-Gordon.

Banks, J. (1994) *Multiethnic education: Theory and practice.* Boston, MA: Allyn & Bacon.

Barrs, M. & Pidgeon, S. (1994) *Reading the difference: Gender and reading in the elementary classroom.* Markham, ON: Pembroke.

Barta, J. & Grindler, M.C. (1996) "Exploring bias using multicultural literature for children." *The Reading Teacher, 50,* 269–270.

Benton, M. (1978) "Poetry for children: A neglected art." *Children's Literature in Education, 9*(3), 111–124.

Bishop, R.S. (2003) "Reframing the debate about cultural authenticity." In D.L. Fox & K G. Short (Eds.), *Stories matter: The complexity of cultural authenticity in children's literature.* (pp. 25–37). Urbana, IL: NCTE.

Blasingame. J. (2007) *Books that don't bore'em.: Young adult books that speak to this generation.* New York, NY: Scholastic.

Booth, D. (1992) *Censorship goes to school.* Markham, ON: Pembroke.

— (2001) *Reading and writing in the middle years.* Markham, ON: Pembroke

— (2002) *Even hockey players read: Boys, literacy and learning.* Markham, ON: Pembroke Publishers.

Booth, D. & Lundy, K.G. (2006) *In graphic detail: Using graphic novels in the classroom.* Markham, ON: Scholastic.

Booth, D., & Moore, B. (2003) *Poems please!: Sharing poetry with children* 2nd Ed. Markham, ON: Pembroke Publishers.

Botelho, M.J. (2004) *Reading class: Disrupting power in children's literature.* Unpublished doctoral dissertation. University of Massachusetts, Amherst.

Brownlie, F. (2005) *Grand conversations, thoughtful responses: A unique approach to literature circles.* Winnipeg, MB: Portage & Main Press.

Burns, B. (1998) "Changing the classroom climate with literature circles."
Journal of Adolescent & Adult Literacy, 42(2), 124–129.

Butzow, C.M. & Butzow, J.W. (2000) *Science through children's literature: An integrated approach.* Englewood, CO: Teacher Ideas Press.

Cai, M. (1998) "Multiple definitions of multicultural literacy: Is the debate really just 'ivory tower' bickering?" *The New Advocate, 11,* 311–324.

— (2002) *Multicultural literature for children and young adults: Reflections on critical issues.* Westport, CT: Greenwood Press.

Camp, D. (2000) "It takes two: Teaching with twin texts of fact and fiction." *The Reading Teacher, 53,* 400–408.

Campbell, J. (1988) *The power of myth.* New York, NY: Anchor Books.

Carter, B. & Abrahamson, R.F. (1990) *Nonfiction for young adults: From delight to wisdom.* Phoenix, AZ: Oryx.

Caswell, L.M. & Duke, N.K. (1998) "Non-narrative as a catalyst for literacy development." *Language Arts, 75,* 108–117.

Chambers, A. (1975) "Why bother?" *Horn Book Magazine,* 51.2, 174–184

Ching, S.H.D. (2005) "Multicultural children's literature as an instrument of power." *Language Arts, 83*(2), 128–136.

Cianciolo, P.J. (2000) *Informational picture books for children.* Chicago, IL: American Library Association.

Clay, M.M. (1991) *Becoming literate: The construction of inner control.* Portsmouth, NH: Heinemann.

— (2000) *Concepts about print.* Toronto, ON: Pearson Education.

Colby, S.A., & Lyon, A. (2004) "Heightening awareness about the importance of using multicultural literature." *Multicultural Education, 11*(3), 24–28.

Cowan, T.L. (2002) "Subverting normal: The anti-fairytale in Linda Holeman's 'Toxic Love' and Wendy A. Lewis's 'You never know'." *Canadian Children's Literature, 108,* 27–38.

Crook, P.R. & Lehman, B.A. (1991) "Themes for two voices: Children's fiction and nonfiction as 'whole literature.'" *Language Arts, 68,* 34–41.

Culler, J. (1997) *Literary theory: A very short introduction.* Oxford, UK: University Press.

Cummins, J. (2001) *Negotiating identities: Education for empowerment in a diverse society.* 2nd Edition. Los Angeles, CA: California Association for Bilingual Education.

Dane Bauer, M. (1991) "An author's letter to teachers." *The Horn Book, 67*(1), 111–116.

Daniels, H. (2002) *Literature circles: Voice and choice in book clubs & reading groups* 2nd Ed. Portland, ME: Stenhouse.

— (2006) "What's the next big thing with literature circles?" *Voices from the Middle, 13*(4), 10–15.

Darling, L.F. (1996) "Deepening our global perspective: The moral matters in trickster tales." *Canadian Social Studies, 30,* 180–182.

Day, C. (2003) *Reading and responding in literature circles.* Marrickville, AU: Primary English Teaching Association.

Donovan, C.A. & Smolkin, L.B. (2001) "Genre and other factors influencing teachers' book selections for science instruction." *Reading Research Quarterly, 36,* 412–440.

Dresang, E.T. (1999) *Radical change: Books for youth in a digital age.* New York, NY: H. W. Wilson.

Duke, N.K. (2000) "3.6 minutes per day: The scarcity of informational texts in first grade." *Reading Research Quarterly, 35,* 202–224.

Elliabbad, Mohieddin (1999/2006) *The illustrator's notebook..* Toronto, ON: Groundwood Books.

Finazzo, D. (1997) *All for the children: Multicultural essentials of literature.* Albany, NY: Delmar Publishing (ITP).

Fink, R. (1995/96) "Successful dyslexics: A constructivist study of passionate interest." *Journal of Adolescent and Adult Literacy, 39*(4), 268–280.

Fountas, I.C., & Pinnell, G.S. (1996) *Guiding readers and writers (grades 3–6).* Portsmouth, NH: Heinemann.

Fredericks, A.D. (2003) "Evaluating and using nonfiction literature in the science curriculum." In R. A Bamford & J. V Kristo (Eds.), *Making facts come alive: Choosing and using nonfiction literature K-8,* (pp. 141–155). Urbana, IL: NCTE.

Freedman, R. (1992) "Fact or fiction?" In E. B. Freeman, C. G. Person (Eds.), *Using nonfiction trade books in the elementary classroom: From ants to zeppelins.* (pp. 2–10). Urbana, IL: NCTE.

— (1998) "On telling the truth." *Booklist, 95,* 224–225.

Frye, N. (1964) *The educated imagination.* Bloomington, IN: Indiana University Press.

Fox, D.L. & Short, K.G. (2003) *Stories matter: The complexity of cultural authenticity in children's literature.* Urbana, IL: NCTE.

Gates, H.L. (2003) "'Authenticity,' or the lesson of Little Tree." In D.L. Fox & K G. Short (Eds.), *Stories matter: The complexity of cultural authenticity in children's literature.* Urbana, IL: NCTE.

Gilles, C. (1990) "Collaborative literacy strategies: 'We don't need to have a circle to have a group.'" In K. Short & K. Pierce (Eds.), *Talking about books: Creating literate communities* (pp. 55–68). Portsmouth, NH: Heinemann.

Goodman, K. (1970) "Behind the eye: What happens in reading." In K. Goodman & O. S. Niles. (pp. 3–38). *Reading: Process and program.* Urbana, IL: NCTE.

Gorman, M. (2004) *Getting graphic: Using graphic novels to promote literacy with preteens and teens.* Worthington, OH: Linworth Publishing, Inc.

Hade, D.D. (1997) "Reading multiculturally." In V. J. Harris (Ed.), *Using multiethnic literature in the K-8 classroom* (pp. 233–256). Norwood, MA: Christopher-Gordon Publishers.

Harrison, D.L., & Holderith, K. (2003) *Using the power of poetry to teach language arts, social studies, math, and more: Engaging poetry lessons, model poems, and writing activities that help students learn important content.* New York, NY: Scholastic.

Harste, J.C., Short, K.G., & Burke, C. (1988) *Creating classrooms for authors: The reading-writing connection.* Portsmouth, NH: Heinemann.

Harwayne, S. (1992) *Lasting impressions: Weaving literature into the writing workshop.* Portsmouth, NH: Heinemann.

Hepler, S. (1998) "Nonfiction books for children: New directions, new challenges." In R. A. Bamford & J. V. Kristo (Eds.), *Making facts come alive: Choosing quality nonfiction literature K-8* (pp. 3-17). Norwood, MA: Christopher-Gordon.

Hoggart, R. (1970) "Why I value literature." In *Speaking to each other,* Vol 2 (pp 11–19). London, UK: Clark, Irwin.

Huck, C. (1990) "The power of children's literature in the classroom." In K.G. Short & K.M Pierce (Eds.), *Talking about books: Creating literate communities* (pp. 3–15). Portsmouth, NH: Heinemann

Huck, C. S., Hepler, S., Hickman, J., & Kiefer, B. Z. (1997) *Children's literature in the elementary school* 7th Ed. Madison, WI: Brown & Benchmark.

Hunt, L. (1970) "The effect of self-selection, interest and motivation upon independent, instructional and frustration levels." *The Reading Teacher, 24,* 416.

Jensen, J.M. (2001) "The quality of prose in Orbis Pictus Award books." In M. Zarnowski, R.M. Kerper, & J.M. Jensen (Eds.), *The best in children's nonfiction* (pp. 3–12). Urbana, IL: NCTE.

Johnson, E., Sickels, E.R., Sayers, F.C., & Horovitz, C. (1977) *Anthology of children's literature* 5th Ed. Boston, MA: Houghton Mifflin.

Keehn, S., & Roser, N. (2002) "Fostering thought, talk, and inquiry: Linking literature and social studies." *The Reading Teacher, 55*(4), 416–426.

Knoeller, C.P. (1994) "Negotiating interpretations of text: The role of student-led discussions in understanding literature." *Journal of Reading, 37,* 572–580.

Kropp, P. (2000) *How to make your child a reader for life*: Toronto, ON: Random House.

Kozak, G. (2005) *The impact of non-fiction read-alouds on reading interest and engagement: A study of two fourth grade students.* Unpublished Master's Research Paper: OISE/University of Toronto. August.

Kuta, K.W. & Zernial, S. (2000) *Novel ideas for young readers.* Englewood, CO: Teacher Ideas Press.

Landt, S.M. (2006) "Multicultural literature and young adolescents: A kaleidoscope of opportunity." *Journal of Adolescent & Adult Literacy, 49*(8), 690–697.

Lasky, K. (2003) "To Stingo with love: An author's perspective on writing outside one's culture." In D.L. Fox & K G. Short (Eds.), *Stories matter: The complexity of cultural authenticity in children's literature.* (pp. 84–92). Urbana, IL: NCTE.

Leggo, C. (2003) "Unraveling the fear of poetry/reveling in the pleasure of poetry." In S. Peterson (Ed.), *Untangling some knots in K-8 writing instruction* (pp. 96–107). Newark, DE: International Reading Association.

Lutz, D. (1996) "Science is what scientists do, or Wetenschap is wat wetenschappers doen." *The Horn Book Magazine, 72*(2), 166–173.

McDowell, M.B. (1977) "New didacticism: Stories for free children." *Language Arts, 54*(1), 41–47, 85.

McGee, L. M., & Tompkins, G. (1995) "Literature-based reading instruction: What's guiding the instruction?" *Language Arts, 72*(6), 405–414.

Moloney, J. (2000) *Boys and books: building a culture of reading around our boys.* Sydney NSW: ABC Books.

Moss, B. (1991) "Children's nonfiction trade books: A complement to content area texts." *The Reading Teacher, 45,* 26–32.

— (1995) "Using children's nonfiction tradebooks as read-alouds." *Language Arts, 72,* 122–126.

National Council of Teachers of Mathematics (1989) *Curriculum and evaluation standards for school mathematics.* Reston, VA: Author.

National Council of Teachers of English (1981) *The student's right to read.* http://www.ncte.org/about/over/positions/category/cens/107616.htm

— (1998) *Guidelines for dealing with censorship of nonprint and multimedia materials.* http://www.ncte.org/about/over/positions/category/cens/107611.htm

Newkirk, T. (2002) *Misreading masculinity: Boys, literacy and popular culture.* Portsmouth, NH: Heinemann.

Nicoll, V. & Roberts, V. (1993) *Taking a closer look at literature-based programs.* Newton, NSW: Primary English Teaching Association.

Nieto, S. (2000) "Multicultural education and school reform." In J. Noel. (Ed.). *Notable selections in multicultural education* (pp. 299–307). Guilford, CT: Dushkin/McGraw-Hill.

Nilsen, A.P. (1971) "Women in children's literature." *College English, 32*, 918–926.

Norton, D.E. (2005) *Multicultural children's literature: Through the eyes of many children*. 2nd Ed. Upper Saddle River, NJ: Pearson Merrill Prentice Hall.

Odean, K. (1998) *Great books for boys*. New York, NY. Random House.

Ontario Ministry of Education (2004) *Me read? No way!: A practical guide to improving boys' literacy skills*. Website http://www.edu.gov.on.ca

Pappas, C.C. (1991) "Fostering full access to literacy by including information books." *Language Arts, 63*, 449–462.

— (1993) "Is narrative "primary"? Some insights from kindergarteners' pretend readings of stories and information books." *Journal of Reading Behavior 25*, 97–129.

— (2006) "The information book genre: Its role in integrated science literacy research and practice." *Reading Research Quarterly, 41*(2), 226–250.

Paterson, K. (1989) *The spying heart: More thoughts on reading and writing books for children*. New York, NY: E.P. Dutton.

Pirie, B. (2002) *Teenage boys and high school English*. Portsmouth, NH: Boynton/Cook.

Rice, D.C. (2002) "Using trade books in teaching elementary science: Facts and fallacies." *The Reading Teacher, 55*(6), 552–565.

Rochman, H. (1993) *Against borders: Promoting books for a multicultural world*. Chicago, IL: American Library Association.

Rosen, H. "The nurture of narrative." In *Stories and meanings* (pp. 6–21) Sheffield, UK: National Association of the Teaching of English.

Rosenblatt, L. (1978) *The reader, the text, the poem: The transactional theory of the literary work*. Carbondale, IL: Southern Illinois University Press.

Roser, N., & Martinez, M. (1995) *Book talk and beyond: Children and teachers respond to literature*. Newark, DE: International Reading Association.

Saxby, M. (1996) "Myth and legend." In P. Hunt (Ed.), *International companion encyclopedia of children's literature*. (pp. 166–176). London, UK: Routledge.

Schmidt, P.R. (1999) "Know thyself and understand others." *Language Arts 76*, 332–340.

Seto, T. (2003) "Multiculturalism is not Halloween." In D.L. Fox & K G. Short (Eds.), *Stories matter: The complexity of cultural authenticity in children's literature*. (pp. 93–97). Urbana, IL: NCTE.

Sibberson, F. & Szymusiak, K. (2000) *Still learning to read; Teaching students to read in grades 3–6*. Portland, ME: Stenhouse Publishers.

Sierra, J. (1992) *Cinderella*. Phoenix, AZ: Oryx Press.

Simon, S. (1982) "Using science trade books in the classroom." *Science and Children, 19*(6), 5–6.

Smiley, J. (2005) *13 Ways of looking at the novel*. New York, NY: Alfred A. Knopf.

Smith, M.W. & Wilhelm, J. D. (2002) *Reading don't fix no chevys*. Portsmouth, NH: Heinemann

Smolkin, L.B. & Donovan, C.A. (2005) "Looking closely at a science trade book: Gail Gibbons and multimodal literacy." *Language Arts, 83*(1), 52–62.

Stotsky, S. (1999) *Losing our language: How multicultural classroom instruction is undermining our children's ability to read, write, and reason*. New York, NY: The Free Press/Simon & Schuster.

Stott, J.C. (1984) *Children's literature from A to Z: A guide for parents and teachers*. New York, NY: McGraw-Hill Book Company.

Sullivan, E. (2001) "Some teens prefer the real thing: The case for young adult nonfiction." *English Journal, 90*(3), 43–47.

Swartz, L. (2006) *The Novel Experience: Steps for choosing and using fiction in the classroom*. Markham, ON: Pembroke Publishers.

Terry, A. (1984) *Children's poetry preferences: A national survey of the upper elementary grades*. Urbana, IL: National Council of Teachers of English.

Thompson, S. (1977) *The folktale*. Berkeley, CA: University of California Press.

Tompkins, G.E., Bright, R.M., Pollard, M.J., & Winsor, P.J.T. (2005) *Language arts content and teaching strategies 3rd Canadian Edition*. Toronto, ON: Pearson/Prentice Hall.

Vardell, S. (1991) "A new 'Picture of the World': The NCTE Orbis Pictus Award for Outstanding Nonfiction for Children." *Language Arts, 68*(6), 474–479.

Vasquez, V. (2003) *Getting beyond "I like the book": Creating space for critical literacy in K-6 classrooms*. Newark, DE: International Reading Association.

Woodson, J. (2003) "Who can tell my story?" In D.L. Fox & K G. Short (Eds.), *Stories matter: The complexity of cultural authenticity in children's literature*. (pp. 41–45). Urbana, IL: NCTE.

Weiner, S. (2006) *The 101 Best graphic novels* 2nd Ed. New York, NY: Nantier Beall Minoustchine Publishing.

Whitin, D.J. (2002) "In my opinion: The potentials and pitfalls of integrating literature into the mathematics program." *Teaching Children Mathematics, 8*, 503–504.

Wooldridge, S.G. (1996) *Poemcrazy: Freeing your life with words*. New York, NY: Three Rivers Press.

Yoder, C. (1999) "Tales of a revolutionary voyage." In S. Tierney, (Ed.), *Children's writer guide* (pp. 271–282). West Redding, CT: Institute of Children's Literature.

Yokota, J. (Ed.) (2001) *Kaleidoscope: A multicultural booklist for grades K-8* 3rd Ed. Urbana, IL: NCTE.

Zarnowski, M. (2003) "It's more than dates and places: How nonfiction contributes to understanding social studies." In R.A. Bamford & J.V. Kristo (Eds.), *Making facts come alive: Choosing quality nonfiction literature K-8* (pp. 121–139). Norwood, MA: Christopher-Gordon.

Books About Children's Literature

Anderson, N.A. (2006) *Elementary children's literature: The basics for teachers and parents 2nd Ed.* Columbus, OH: Pearson.

Baker, D. & Setterington, K. (2003) *A guide to Canadian children's books.* Toronto, ON: McClelland & Stewart.

Bainsbridge, J. & Pantaleo, S. (1999) *Learning with literature in the Canadian classroom.* Edmonton, AB: University of Alberta Press.

Blasingame, J. (2007) *Books that don't bore 'em.: Young adult books that speak to this generation.* New York, NY: Scholastic.

Booth, David & Barton, B. (2000) *Story works.* Markham, ON: Pembroke Publishers.

Butler, D. (1998) *Babies need books: The joy of books with children from birth to six.* Portsmouth, NH: Heinemann.

Codell, E.R. (2003) *How to get your child to love reading: For ravenous and reluctant readers alike.* New York, NY: Algonquin Books.

Fitch, S. & Swartz, L. (2008) *The poetry experience: Steps for choosing and using poetry in the classroom.* Markham, ON: Pembroke Publishers.

Galda, L. & Cullinan, B.E. (2001) *Literature and the child,* 5th Ed. Belmont, CA: Wadsworth.

Huck, C.S., Hepler, S., Hickman, J. & Kiefer, B.Z. (2000) *Children's literature in the elementary school* 7th Ed. Madison, WI: McGraw-Hill College.

Jacobs, J.S. & Tunnell, Michael O. (2004) *Children's literature briefly.* Columbus, OH: Pearson.

Jobe, R. & P. Harte (1991) *Canadian connections: Experiencing literature with children.* Markham, ON: Pembroke Publishers.

Jobe, R. & M. Dayton-Sakari (2002) *Info-kids. How to use non-fiction to turn reluctant readers into enthusiastic learners.* Markham, ON: Pembroke Publishers.

Lesesne, T.S. (2003) *Making the match: The right book for the right reader at the right time, Grades 4–12.* Portland, ME: Stenhouse.

Lynch-Brown, C & Tomlinson, C.M. (2008) *Essentials of Children's Literature* 6th Ed. Columbus, OH: Pearson.

Norton, Donna E. (2007) *Through the eyes of a child: An introduction to Children's Literature* 7th Ed. Columbus, OH: Pearson.

Sibberson, F. & Szymusiak, K. (2000/2008) *Still learning to read; Teaching students to read in grades 3–6.* Portland, ME: Stenhouse Publishers.

Spufford, F. (2002) *The child that books built.* London, UK: Faber and Faber.

Swartz, L. (2006) *The novel experience: Steps for choosing and using fiction in the classroom.* Markham, ON: Pembroke Publishers.

Temple, C., Martinez, M. & Yokota, J. (2006) *Children's books in children's hands: An introduction to their literature.* Columbus, OH: Pearson.

Weiner, S. (2006) *The 101 best graphic novels* 2nd Ed. New York, NY: Nantier Beall Minoustchine Publishing.

Index